The Qur'ān and its Exegesis

Other books on Islamic Studies published by Oneworld:

City of Wrong: A Friday in Jerusalem, M. Kamel Hussein (trans. Kenneth Cragg), ISBN 1-85168-072-1
Companion to the Qurán, William Montgomery Watt, ISBN 1-85168-036-5
Defenders of Reason in Islam: Mu'tazilism from Medieval School to Modern Symbol, ISBN 1-85168-147-7
The Event of the Qur'án: Islam in its Scripture, Kenneth Cragg, ISBN 1-85168-067-5
The Faith and Practice of Al-Ghazálí, William Montgomery Watt, ISBN 1-85168-062-4
Islam and the West, Norman Daniel, ISBN 1-85168-129-9
Jesus in the Qur'án, Geoffrey Parrinder, ISBN 1-85168-094-2
Muhammad: A Short Biography, Martin Forward, ISBN 1-85168-131-0
Muslims and Christians Face to Face, Kate Zebiri, ISBN 1-85168-133-7
Muslim Devotions: A Study of Prayer-Manuals in Common Use, Constance E. Padwick, ISBN 1-85168-115-9
On Being a Muslim: Finding the Religious Path in the Modern World, Farid Esack, ISBN 1-85168-146-9
Qur'án, Liberation and Pluralism, Farid Esack, ISBN 1-85168-121-3
Rabi'a: The Life and Work of Rabi'a and Other Women Mystics in Islam, Margaret Smith, ISBN 1-85168-085-3
Rúmi: Poet and Mystic, Reynold A. Nicholson, ISBN 1-85168-096-9
A Short History of Islam, William Montgomery Watt, ISBN 1-85168-109-4
A Short Introduction to Islamic Philosophy, Theology and Mysticism, Majid Fakhry, ISBN 1-85168-134-5
Voices of Islam, John Bowker, ISBN 1-85168-095-0

THE Qur'ān AND ITS EXEGESIS

Selected Texts with Classical and Modern Muslim Interpretations

Helmut Gätje

Translated and edited by Alford T. Welch

ONEWORLD
OXFORD

THE QUR'ĀN AND ITS EXEGESIS: SELECTED TEXTS WITH CLASSICAL AND MUSLIM INTERPRETATIONS

Oneworld Publications
(Sales and Editorial)
185 Banbury Road
Oxford OX2 7AR
England

Oneworld Publications
(U.S. Marketing Office)
PO Box 830, 21 Broadway
Rockport, MA 01966
U.S.A.

Translated from the German
Koran und Koranexegese
First published in Great Britain by Routledge Ltd

Reprinted 1997

A CIP record for this book is available
from the British Library

ISBN 1-85168-118-3

Printed and bound in Finland by WSOY

CONTENTS

II. MUḤAMMAD

III. SALVATION HISTORY

IV. ISLAM, THE 'BOOK RELIGIONS', AND PAGANISM

V. GOD

VI. ANGELS, SPIRITS, AND MANKIND

VII. ESCHATOLOGY

VIII. DUTIES AND PROHIBITIONS

IX. DOGMATICS

X. MYSTICAL AND PHILOSOPHICAL QUR'ĀNIC EXEGESIS

XI. SHĪ'ITE QUR'ĀNIC EXEGESIS

XII. MODERN QUR'ĀNIC EXEGESIS

PREFACE TO THE GERMAN EDITION

This selection of texts on Qur'ānic exegesis is intended to provide for the non-orientalist reader an impression of the exegetic activity of the Muslims. In accordance with this goal, an attempt has been made to present clearly certain general features of Qur'ānic exegesis within Islam without complicating the issue by presenting too great a number of individual peculiarities. A wealth of exegetical works on the Qur'ān have been produced within Islam, a large part of which have been treated recently by Muḥammad Ḥusain adh-Dhahabī in the extensive Arabic work *At-tafsīr wa-l-mufassirūn* ('Exegesis and the Exegetes'), 3 vols, Cairo 1381 A.H./1961–2. Although there is still much to be said with regard to Qur'ānic exegesis, the present work is concerned much less with an elaboration of this topic as with a presentation of representative Muslim thought.

Central to the selection are important representatives of 'classical' Sunnite exegesis, who, however, are accompanied by representatives of other points of view. The fact that Zamakhsharī occupies a large part of the text is due not only to his significance but also to the fact that his texts are well suited for a selection of this type. Ṭabarī, for example, is frequently too verbose. On the other hand, Baiḍāwī is more often included because he often skilfully makes Zamakhsharī's text more concise or, for dogmatic reasons, offers another interpretation. In making the selections, care had to be taken not to assume too great a knowledge of Islam on the part of the reader. For this reason the texts have been arranged topically rather than according to the individual exegetes. The texts themselves will receive varying interest. For the most part they reflect the straightforward, technical course of the exegesis, but some have been abbreviated, specifically those of little significance to the non-orientalist.

The individual texts are usually preceded by the Qur'ānic verses, printed in italics. In the Muslim texts themselves this is not always the case, since the exegetes and their pupils knew the Qur'ānic passages by heart and thus could limit themselves to brief allusions. For the German version of the Qur'ānic text, the translation by Rudi Paret has been used, with certain exceptions. Deviations resulted necessarily from the content of the commentaries, and occasionally minor alterations have been made without any indication to the reader. To justify each change would have demanded too much space. Thus, if the reader wants to delve more deeply into the subject, he will do well to consult Paret's translation. In translating the commentaries, I have proceeded somewhat more freely than Paret has in relation to the Qur'ānic texts. Again, too many explanations would have been necessary otherwise. On the whole the footnotes are limited in general to references that are essential for an immediate understanding of the texts. Some supplementary material is also to be found in the form of brief notes that have been incorporated into the index. The usual eulogies that follow certain names in Arabic texts have been omitted in the translation.

The Qur'ānic references are cited according to the so-called Kūfic verse numbers (see p. 27). The verse numbers of the Flügel edition, which is still widely used in the West, have been indicated following a diagonal whenever they differ from the Kūfic numbers. When such an indicator is not present, the numbers agree. Dates refer to the Christian calendar unless otherwise indicated; the Islamic calendar dates from the Hijra (see p. 10). The bibliography at the end is intended only to give the reader a very general basis for orientation and at the same time signify those writings and editions which were utilized the most by the author. For the introduction I owe much to these and other writings, without mentioning them specifically. Now and then I have also adopted unconsciously certain modes of expression.

A considerable length of time has elapsed since this book was written, and it is obvious that during this time new contributions to the subject have been published. In the realm of newly published contributions to Qur'ānic research, I would like to direct the reader's attention first of all to Paret's commentary to his translation of the Qur'ān (Rudi Paret, *Der Koran: Kommentar und Konkordanz*, Stuttgart, 1971), and then also to Nabia Abbott, *Studies in*

Arabic Literary Papyri, Vol. II, *Qur'ānic Commentary and Tradition*, Chicago, 1967, a book which provides us with new knowledge on the problem of written documentation in early Islamic times.

In addition to the editor of the Bibliothek des Morgenlandes and the publishing house, my thanks go also to Professor Paret, who not only motivated me to do research on this subject but also was kind enough to read the manuscript and make several comments concerning its content. Points of information raised by specific questions were provided to me by Professor Spitaler. Special thanks go to Herr Dr Khoury and Frau Dr Jacobi, who were unselfish with their help in selecting and interpreting the texts, and thus have contributed significantly to the completion of this book. Finally, the members of the local Institut für Orientalistik have assisted me in correcting the manuscript. Their part too should be mentioned specifically at this point.

Saarbrücken Helmut Gätje
1971

PREFACE TO THE ENGLISH EDITION

This edition of Helmut Gätje's *Koran und Koranexegese* provides for the English-speaking world a valuable collection of classical and modern Muslim interpretations of key passages of the Qur'ān. Because of its topical arrangement, this collection provides a survey of Muslim faith based on original Arabic sources that have been inaccessible to the majority of English readers. This work will thus be just as valuable to the general reader who has an interest in Islam as to the specialist. This English edition is based on both the German and the original Arabic texts. A literal rendering of the German would not have provided the best English translation of the original Arabic.

For the English version of the Qur'ānic text, the translation by Arthur J. Arberry, *The Koran Interpreted* (London: Allen & Unwin, 1955), has been used, with certain exceptions. It should be noted that Arberry's title is misleading to the general reader. It reflects the orthodox Muslim view that the Arabic text of the Qur'ān *is* the Qur'ān, and that any rendering into another language is an 'interpretation' and not a 'translation'. Arberry's version is, in fact, closer to the Arabic than most English translations. While this has the advantage of accurately reflecting the Arabic text, at times it results in ambiguity (reflecting the ambiguity of the Arabic) or rather awkward English, as for instance in the literal rendering of Arabic idioms. As with Helmut Gätje's use of Rudi Paret's translation of the Qur'ān (see the Preface to the German Edition), alterations were necessitated, sometimes by the content of the commentaries, and at other times for reasons of style followed in the English edition. Occasionally, significant interpretations in the translations by Arberry and Paret, when not followed in the English edition, are cited in footnotes.

In all Qur'ānic references the verse numbers of the Egyptian standard edition are given first, followed after a diagonal by the numbers of the European edition by Gustav Flügel, where they differ. In the Qur'ānic quotations at the beginning of each section of commentary, the verse numbers have not been included in the text of the translations. The reader can determine the exact location of each verse, however, since the last line of each verse (according to the Egyptian standard edition) is indented, except where the quotation consists of only one verse.

Numerous transliterations of Arabic terms appearing in Gätje's text have been omitted in the English edition, when it seemed that they were included only because they appear in Paret's translation of the Qur'ān, which is adopted by Gätje, and when they are not essential for understanding the commentary. On the other hand, transliterations of Arabic terms not included in Gätje's translation of the commentaries have sometimes been added in the English edition, where it seemed necessary for proper understanding of the text. A standard method of transliteration followed by English-speaking orientalists and in English editions of the Islamic World Series has been adopted.

The translator and editor of the English edition has added notes (in square brackets), which provide references to English literature and to other works that have appeared since the publication of the German edition. A new and expanded bibliography with annotations has also been prepared for the English edition. It is designed for the English-speaking reader, but also includes classic and standard works in other languages. An attempt was made to include all English editions of works cited by Gätje where they exist. The list of Arabic works includes only the editions used by Gätje. The equivalent Western dates have been added to citations of oriental works.

Certain corrections and improvements in the translation mentioned in reviews of the German edition have been made in the English edition. For these improvements we are especially indebted to Professor Rudi Paret and Professor A. F. L. Beeston.

East Lansing, Michigan Alford T. Welch
1975

INTRODUCTION

1. ARABIA BEFORE ISLAM

With the founding of a new religion in the first half of the seventh century, Muḥammad created the pre-conditions for the entrance of the Arabs into world history and the founding of the Islamic world empire. The fact that Arabia had remained outside the mainstream of world history until then had to do with the geographical position and nature of the land: the Arabian peninsula consists for the most part of desert regions and is difficult to reach from the neighbouring cultural centres of Palestine, Syria, and Mesopotamia. The peninsula's climate is determined essentially by the paucity and irregularity of precipitation during the hot season. Periodic summer rains fall only in the higher mountain altitudes of southern Arabia, making self-reliant agriculture possible only through the use of dams. Here, in the first century B.C., separate states developed, whose survival was supported by their role as middlemen in the trade between the Mediterranean region and the Indian Ocean.[1] Trade with the Mediterranean was accomplished in part via the Red Sea and in part on land via the so-called 'incense route' along the east coast of the Red Sea. The significance of these states, whose inhabitants differed from the remaining populace of the peninsula also in their language,[2] had, of course, by the time of Muḥammad already largely diminished. After an intervening period of Ethiopian rule, southern Arabia had by that time become a Persian province.

Other attempts to establish states had occurred in the border regions of the Fertile Crescent.[3] In contrast, the interior desert regions of Arabia offered only poor prospects for the founding of states of longer duration. Here there were settled tribes in separate oases, while the Bedouins lived a partially or fully nomadic existence based on the herding of animals. In general, both among the Bedouins and the settled peoples, there existed a division into tribes and clans, each of which elected a chief. The peculiar conditions of the severe Bedouin way of life often led to conflict and feuding, which however did not result in the total absence of a common culture. Rather, common religious and judicial customs had developed, among which was the significant 'truce' during four months of the year.[4] During this time of 'sacred peace' one could safely undertake the pilgrimage to various religious sites and at the same time conduct trade without being disturbed. Around the religious sites themselves, there was a 'protected area' (*ḥimā*) or 'holy area' (*ḥaram*), in which neither the spilling of blood nor the apprehension of criminals was permitted.

A special beneficiary of these religious and judicial customs was the city of Mecca, which lay on the incense route and lived almost exclusively from trade. From here the inhabitants, who belonged largely to the Quraish tribe, sent out caravans in various directions and thus came into contact with the cultural centres of the north. Inside its walls Mecca sheltered one of the most significant religious sites, the cube-shaped structure of the Ka'ba (cube), in which lies a black meteorite. In addition, various other holy places, which became centres of annual pilgrimage, were to be found in the surroundings of Mecca.

An important basis for the continuation of an encompassing culture was achieved through the formation of a common Arabic literary language. This language probably originated with a single dialect, and only gradually became a kind of common 'standard' language which differed from the daily speech patterns of the Bedouins, and yet has remained to a certain degree in living contact with the dialects. With this elevated speech, which did not pose insurmountable demands in terms of one's ability to differentiate linguistically, Arabic had entered a mature phase, and even if the language of Muhammad deviates from this language in many ways, a certain influence is unmistakable. From the poetry of the pre-Islamic Arabs various individual examples have survived, partly because the language of these poems was later used to gain philological understanding of the Qur'ān.

A frequently recurring theme in these poems is the representation of relentless fate, which one cannot escape but, rather, can only face with patience and manly courage. One finds next to nothing in the poems concerning specific religious concepts of pre-Islamic items, the so-called period of 'ignorance' (*jāhiliyya*). This may be related to the fact that the inherited religious concepts had already lost much of their efficacy by this time. Also, since Muslim descendants of the ancient Arabs essentially showed interest in the pagan religious concepts only to the extent that they were mentioned by Muḥammad, we know little about the details of the pre-Islamic forms of religion in Arabia. Also, the older inscriptions that have survived in various regions in Arabia do not convey a complete picture. Nevertheless, it is certain that a series of masculine and feminine gods were worshipped, sometimes belonging to individual tribes and having their place of residence at specific locations. In Mecca, the worship of the three goddesses al-Lāt, al-'Uzzā, and Manāt,[5] as well as the tribal god Hubal continued until the time of Muḥammad, when these cults were partly incorporated into that of Allāh. Significant in this connection is that a more general term for 'God' had developed already in pre-Islamic times with the word Allāh, which came from *al-ilāh* (the god). This term could at first be applied to the specific tribal god, but also offered the linguistic basis for the concept of a High God. Next to the gods stood the spirits (*jinn*[6]), which were viewed as half 'worldly' and half 'otherworldly' beings and which could enter into direct contact with certain individuals. The soothsayers or seers (*kuhhān*, sing. *kāhin*), who could interpret dreams, make prophecies, and do various other kinds of supernatural things, are said to have been inspired by such spirits. These seers clothed their pronouncements in the form of a rhymed prose called *saj'* and showed themselves through their speech and the content of their statements to be the mouthpieces of their specific spirits. The legitimacy of the pronouncement was strengthened by impressive oaths. Also the poets, who were called 'knowing ones' (*shu'arā'*, sing. *shā'ir*), brought one into contact with the spirits.

The fact that the traditional religious views of the Arabs had already lost some of their vitality by Muḥammad's time may be attributed to a certain inherent destiny. However, one cannot view this development without relating it to the incursions of Judaism and Christianity, which had penetrated into the Arabian interior in spite of all the hostile conditions for propagation. Apparently, after the destruction of Jerusalem by Titus (70 A.D.) and the unsuccessful rebellion of Bar Kochba (135 A.D.), large groups of Jews immigrated to Arabia, where they settled in closed units and remained faithful to the strict monotheism of their religion, despite their adoption of the Arabic language and way of life.

Christianity penetrated into Arabia from the surrounding cultural centres. Syria, Palestine, and Egypt were provinces of Christian Byzantium, and the majority of the populace under Persian rule in Mesopotamia was also Christian. In addition, there was the influence from Ethiopia, which had elevated Monophysite Christianity to the status of a state religion in the fourth century, and had been especially influential in southern Arabia. The influence of Christianity was naturally strongest in the border areas and in the newer, developing Arab states situated there. In Arabia itself there seems to have been only a single Christian community of duration, and that was in the southern part of the land (Najrān). Eremites, who travelled into the desert to evangelize, were important for the spread of the Christian faith. They belonged mostly not to the Byzantine state religion, but were rather members of the Monophysite or Nestorian confessions. Although these missionaries, whose ascetic piety commanded the respect of the heathen Arabs, had few direct successes to show for their work, they had the effect, together with the Jews, that a number of Arabs became inclined toward monotheistic and eschatological concepts. Such ancient Arab seekers of God, who confessed formally to neither Christianity nor Judaism, are designated (in the Qur'ān) with the word *ḥunafā'* (sing. *ḥanīf*), the actual meaning of which is still not completely clear today.[7] In Mecca and Medina, Muḥammad's centres of influence, there were no united Christian communities, but probably single individuals of this faith, who belonged for the most part to the slave class and could rarely show evidence of a higher educational niveau.

2. MUḤAMMAD AND HIS TEACHINGS

Muḥammad, who for the devout Muslim stands as the 'seal' (*khātam*) at the end of a line of prophets and is usually designated simply as 'the Prophet' (*an-nabī*) or 'the messenger of God' (*rasūl Allāh*),[8] was born in Mecca around 570 as the posthumous son of 'Abd Allāh ibn 'Abd al-Muṭṭalib of the clan of Hāshim of the tribe Quraish. Then, when he was six years old, his mother Āmina died, and the orphan, Muḥammad, grew up at first under the guardianship of his grandfather 'Abd al-Muṭṭalib, and then of his father's brother Abū Ṭālib (died 619), whom he is supposed to have accompanied on a business trip to Syria. As a young man Muḥammad entered into the services of the rich merchant widow Khadīja, whom he married when he was approximately twenty-five years old. Although Khadīja was considerably older than Muḥammad, the marriage progressed very happily and was blessed with several children, of whom however only the daughters survived beyond early youth.[9] It appears that Muḥammad did not at first enter into the public life of his native city in any special way.

We know very little concerning the inner development that led Muḥammad, at the age of forty or more, to go before his countrymen with religious revelations. According to the Muslim tradition, the calling occurred suddenly; however, it is known that Muḥammad had occupied himself with religious questions for some time previously, either consciously or unconsciously. The decisive point for Muḥammad's mission as a prophet originated, of course, with the conviction that he was a chosen 'messenger' (*rasūl*) of God who was given responsibility in matters of faith, not only for himself but also for his people. In this awakening lies the actual experience of his calling which occurred once initially and then led to a continuing awareness of mission. Traditional Muslim accounts, according to which an interruption (*fatra*) is supposed to have occurred after the first revelations, show that this consciousness of mission established itself only gradually.

In the Qur'ān itself it is stated that the Qur'ān was sent down in the month of Ramaḍān (Sūra 2:185/181), and also in 'the night of destiny' (Sūra 97:1), and in 'a blessed night' (Sūra 44:3/2).[10] These passages seem to indicate that the first revelations were experienced in this night. The oldest part of the revelation is traditionally held to be Sūra 96:1–5 or Sūra 74:1–7.[11] The accuracy of this view remains unverified, considering, among other things, the possibility that the oldest parts of the revelation have not even survived. In any case, the certainly very old beginning of Sūra 96 contains in the command 'Recite!' (*iqra'*) directed to Muḥammad a leitmotif of the whole revelation, which also at other points proclaims again and again that Muḥammad is not to speak in his own name but rather to repeat something that has been conveyed to him word for word. The revelation thus involves a recitation or something to be recited; and this indeed is the meaning of the probably originally Aramaic word *qur'ān*, which came to signify the revelation in its totality as well as single parts of it. With such a concept concerning the form and content of the revelation, the possibility arose of using parts of the revelation as liturgical texts in the worship service.

Externally, all of Muḥammad's revelations were clothed in the form of rhymed prose (*saj'*), the effect of which may be exemplified here by the following translation of Sūra 93:

> I swear by the splendour of the light,
> And by the silence of the night,
> That the Lord shall never forsake thee,
> Nor in His hatred take thee;
> Truly for thee shall be winning
> Better than all beginning.
> Soon shall the Lord console thee, grief no longer control thee,
> And fear no longer cajole thee.
> Thou wert an orphan boy, yet the Lord found room for thy head,
> When thy feet went astray, were they not to the right path led?
> Did He not find thee poor, yet riches around thee spread?
> Then on the orphan boy, let thy proud foot never tread,
> And never turn away the beggar who asks for bread,
> But of thy Lord's bounty ever let praise be sung and said.[12]

While the distance between rhymes is relatively short in the older parts of the Qur'ān, which are spoken in a lively, passionate style for the most part, it increases gradually in the later parts, and, correspondingly, the style becomes more copious and more tranquil. In his use of rhymed prose Muḥammad was influenced by the ancient Arab soothsayers (*kuhhān*, sing. *kāhin*). The same is true for some conspicuous oaths which are found in the earliest revelations.

The question concerning the basic themes of the earliest revelations has been answered in various ways. Without doubt Muḥammad was at an early stage moved by the belief in a last judgment, where man would be held responsible for his actions. This idea is quite impressively described. Scenes from the end of the world are supposed to convey to the listeners the horrors which the evil-doers will one day experience. After the end of the world comes the resurrection of the dead and the judgment; and then the stay in paradise or hell follows. Later in the Qur'ān, these thoughts are expanded. This is true also for the image of the almighty and benevolent God, which apparently already at an early time co-existed with that of the judging and punishing God. God created heaven and earth as well as all creatures, concerning which the Qur'ān places special emphasis on the creation of man. The process of the creation is not terminated with a single act but rather repeats itself constantly in the genesis and development of new life. This serves also as a sign that God can resurrect the dead. God's goodness reveals itself especially in that he sends rain to the arid land and thus creates nourishment for man. For all this he deserves praise. Man is to surrender himself to God completely (*aslama*, infinitive *islām*) and in so doing becomes a Muslim. His relationship to God corresponds to that of a slave or servant (*'abd*) to his master (*rabb*), who stands by him as a protector or patron (*maulā*[13]), friend (*walī*) or helper (*nāṣir*), on whom one can depend. In contrast to the believer (*mu'min*), is the unbeliever (*kāfir*), a man who does not acknowledge the oneness of God, but rather associates (*ashraka*, participle *mushrik*) other gods with him. It seems that Muḥammad conceived the thought of a single God quite early; however, the strong emphasis upon this concept probably first arose during the confrontation with the pagan Meccans.

Much is to be found even in Muḥammad's earliest revelations that would not have been thinkable without the emanations of Christianity and Judaism. This is even more the case with some of the later revelations. If one assumes, contrary to the traditional Muslim accounts that say otherwise, that the merchant Muḥammad could read and write, it is remarkable that the assimilation of Jewish and Christian thought occurred exclusively by way of mouth. Disregarding the fact that a corresponding literature in translation could hardly have existed, the direct borrowing of aspects of the older texts of revelations would have been irreconcilable with Muḥammad's sense of mission. When the text of the Qur'ān in places resembles the biblical tradition fairly closely, Muḥammad was never so conscious of such a resemblance as to have considered the content of his revelation not to be an inspiration conveyed to him personally.

Yet Muḥammad naturally knew that the Jews and Christians possessed scriptures. From a certain point onwards he held the conviction that the essential contents of these texts were identical with the contents of his revelations and that, with the Qur'ān, God had in a certain sense provided an Arabic equivalent to the other scriptures. The Qur'ān also, like the older books of revelations, is a holy scripture that has its origin in a heavenly archetype (*umm al-kitāb*[14]). Muḥammad reproduces the content of this text faithfully in his revelations.

With this conviction, Muḥammad gained at the same time a special understanding of his own historical situation. History is the history of salvation, and the men of God of the Hebrew Bible, as well as Jesus, are prophets or messengers whom God sent to mankind from time to time in order to inform them of his laws and warn them against disbelief. Several times already in this world, that is, even before the Last Judgment, God has inflicted devastating punishment upon disbelievers, as for example in the story of the Flood. Muḥammad himself is the last in this series of prophets. He repeats and confirms their revelations. So it is understandable if Muḥammad many times saw the older prophets in the light of his own situation. They experienced similar things in their confrontations with the disbelievers as he did with the pagan Arabs. Through this view of things Muḥammad gained courage and hope for God's support.

Although one might assume that Muḥammad would manifest a special interest in the fate of his predecessors, the amount of biblical material reproduced in the Qur'ān, taken on the whole, is relatively small. The material extends in time from the creation story and the expulsion from paradise, and the legends of Cain and Abel,[15] Noah and the Flood, Abraham and his sons, Moses and Aaron, Joseph and his brothers, as well as further references to figures in the Hebrew Bible, to Jesus, of whom Muḥammad knew well only the apocryphal version of his birth and childhood. Taken independently, references to such materials are of varying scope and significance. The Qur'ānic accounts differ in places quite substantially from the biblical accounts and often prove to be very sketchy.[16]

At first, Muḥammad recited his revelations to a small circle of friends and relatives and only later went before a larger public. Among the first adherents to the new faith were Muḥammad's wife Khadīja, his cousin and later son-in-law 'Alī ibn Abī Ṭālib, and Muḥammad's client (*maulā*) and adopted son Zaid ibn Ḥāritha. Along with others, the rich and upright merchant Abū Bakr allied himself with them and stood by Muḥammad faithfully during all attacks and dangers and later became the first successor (*khalīfa*, 'caliph') to Muḥammad, assuming leadership of the community (*umma*[17]) of believers. At first the Meccans did not give Muḥammad's revelations any special attention. This changed, however, when Muḥammad began energetically to oppose polytheism and the worship of idols. The Meccans now had to be concerned about their religious festivals and the profitable business that accompanied them. In spite of increasing opposition, Muḥammad remained steadfast, with the possible exception of a temporary compromise. In his polemic against paganism, he proceeded from the assumption that his opponents recognized the existence of God, but associated other gods with him. In relation to this, Muḥammad pointed to the chaos which, among other things, would follow for the world as a result of such polytheism. Occasionally, the Qur'ān refers to the idols as totally worthless (*bāṭil*), but in general they seem to be regarded as angels, satans, or spirits (*jinn*). But they are clearly not gods.

The Meccans reacted to Muḥammad's revelations first of all by attempting to make him look ridiculous and by rejecting his claim to be a prophet. They portrayed him as one possessed by a spirit (*majnūn*), a sorcerer (*sāḥir*), a wizard (*masḥūr*), a seer of the old order (*kāhin*), and also as a poet (*shā'ir*). Countering these accusations Muḥammad pointed above all to the character of his revelation, which was so structured that no being except God could have produced it. So, the Qur'ān became a miracle (*mu'jiza*[18]) that prohibited Muḥammad's opponents from doubting his mission. The Qur'ān was the 'sign of proof' for Muḥammad in the same sense that the miracles were proofs for Jesus and the other prophets. Muḥammad himself did not perform any other miracles.[19] Just as this line of thought had little impact, the references to the coming judgment and the punishments to be expected seem to have made little impression on the opponents. Muḥammad was challenged to name the exact time of the judgment and was ridiculed. Meanwhile things went further. Means of persecution based on social superiority were put into effect and other types of oppression were employed against the believers. Muḥammad himself was protected by his clan, which had to endure a prolonged boycott as a consequence.

To escape the growing pressure, more than a hundred faithful men and women emigrated to Christian Ethiopia in the year 615. During this time of oppression Muḥammad won the allegiance of a significant individual, 'Umar ibn al-Khaṭṭāb, who subsequently became the second caliph, but in 619 Muḥammad lost his wife and his uncle Abū Ṭālib in death. In about 620 Muḥammad tried in vain to win the tribe of Thaqīf in the neighbouring city aṭ-Ṭā'if to his cause. He was successful, however, with the two chief tribes of Yathrib, a place which through the influence of the Jews who settled there was also called by the originally Aramaic name al-Madīna, 'the city, the court district', which was later construed as 'the city of the Prophet' (*madīnat an-nabī*). These tribes in Medina accepted the obligation for the defensive and offensive protection of Muḥammad and a group of about seventy Meccans who emigrated to Medina by September of 622. The Islamic system of dating stems from this emigration (*hijra*).

Through the stubborn opposition of the Meccans, Muḥammad became firmly convinced that such an obstinacy would be impossible if God himself had not wanted it. God not only allows the disbelievers to wander astray, but actually leads them astray and has determined from the beginning that they shall be damned. Having reached this conviction in predestination while in Mecca, a teaching which of course does not appear uniformly in all parts of the Qur'ān, Muḥammad carried it with him to Medina and reiterated it there.

In contrast to Mecca, which was largely inhabited by a single tribe, Medina had a relatively loose political structure. The inhabitants earned a living through agriculture and the cultivation of palms and were divided into various tribes. In this way they became more and more involved in feuding and thus had reason to look for an arbiter who stood above the factions; this they hoped to find in Muḥammad. Also, in Medina alongside the chief tribes of Aus and Khazraj, who became the 'helpers' (*anṣār*) of the Prophet, three Jewish tribes had been living for a long time. Thus, the concepts of monotheism were not so strange to the Arab populace of this city as they had been to the Meccans. At first Muḥammad encouraged the 'emigrants' (*muhājirūn*) to fraternize with the newly converted 'helpers', and then he issued a communal decree which banned any feuding in the region of Medina and made all inhabitants responsible for the defence of the total community. Muḥammad, as the Messenger of God, was the final judge in all disputes. Through such regulations, which were also valid for the disbelievers and Jews of Medina, the old tribal ordinances were not in fact suspended but probably in actuality were made powerless. Muḥammad came inevitably to assume a political role in Medina, and he so mastered this role that the union of religion and politics in the widest sense became the continuing feature of Islamic communal government.

A severe disappointment met Muḥammad in Medina at the hands of the Jews. It appears that shortly before the emigration Muḥammad had introduced the Friday worship service under the influence of the Jewish Sabbath, without intending a complete cessation of all work. Jewish influences also appeared in fasting and in the form of prayers, which were for a time performed facing in the direction of Jerusalem. When, in spite of all this, the majority of the Jews still did not want to recognize the prophetic mission of Muḥammad, he became convinced that they had falsified the revelation conveyed to them, a claim for which he found support in various examples from biblical stories. Muḥammad remained friendly towards the Christians for a longer time; yet in the course of time he criticized them too, primarily for dogmatic reasons. For example, Muḥammad held the doctrine that Christ was the Son of God to be polytheistic. Also, under Docetic influence, he rejected the fact of Jesus' crucifixion. Yet, the Jews and the Christians, along with the so-called Sabaeans and the Zoroastrians,[20] came to enjoy a special position in later Islam as members of a book-religion (*ahl al-kitāb*, literally 'people of the book'). In general, after payment of a tribute (*jizya*) they could remain true to their faith and were then viewed as wards (*dhimmiyyūn*, sing. *dhimmī*).

Following the confrontation with Judaism, which led to the expulsion, and even the violent elimination, of Medinan Jews, the direction of prayer (*qibla*) was re-oriented towards Mecca rather than Jerusalem. For Muḥammad, who now once again leaned more strongly upon the Arab culture, the relationship of the holy places of Mecca to the earlier salvation-history came to be represented in the claim that the 'Ḥanīf',[21] Abraham, with his son Ishmael, had built the foundation walls of the Ka'ba. Henceforth, Mecca became the central place of worship of Islam, and in this way various heathen rites came to an end. The pilgrimage (*ḥajj*) to Mecca is still today an obligation (*farḍ*) for every Muslim who is able to make such a trip. As further basic duties that the individual must perform, Islam has the confession (*shahāda*) that there is no god except God (Allāh) and that Muḥammad is the Messenger of God, the ritual prayer (*ṣalāt*[22]) to be performed five times daily, fasting (*ṣaum*) during the day in the month of Ramaḍān, and the payment of alms (*zakāt*[23]).

With the change of the *qibla* towards Mecca, a firm political goal was also established at the same time: the conquering of the Holy Places. From the fight for Mecca, which was directed against unbelievers, the idea of the holy war (*jihād*) developed. This became a duty for the community of believers, from which the individual could escape only when there were enough other fighters available.[24] Of course, a desire for booty also came into play in the military undertakings that followed. Muḥammad himself received one-fifth of the booty from each raid.

In the fight against the Meccans and in other campaigns, Muḥammad showed himself to be a patient and resolute politician, who however was not unaware of the dangers posed to him by the 'hypocrites' (*munāfiqūn*) in Medina, who confessed in public to be Muslims but were actually unconverted. Despite many setbacks, in March of 628 in Ḥudaibiya not far from Mecca, Muḥammad was able to conclude a treaty that granted him the right to make the pilgrimage the following year. In January of 630 Mecca fell to him without bloodshed, after he had previously met defeat in a campaign against the Byzantines. The following 'Year of the Deputations' saw many Arab legations in Medina, who declared that their tribes were joining the theocratic community of the Prophet. In February and March of 632 Muḥammad undertook the last pilgrimage and firmly established on this occasion the Islamic calendar, in so far as it proceeds strictly according to the lunar year without inserted months.[25] A little later the Prophet became ill and died on the 7th or 8th of June 632 in Medina in the arms of his old companion Abū Bakr and his daughter 'Ā'isha, whom Muḥammad had married in Medina along with several other women and to whom he was especially close.

In the Christian occident, Muḥammad was considered for a long time merely as a heretic; later, however, he was accused of having been a deceiver who used the revelation solely as means to an end. Further, it was suggested that he had spread his religion with the sword and had shied away neither from breaking treaties nor from assassination. Also, his alleged sensuality and the large number of his marital or semi-marital relationships were held up against him. Although there may be some validity to these allegations, the historian must not concern himself with judging Muḥammad according to the values of Christian morality. One must view him in the context of his times and consider the conditions that prevailed in Arabia at that time. Measured by these standards, Muḥammad fulfilled a thoroughly moral mission. For example, he put limits on polygamy, and from a certain point onwards he restricted his own desire for marriage. He lessened blood revenge and also tried to alleviate the lot of slaves. And the fact that he held fast to the essential content of his mission even in the face of severe and depressing setbacks can be taken as proof of an inner truthfulness.

3. ISLAM AFTER MUḤAMMAD

After the death of Muḥammad, who had given no instructions regarding his succession in the leadership of the community, there was a series of defections, together with the appearance of various other prophets in the Arabian peninsula. Thanks to the determined intervention of the Prophet's Companions, Abū Bakr and 'Umar ibn al-Khaṭṭāb, this dangerous crisis was surmounted. Abū Bakr was appointed as the first successor (*khalīfa*) of the Prophet, and after his death (on 22 August 634), 'Umar assumed the leadership of the community. Of special significance in overcoming this first crisis, which was later followed by others, was the unifying influence which the large military expeditions exerted upon the Arabs. Within a few years the Byzantine provinces of Syria, Palestine, and Egypt, as well as the Persian territory in Mesopotamia, were conquered; and around the middle of the seventh century the Sassanid empire completely ceased to exist. With this and other vast conquests which followed, the external foundations for the development of Islam as a world religion were laid. One may ask whether Muḥammad himself had striven towards such a development. Whereas at first he considered himself to be an envoy to the Arabs, later he gradually went beyond this limitation in his confrontations with the Jews and Christians and in the founding of the theocracy. He came to regard himself as the envoy to all unbelievers, and for this reason one can say that his successors acted completely according to his wishes. On the other hand, the expansion of Islam into a number of areas with ancient cultures had internal repercussions upon Islam which neither Muḥammad nor his first successors could have foreseen. Also, with the exception of the position of their language, the Arabs were unable to retain an enduring position of pre-eminence in the new cultural situation.

After the assassination of 'Umar by a Persian slave (on 23 November 644), arguments regarding the question of succession ensued. 'Uthmān ibn 'Affān, one of the Quraish of the clan of Umayya, was chosen to succeed 'Umar; but opposition arose immediately and led eventually to 'Uthmān's murder by Muslim opponents on 17 June 656 while he was at prayer in Medina. 'Uthmān's successor was the son-in-law and cousin of the Prophet, 'Alī ibn Abī Ṭālib, who, however, was not universally acknowledged and who had an especially energetic opponent in the Umayyad governor of Syria, Mu'āwiya. In the midst of severe internal strife 'Alī was fatally assaulted on 22 January 661. Mu'āwiya then established control of the caliphate, which remained for nearly a century in the hands of relatives of the family of Umayya, who resided in Damascus. The consequences of this struggle lasted for a long time. While the majority of Muslims acknowledged the caliphate of the Umayyads, or at least considered permissible any choice for caliph so long as he was from the tribe of Quraish, the supporters of 'Alī, who obtained recruits mainly from regions of Iraq and Persia, continued to maintain the view that the political and religious leader (*imām*[26]) of the community (*umma*) must be a member of the family of the Prophet. Following 'Alī this could only mean one of his descendants from his marriage to Muḥammad's daughter, Fāṭima. This would include only al-Ḥasan, who for his part renounced claim to the title of caliph, and al-Ḥusain, who met his death on 10 October 680 at Karbala in Iraq in a battle over the caliphate. One refers to the supporters of 'Alī and his family as Shī'ites, from the Arabic expression *shī'at 'Alī* (party of 'Alī). Over against them stand the Sunnites, the 'people of the tradition and the community' (*ahl as-sunna wa-l-jamā'a*[27]).

The Shī'ites split up later into various sects. One small group, called the Zaidites after a great-grandson of 'Alī, Zaid ibn 'Alī (died 740), made no distinction between the descendants of al-Ḥasan and al-Ḥusain regarding the caliphate and, in their theology, stood relatively close to the Sunnites. The majority of the Shī'ites, on the other hand, believed in a hereditary imāmate and in the divine knowledge being transmitted from the father to the oldest son within the descendants of al-Ḥusain. Now when Ismā'īl, the son of the sixth imām, died in 762 before his father, a further schism resulted. A minority, in fact, denied that Ismā'īl had died before his father and saw in him or in his son Muḥammad ibn

Ismā'īl a legitimate imām. Some regarded Ismā'īl, and others his son Muḥammad, as the last and seventh imām, who had gone into seclusion in order to return at the end of time as Mahdī ('rightly guided one'). These Ismā'īlites are called the 'Seveners' (*sab'iyya*). Other followers of Ismā'īl and his son carried the line of imāms further to the descendants of Muḥammad ibn Ismā'īl, who lived in strict seclusion until, with the founder of the Fāṭimid dynasty, 'Ubaid Allāh (died 934), a line of public imāms began again in the tenth century. In addition, other factions developed within the realm of the Ismā'īliyya. In contrast to the Ismā'īlite lines within the Shī'a, who leaned in part very strongly on gnostic speculations and spread their doctrines as secret knowledge, the large group of the 'Twelvers' (*ithnā 'ashariyya*) or Imāmites continued the line of imāms after the death of Ismā'īl with his brother Mūsā al-Kāẓim (died 799), down to 'Alī Muḥammad al-Mahdī, who, as the twelfth imām, is supposed to have been carried away in 874. They also conceded divine inspiration to the imāms and, along with it, authority in doctrinal matters, which they more or less unhesitatingly used for their political goals in reference to contemporary events.

Although the Shī'ites, who today live for the most part in Iran, Iraq and the Yemen, have always been outnumbered by the Sunnites, politically they have played no small role and, from time to time, have ruled regions which are Sunnite today. As opponents of the Umayyad caliphs, they also supported the 'Abbāsid revolutionary movements, then saw themselves deceived of course when the 'Abbāsids, who descended from al-'Abbās, a paternal uncle of Muḥammad, claimed the caliphate for themselves (750). Whereas the Arabs had been the chief supporters of the Umayyads and the most prominent element of the realm, now the Persian element moved more strongly into the forefront. The relocation of the caliphate from Damascus to Baghdad, where court was held in a way that showed many similarities with older Persian customers, can be seen as a symbol of this change.

Under the 'Abbāsids, Islamic culture reached its highest point of development, together with a gradual consolidation, and then fell into a phase of stagnation. Politically, the history of the 'Abbāsids shows many changes in the structure of the empire, which lost much of its internal strength in the course of time. In their rule of the empire the caliphs utilized to an increasing degree Turkish mercenaries who streamed in by way of Persia. In this empire they played a role with stages that are comparable in many respects to those of the Germanic migrations into Rome. The end of this development was the leading position of the Ottoman Turks as they established themselves in the thirteenth and fourteenth centuries. The gradual decay of the Ottoman empire, the intervention of the Western great powers in the Islamic territories, and the counter-movements having more or less nationalistic tendencies bring the development up to the present.

The collection of divine revelations in the Qur'ān serves Muslims as the primary source for their religious doctrines. However, the fact that Muḥammad was not a systematic thinker but rather allowed himself to be guided by inspirations had as a consequence the fact that the Qur'ān provided a general outline of the faith but left certain questions unanswered, or even seemed to answer them in contradictory ways. Therefore, the problem arose of going beyond the Qur'ān to the will and opinions of the Prophet and, when necessary, to approximate his 'custom' (*sunna*). Verification for such a *sunna* is testified to by a number of trustworthy reporters who have transmitted the respective 'traditions' (*aḥādīth*, sing. *ḥadīth*[28]) from the time of the Prophet. In its final form, then, a specific Tradition (*ḥadīth*) consists of a chain of witnesses (*isnād*), which must be without gaps, and the content (*matn*) which is transmitted. The same is also true for Traditions regarding deeds and statements of the Companions of the Prophet, since they were supplementarily consulted.[29] The fact that much of dubious reliability is present within the voluminous material of the Tradition, and in reality does not go back to Muḥammad or his Companions but rather conveys the opinions of the transmitters, did not escape the Muslims and led to the development of a Ḥadīth criticism, which is of course essentially a critique of the transmitters. The material resulting from this criticism is to be found in various collections of the ninth century, which later enjoyed an almost canonical reputation. As a historian, however, one can depend on this material only in a limited sense.

The external form of the Tradition, in conjunction with Muslim accounts, led to the assumption that the transmission was achieved for a long period of time chiefly by way of mouth and that the plans for collections of the Traditions did not begin until about two hundred years after Muḥammad's death. On the other hand, it has recently been shown that the Companions of the Prophet and their immediate successors already possessed written accounts, which were then compiled in notebooks in the first half of the eighth century. The Traditions are now believed to have been arranged according to content since about the middle of the eighth century; then, in the ninth century they were compiled according to the Companions of the Prophet, who are named as competent authorities for the individual Traditions. Of course, there still remain many open questions concerning the transition from verbal to written transmission.

To the extent that the contents of the Tradition refer to the external living conditions of Muḥammad and the development of his community, it became the basis of the *sīra*, or official biography of the Prophet, and the related historical account. Regarding questions of faith, cult, law, and interpretation of the Qur'ān, the Tradition was able to attain normative stature. Of course, by no means are all of the questions answered or unambiguously resolved regarding this material; the Tradition itself often reflects different points of view. With the Tradition as starting point, an intellectual development proceeded, which found its outcome in the various sciences. In this respect, the Shī'ites have gone their own way on many occasions, which can only be mentioned in passing here.

Of concrete significance were especially questions of law (*fiqh*[30]), which had the character of religious law (*sharī'a*) in medieval Islam and encompassed all relationships concerning private and public life as well as matters pertaining to ritual. While earlier it was common to decide doubtful cases in these and in other areas according to individual opinion (*ra'y*[31]), later the so-called 'decision by analogy' (*qiyās*) established itself. This consists in referring back to a rule which was devised for a similar case in order to decide a current case. Finally, the consensus (*ijmā'*) of the scholars also came to be taken as a practical authority concerning decisions of law and faith, proceeding from a Tradition according to which the Prophet said that his community would never agree on a mistake. The issue of consensus was determined negatively by the absence of objections. Often an original consensus, by which the Shī'ites and other sects remained excluded, was considered as continually binding, and any 'independent investigation' (*ijtihād*) based on the Qur'ān and Tradition was regarded as inadmissible. Since about 300 according to Islamic dating the 'gate of *ijtihād*' has been closed, according to prevailing opinion, and complete dependence (*taqlīd*[32]) on the older authorities is to be maintained. For newly arising questions the office of the Muftī (from *aftā*, 'to deliver an opinion, decide a legal question') was created. The Muftī renders a legal judgment (*fatwā*) for each case.

Although complete agreement concerning details of the law and questions of method has never been achieved, four 'legal rites' (*madhāhib*, sing. *madhhab*) have established themselves as predominant. They are attributed to four important teachers of law, namely Abū Ḥanīfa (died 767), Mālik ibn Anas (died 795), ash-Shāfi'ī (died 820), and Aḥmad ibn Ḥanbal (died 855). One speaks, therefore, of Ḥanafites, Mālikites, Shāfi'ites, and Ḥanbalites. These legal rites, which also represent at the same time certain forms of theology, have validity in various regions of the Muslim world, although the choice of the rite is made freely by each Muslim. The adoption (*taqlīd*) of a legal decision from another legal school is also considered permissible. The law is essentially casuistic and categorizes the human actions according to a religious doctrine of duties as: required or necessary (*farḍ*, *wājib*), recommended (*mandūb*, *mustaḥabb*), allowed or permissible (*mubāḥ*, *ḥalāl*, *jā'iz*), objectionable (*makrūh*), and forbidden (*ḥarām*).

Traces of the dogmatic development which led to the formation of an Islamic theology are identifiable at an early date, although our knowledge of the details at many times is incomplete. The struggles described above concerning the successor of 'Uthmān in the caliphate, which led to the formation of the Shī'a, had in fact primarily a political basis, although questions of faith were also involved. A group of believers broke away from 'Alī during the struggle, with the justification that neither he nor his opponent Mu'āwiya possessed the moral qualification to be caliph. According to the view of 'those who went out' (the Khārijites), the most worthy one in the community has a claim to the caliphate, completely independent of his descent. Indeed, faith and works are linked in such a way that anyone who has committed a serious sin is not only a sinner but absolutely an unbeliever. In contrast to this development, which continued to evolve further outside Sunnite Islam, 'those who postpone' (the Murji'ites) leave the decision concerning a man's faith undecided. God alone is to judge and decide. Also the problem of freedom of will was already voiced at an early date. On ethical grounds, the Qadarites represented the view that divine predetermination (*qadar*) is limited to the extent that a man creates his deeds himself. They designated their opponents as 'followers of blind necessity (*jabr*)' (Jabrites).[33] When Christian concepts and, more significantly, philosophical thought of Greek origin were incorporated into the course of further dogmatic discussions, there is much to support the point of view that the motivation for such discussions originated in Islam itself. In the early 'Abbāsid period there was an extensive treatment of various difficult questions, in which especially the so-called Mu'tazila—a name which remains uncertain—took part.

The theology of the Mu'tazilites shows strong rationalistic features, and, correspondingly, the place of the intellect (*'aql*) in determining faith is emphasized. The Mu'tazilites took man's freedom of will so seriously that they limited God's omnipotence through the principle of justice (*'adl*). God is obligated to reward the good and to punish evil. In this world he can, in fact, help (*waffaqa*) man's good strivings to succeed, but man creates his deeds himself. According to the Mu'tazila, the acknowledgment of monotheism (*tauḥīd*) means that the very being of God is one in the strictest sense and that no eternal attributes may be ascribed to him that would supplement this being. What appears to us as an attribute is in reality not different from God himself. The Qur'ān as the speech of God was created in 'time' as an additional attribute and therefore does not exist from eternity, as is many times assumed. Corresponding to this strict interpretation, the Mu'tazilites, who of course do not agree on all details, turn away from any anthropomorphic concepts of God. Therefore, when God's seeing or hearing or God's hands and feet are spoken of in the Qur'ān, or even the idea that man sees God, one must not take this literally but rather must think of it as a kind of metaphor. In their argumentation the Mu'tazilites drew from Greek logic and introduced a speculative dialectic into theology, which is called *kalām* (speech, discussion). The word subsequently became the term used simply to designate theology, and theologians are called *mutakallimūn*.

For many believers, of course, the dialectic of the Mu'tazilites was too subtle and incomprehensible, and so the demand was voiced that one should accept the Qur'ān's portrayal of God as it is, without further asking 'how?' (*bi-lā kaifa*, literally 'without how'). Finally, a kind of synthesis theology became established in Sunnite Islam, as taught by al-Ash'arī (died 935). Al-Ash'arī himself originally came from the Mu'tazila but then moved towards orthodoxy and fought for this standpoint with the methods of dialectic reasoning. According to al-Ash'arī and his school, man does not possess freedom of will in the strict sense. He has merely the capacity to acquire (*kasaba*), through an act of acceptance, the actions that have been created for him. The concept of God must not be made completely void, as most Mu'tazilites have done in a practical sense; yet one must keep imagined concepts of God, which encroach upon the dignity of God, at a distance.

The doctrine of faith and duties which was developed by the theologians and legal experts of Sunnite Islam has in many ways the sober features of a legal piety, which perhaps corresponds to the essential nature of the Arabs but not to other characteristics, which lean towards a warmer, more emotional religiosity. Movements towards an inwardness of religion have been important in Islam to various degrees, not least in the faith of the common people. After theologians had idealized Muḥammad's image and accorded him sinlessness ('*iṣma*[34]) and intercession (*shafā'a*[35]) with God, the people embellished this image with all kinds of added features which made possible a stronger personal devotion to the Prophet. Also in popular Islam there are a number of pious saints (*auliyā'*, sing. *walī*) who, since they are not prophets, did not perform any 'miracles of proof' (*mu'jiza*), but many did, however, perform a number of 'personal miracles' (*karāmāt*, sing. *karāma*).[36]

Islamic mysticism has expressed in various ways the desire to break down the barrier which stands between man and God as a consequence of dogma. Proceeding out of early Islamic thought and ascetic practices, mysticism in its numerous forms was without doubt influenced by Christian, Persian, late Hellenistic, and probably also Buddhist thought. Its Arabic name *at-taṣawwuf* (as well as the alternative name, *aṣ-ṣūfiyya*) refers to the woollen cowl (*ṣūf*) of the older ascetics (*ṣūfī*). The path by means of which the Sūfīs seek to come closer to God, or even to become one with him, consists of pious exercises and contemplations, which are performed singly or together with brothers of the order. To the extent that mysticism still recognizes legal piety at all, this is now a preliminary step along a path of development which in various stages leads deeper and deeper into the secrets of divine knowledge by means of divine enlightenment. Corresponding to this, the mystics seek a deeper, inner meaning of the Qur'ān, beyond the external meaning, as interpreted by the traditional exegesis, sometimes even attempting to grasp this inner sense with clearly cabbalistic methods.

Al-Ghazzālī[37] (died 1111), probably the most significant Islamic thinker, deserves the credit for having made the inward-turning piety of mysticism, in a moderate form, fruitful for Islamic theology. Al-Ghazzālī, after an intense involvement with the thought of traditional Greek philosophy, arrived at the brink of complete scepticism concerning the human intellect and then came to believe that the intuitive certainty of faith alone could convey truth. The law must be fulfilled, but it must be fulfilled with the right intentions and in purity. Al-Ghazzālī employed dialectical methods in presenting his theology and also claimed for himself the right of 'independent investigation' (*ijtihād*) which had been curtailed by the orthodoxy, but he became an opponent of traditional philosophy and did decisive damage to this aspect of Islam. With his theology, which is presented above all in the extensive work *Iḥyā' 'ulūm ad-dīn* ('The Revival of the Religious Sciences'), Muslim dogma of the Middle Ages reached its high point and at the same time found a certain inner conclusion for a long time to come.

This is not to imply, however, that there has been no development within Muslim theology until the most recent past. When al-Ghazzālī linked his theology to various older movements and joined these together in his own way, this did not in any way relieve all of the existing tensions. Furthermore, one could ask whether the events of the dogmatic and practical development corresponded to the actual intentions of Muḥammad. This question was answered negatively above all by the Ḥanbalite theologian Ibn Taimiyya (died 1328). He proposed a reform of Islam through the elimination of all innovations (*bida'*, sing. *bid'a*[38]), which included for him not only the cults of the prophets and saints but also long-established forms of this older theology. His demands were later revived on the Arabian peninsula by Muḥammad ibn 'Abd al-Wahhāb (died 1791) and led significantly to the so-called Wahhābī movement, which has characterized the present kingdom of Saudi Arabia.

A totally new situation for Islam resulted from the encounter with modern, Western culture. Considering the technical superiority of this culture it was inevitable that certain processes of assimilation would be introduced into Islamic countries. Thus, certain states have modelled parts of their legal systems after the European example, proceeding more or less directly from the existing laws of Western states. This led in fact to a reduction of the scope of the traditional, religious law; yet a major concern was that the new, positive law should not force the believers into actions prohibited by the Islamic religion.

The encounter with Western culture resulted, however, not only in processes of assimilation in certain areas but also in a new attitude towards the native culture and history. The resulting reform movements form the so-called Islamic modernism. To begin with, in the preceding century, educated Indian Muslims became convinced that Islamic religion could come to terms completely with the demands of the modern age. They sought to prove this by means of a rationalistic interpretation of Muḥammad's revelation and proceeded in such a manner that they regarded certain rulings as final and timeless, but others, as conditioned by time and thus antiquated. These Muslims adopted a critical attitude towards the older theology since it had made the mistake of treating relative matters as absolutes.

Of special significance for the reform movements in Islam was the activity of Jamāl ad-Dīn al-Afghānī (died 1897), who came from Persia and won an important following specifically in the Egyptian scholar Muḥammad 'Abduh (died 1905) and his pupil Muḥammad Rashīd Riḍā (died 1935). All three viewed the liberation of all Islamic peoples from foreign rule as an essential prerequisite for the revival of Islam; however, they presented varying view-points regarding the question of the formation of a united pan-Islamic dominion or individual, national states.

Whereas the Indian reformers expounded their thoughts largely under the influence of a civilizing belief in progress, the Egyptians were led more by theological considerations, whereby of course they also acknowledged that Islam as a world religion is valid for all times and all cultural circumstances. In order to perceive the true essence of Islam, which has been lost in the course of time, one must free oneself from the blind dependence (*taqlīd*) on traditional interpretation and return to the religion of the forefathers (*salaf*[39]). The Qur'ān and the Tradition are sources, the latter, however, only to the extent that it can be proved to be authentic. These sources must be opened anew through 'independent research' (*ijtihād*). The application of the religious tenets to practical life is guided according to the needs of the common welfare (*maṣlaḥa*) and cannot be presented as binding for all times; indeed, certain rulings are intentionally made only for a definite time. Among these is, for example, polygamy, which must yield in Islam, when conditions demand it. The old system of the legal schools is to be discarded along with the illegitimate innovations (*bida'*). The law is thus fulfilled only when one accepts the ethical demands that stand behind it. In other areas one recognizes here the influence of al-Ghazzālī. But there are also clear similarities with the spiritual fathers of the Wahhābīs as the first 'reformers' of a theological bent. The intellectual discussion within Islam continues. It proceeds in part from quite divergent points of view. The most recent past has shown in the meantime that Islam is not willing to sacrifice its essential identity and that it is beginning to win new strength from this conviction.

4. THE HISTORY OF THE TEXT OF THE QUR'ĀN

Although the Qur'ān is considered by the believing Muslim to be the exact reproduction of a heavenly document, it is for us a literary document in which are collected the revelations which Muḥammad presented as divine inspiration in the period from about 610 to his death. In general there is no doubt about the genuineness of the revelations that have been handed down, even if many details concerning the exact wording are problematic. It may be assumed that the Qur'ān in its present form contains the greatest part of the revelations which actually occurred; on the other hand, one cannot support the claim that it includes all of the revelations. Through the Muslim Tradition, a few shorter pieces are known to us, which are expressly designated as original parts of the revelation, yet are not in the Qur'ān. Of course, the genuineness of such additions is sometimes difficult to prove at all, and sometimes may be proved only in a tentative manner. Above and beyond this, it has been concluded, from a selection of warnings, commands, and elucidations that Muḥammad is supposed to have given on various occasions, that he received still other revelations in addition to the Qur'ān. Perhaps this is why he was sometimes himself in doubt.

Granted that certain revelations, especially some from the

first part of his ministry, may have been forgotten, still Muḥammad seems to have begun quite early the practice of reciting passages from the Qur'ān to his followers for as long as necessary until they knew them by heart. This type of transmission had its model in the propagation of ancient Arabic poetry, since the art of writing was not widespread in pre-Islamic Arabia. On the other hand, his does not preclude the possibility that written copies of poems already existed in pre-Islamic times. Muḥammad also probably dictated connected sections of the revelation to be written down even before his departure for Medina. To a certain degree, things remained in flux, of course, since the Prophet often referred back to older parts of the Qur'ān during his revelations and, when necessary, modified, expanded, or even nullified them.

The need for establishing the written form and collecting the revelations arose, if not before, at least by the time of the death of Muḥammad, when the source of the revelation was exhausted and one had to rely on the material which had been previously given. With this in mind, according to prevailing tradition, the later caliph 'Umar is believed to have commissioned Muḥammad's secretary Zaid ibn Thābit (died ca. 655) to produce a written collection even during the lifetime of Abū Bakr. He then gathered more or less comprehensive documents recorded on various materials and from various sources and referred back to the oral tradition to complete his work. He transferred the content of this collection onto regular 'sheets' (*ṣuḥuf*). After 'Umar's death (644) these are supposed to have come into the possession of his daughter, the Prophet's widow, Ḥafṣa, and to have become the basis of the so-called 'Uthmānic edition of the Qur'ān. The traditional accounts are ambiguous at this point and thus it has been assumed that, in addition to this collection, Zaid perhaps compiled a personal version which then became the basis for the edition named above. However that may be, it is in any case certain that Zaid ibn Thābit played an essential part concerning the production of the Qur'ān in the form in which it appears today.

In addition, in the period of about twenty years between the death of Muḥammad and the compilation of the 'Uthmānic edition of the Qur'ān, there were at least four additional collections or editorial versions which we know of through indirect sources. They go back to: Ubayy ibn Ka'b (died 639 or later) from Medina, a secretary of the Prophet; 'Abd Allāh ibn Mas'ūd (died around

653), a long-time servant of Muḥammad; Abū Mūsā 'Abd Allāh al-Ash'arī (died 662 or later); and Miqdād ibn 'Amr (died 653), one of the earliest adherents to Islam. With the exception of a few additions and omissions, these versions had the same sūras as the 'Uthmānic Qur'ān, although in somewhat different orders.

Complaints that different versions of the Qur'ān were in circulation, which led to disputes and would have seriously endangered the future of Islam, are cited as the impetus for the 'Uthmānic edition of the Qur'ān. Concerning the circumstances under which the 'Uthmānic edition came into being, there are divergent reports. In any case, it is certain that 'Uthmān appointed a commission, to which Zaid ibn Thābit belonged, around 650 or somewhat later in Medina. Probably, the editorial activity of this commission consisted chiefly in copying the text which Zaid ibn Thābit had previously produced. Copies were then made from this Medinan model-codex (*al-imām*) which were then sent to the respective metropolitan centres of Kūfa, Baṣra, and Damascus, and perhaps also to Mecca. During this same period administrative measures were taken to ensure the general acceptance of the 'Uthmānic text. This included especially the destruction of copies of divergent texts. In this way a relatively uniform version of the Qur'ān was established throughout the entire Islamic world, although there has never been a textus receptus which is binding in all details. The Shī'ites use this version also, maintaining of course that individual words and verses or even whole sūras had been added, omitted, or changed in a biased manner. Such accusations, which are tantamount to alleging a conscious falsification to the detriment of 'Alī and his successors, do not stand up under investigation. On the contrary, a so-called 'Sūra of Light', which has been handed down outside the Qur'ān, represents with certainty a Shī'ite falsification.

Reliable information about the fate of the copies of the Qur'ān produced by direction of 'Uthmān is as good as non-existent; however, using traditional Muslim accounts and the later version of the Qur'ān, a number of conclusions can be drawn concerning the state of the 'Uthmānic edition of the Qur'ān. In this edition the material of the revelation is divided into 114 sūras of various lengths which are familiar to us. Smaller units within the sūras are formed by the prose rhymes; these form, essentially, the basis for the division into verses (*āyāt*, sing. *āya*, actually meaning 'sign'[40]), although these were not yet graphically indicated in the 'Uthmānic Qur'ān.

The division of the material into separate sūras seems to have been maintained in general agreement with the older versions. The term *sūra*, the meaning of which is still ambiguous, occurs in the Qur'ān just as the term *āya* does, and it may be assumed that Muhammad himself had already fashioned a number of sūras into final form. This applies especially to the shorter sūras of the older times, which form independent units. On the other hand, the longer sūras are composite, being put together out of various segments of the revelation, usually with the same prose rhyme, and not necessarily agreeing in time, so that in certain circumstances the specific technique of compilation played a role.[41] Having developed in this manner, and being neither chronologically nor contextually similar throughout, the units are arranged in the 'Uthmānic Qur'ān according to the external criterion of length, with the longer sūras coming first, with the exception of the shorter opening sūra. However, to be more exact, one would have to say that this principle of arrangement, which apparently aims not at the number of verses but at the overall length of the sūras, had already existed previously since it is found in earlier versions, and that it has not been applied rigorously. Taking into consideration a few uncertainties, this is roughly the manner in which the present order was established.

The so-called *basmala*, that is, the phrase *bi-smi llāhi r-raḥmāni r-raḥīm* ('in the name of God, the Merciful, the Compassionate'), which is missing only before Sūra 9, serves as an introductory formula and divider for the individual sūras. From the Qur'ānic text (Sūra 27:30) and other sources, it can be established that Muḥammad knew this formula, and therefore it is not improbable that he himself had it placed at the beginning of separate sūras when they were written down. In addition, at the beginning of twenty-nine sūras one finds certain letters or groups of letters, the meaning and significance of which are in dispute. These symbols are considered part of the revelation. The names of the individual sūras were a later supplement to the 'Uthmānic edition of the Qur'ān and were at first probably not titles but rather phrases written at the end. What is involved here is the use of striking words from the beginning or elsewhere in the sūras for the purpose of facilitating reference to specific sūras. Some sūras came to be referred to by more than one name. Muslims usually use these names, which were in general circulation in the second century after the Hijra, when they cite passages of the Qur'ān. Whether or not Muḥammad himself also did so in certain cases must remain uncertain.

Since the 'Uthmānic Qur'ān did not at first have any graphic divisions for the separate verses, there developed later various systems for the division and enumeration of the verses. Means for delineating the verses were already developed in the first century of the Muslim era; however, these were at first used non-uniformly and inconsistently. For the actual division into verses, it was significant, among other things, whether or not the introductory phrase (*basmala*) and the symbols before certain sūras were counted as separate verses or as part of the following contexts. The majority of differences in verse divisions result from differing sub-divisions within the text of the revelation and in the maximum case amount to more than twenty discrepancies in a single sūra. Barely one-fourth of the sūras remain unaffected. While in the West up until the present time, the Qur'ān has usually been quoted according to the inadequate edition by Gustav Flügel (printed in Leipzig since 1834), gradually the so-called Kūfic verse numbering[42] according to the official Cairo edition (printed since 1925) is beginning to establish itself here also.

Although neither a uniformly objective nor a chronological point of view served as a criterion in the arrangement of the material in the 'Uthmānic Qur'ān, the Muslims, too, raised questions concerning the dates and order of the revelations. Not only because it is not unimportant for the understanding of the individual revelations to know when and under what circumstances they occurred, but also because of the Qur'ānic doctrine that certain verses can be abrogated by others, a motive existed for research into the relative chronology. Given the variety of situations and the inner development of many of Muḥammad's views, there occurred in the Qur'ān rulings on various subjects which deviated from one another or even contradicted one another. Now, if one believes that such deviations are inconsistent with the perfection of holy revelation, this problem could be resolved by assuming from the start that a proclaimed decision is made only for a specific period or situation, and that it may later be expanded, refined, or even rescinded by another decision. The application of this principle could not have been so much of a problem for Muḥammad himself as for the later Muslims who in retrospect had to determine the chronological sequence in order to determine which parts of the revelation were abrogating (*nāsikh*) and which abrogated (*mansūkh*).[43]

In determining dates of parts of the Qur'ān, the Muslims referred back to materials of the Tradition, but also employed linguistic and contextual criteria. For a rough, chronological division, the emigration of the Prophet offered a starting point: the distinction between Meccan and Medinan revelations. Beyond this, indexes are to be found in various Traditions in which the sūras are listed according to their chronological order. To a limited extent the internal structure of the sūras has also been taken into consideration. The results of traditional Muslim research are not satisfying, and one must accept the fact that definitive decisions regarding exact dates or even exact chronological order are simply no longer possible. Thus, it is questionable whether even the Prophet himself in his time would have been in a position to indicate the exact sequence of the early Meccan portions of the revelation. Taking these circumstances into account, it may be said that the results presented by Theodor Nöldeke in 1860 in his *Geschichte des Qorāns*, and afterwards by the revisers of this history, are definitive in their major features and also in many details. Nöldeke, following Gustav Weil, distinguished between three Meccan periods of the revelation and one Medinan period. As belonging to the first periods, he counted the 'older, more passionate'; to the third, the 'later, approaching more the Medinan sūras or parts of sūras'; and the second he regarded as a transitional group. Richard Bell, in his English translation of the Qur'ān (1937–9), went even further than Nöldeke. He attempted to isolate the individual segments of the sūras and, within the individual sūras, to arrange the segments chronologically and in relation to one another, as they might have once existed separately, or as they were attached to other materials, in the early period of Islam.[44]

Although not all traces of earlier variants were eliminated with the 'Uthmānic edition of the Qur'ān, this edition still provided a relatively complete uniformity in opposition to deviating variants. However, the 'Uthmānic text was in no sense unambiguous in all details. The Muslims of older times already knew that this text was not absolutely perfect and without mistakes. In addition, the different copies sent to the metropolitan centres of the realm exhibited certain deviations from one another. When once again a number of different variants developed on the basis of the 'Uthmānic Qur'ān, this was due less to scribal errors than to the inadequacy of the contemporary Arabic script. This script derived from the Aramaic and consisted of a number of consonantal symbols with which the vowels could be expressed either not at all or only inadequately. Besides this, certain consonantal symbols had become so similar to each other in the course of their development that diacritical marks were needed to distinguish between them. The origin of these marks goes back to pre-Islamic times; however, they were used only sparingly in the older Qur'ānic manuscripts which for the most part can be positively dated only since the fourth century after the Hijra. Additional symbols for vowels and other sounds are believed to have been developed already in the first century after the Hijra, but they became established only gradually in the orthography of the Qur'ān. Moreover, the copies of the Qur'ān of the first four centuries were written in a style which differed from the usual cursive Arabic. This concise script is called Kūfic.

Considering these inadequacies of older Qur'ānic orthography, it is understandable that the oral tradition remained authoritative at first for individual reading, and only later became fixed in writing. In the first century after the Hijra there developed in Medina, Mecca, Kufa, Baṣra, and Damascus schools of Qur'ānic readers (*qurrā'*, sing. *qāri'*), whose supporters were for the most part active in various areas of Qur'ānic study. While the choice between several possible variants (*qirā'āt*, sing. *qirā'a*) was made at first according to free judgment (*ra'y*[45]) or also according to Traditions, later the variants of the teachers became more influential and a choice was made from among them. Criteria for the reliability of a variant were correct language, assurance based on a Tradition, and the view of the majority, that is, a kind of consensus of the majority. The result was similar to that of law: one did not propagate the exclusivity of a single form of the text, but rather permitted different 'canonical' groups of variants to be valid[46] alongside each other, the knowledge of which belonged to the armour of the Qur'ānic teacher. A saying of Muḥammad was referred to in this connection, according to which God's word had been revealed to the Prophet himself in several ways.

There are different types of variants. In part what is involved are differing interpretations of the consonantal text and, in part, different ways of adding the vowels. But, in addition, there were also interpretive supplements (*ziyādāt*, sing. *ziyāda*[47]), which perhaps were intended as emendations, or perhaps merely as explanatory glosses. Also, the substitution of one word by a better-known synonym was done relatively freely in earlier times. It is understandable that in choosing a variant, the obvious tendency was often to achieve a theologically unobjectionable text.[48]

The history of the text of the Qur'ān shows many interesting connections with linguistics and other branches of the sciences. Endeavours to fix the Qur'ānic text have been of decisive significance for the rise and development of such sciences. Here, also, the crucial phase occurred in the first centuries of Islam. When one evaluates the variants from a philological point of view today, one must say that their large quantity stands in no relationship to their significance in the task of reconstructing the text.

Although the existence of the Qur'ān was known in the West at an early time, it was not until 1143 that Peter the Venerable of Cluny had an initial, complete Western translation into Latin made by the Englishman Robertus Ketenensis. This translation, which was printed exactly 400 years later, was followed by others which were all motivated more or less by missionary and apologetic considerations. Critical studies of the Qur'ān did not come until the period of historical critical research. Among the translations available today, in addition to the English by Richard Bell, above all should be mentioned the French by Régis Blachère (1949–51) and the German by Rudi Paret (1962).[49] Paret's translation is of special significance because, for the first time, it considers very seriously the idea that one must interpret the Qur'ān from within itself as an historical document. Paret therefore searched through the whole Qur'ān systematically for parallel points and interpreted these alongside the material from Muslim commentaries. Regarding its form, the translation is clothed in an easily flowing conversational style in such a way that the intention of the text, above and beyond the linguistic expression, is made clear to the reader by means of parenthetical remarks of various lengths.

5. MUSLIM EXEGESIS OF THE QUR'ĀN

Muḥammad himself declared the Qur'ān to be an inimitable work.[50] The subsequent justification of the resulting miraculous character (*i'jāz*) of the work as conceived by Muslim theology encompasses various points of view, which in part are directly derived from statements from the Qur'ān. Thus, it has been asserted that the Qur'ān contains a number of correct prophecies of future events, that in spite of its considerable volume it exhibits not a single contradiction, and that in its own way it anticipates a number of scientific discoveries. According to Muslim tradition, Muḥammad was uneducated (*ummī*)[51] in the sense that he could neither read nor write, and his compatriots also had no knowledge of the earlier story of salvation; thus, he must have experienced this through a superhuman source. The language of the Qur'ān is also considered to be more or less uniformly unsurpassable. Although opinions concerning the validity and significance of these views, and concerning particulars, may vary, the fundamental existence of the miraculous nature of the Qur'ān has not been doubted by Muslim exegetes. It is obvious that an exegesis which views the Qur'ān with such presuppositions must proceed in many instances in a different direction from that of the historical-critical analysis of the Qur'ānic text, as practised by Western researchers.

According to the Muslim view, the Qur'ān, as God's speech, cannot be translated but, rather, must be studied in its original Arabic form. In fact, there have been isolated attempts to make the Qur'ān accessible in other languages of the Islamic cultural world; yet by far the greatest extent of Muslim literature on the Qur'ān is written in the Arabic language, although the authors of this literature were often of non-Arab origin. Arabic also played a leading role in other areas of Islamic literature, which would have been unthinkable without the significance of the Arabic Qur'ān.

If one conceives of Qur'ānic interpretation in the widest sense, it can be said that it is as old as the revelations of Muḥammad, for every listener had to interpret the revealed text for himself. Problems regarding the form of the text lead directly or indirectly into the realm of exegesis. As long as the Prophet was living, one could turn to him when in doubt and provide an occasion for him to give an explanation or even an elaborating revelation. Thus, it is statements by the Prophet and testimonies of his Companions that stand in the centre of the older exegesis, as religious Tradition (*ḥadīth*) handed down from the first generation of Islam. When, according to Muslim reports, in the early period of Islam doubts were occasionally expressed about an interpretation of the Qur'ān, these were probably directed primarily towards an all too speculative interpretation based on subjective opinion (*ra'y*[52]), and not towards an interpretation based on knowledge (*'ilm*[53]) of authoritative religious Tradition. Meanwhile, the material of the exegetic Tradition grew very soon in such a manner and to such an extent that considerable doubt has often existed concerning its authenticity. In addition, contradictions occur among the statements of various Companions of the Prophet, and even within accounts attributed to the same person. Already in the early exegesis, there was a tendency to interpret as many of the ambiguous passages (*mubhamāt*) of the Qur'ān as possible, if not all of them, including even unimportant details. In this connection there has been talk of fabrications and falsifications; yet one must also consider the possibility of unconscious appropriation and mutual misunderstanding. For the later Muslim exegetes, the contradictions resolve themselves in part by the fact that differing interpretations are accepted alongside one another as admissible and correct.

The scholarly exegesis which developed on the basis of the religious Tradition is designated by the term *tafsīr*[54] (explanation, interpretation). Originally, the word *ta'wīl* was equated with this term; then an additional 'inner' meaning, to be grasped through intuition, came to be accepted by the mystics and others, alongside the 'external' meaning of the Qur'ān as represented by the Tradition-bound exegesis. Within these circles the term *tafsīr* became limited to the 'external' interpretation of the Qur'ān, while the term *ta'wīl* came to designate the 'inner' or allegorical interpretation.

The chief authority on the exegetical Ḥadīth was Muḥammad's cousin 'Abd Allāh ibn 'Abbās (also 'ibn al-'Abbās', died around 688), who is therefore held to be the actual originator of traditional exegesis. Although at the time of the death of the Prophet, Ibn 'Abbās was at most fifteen years old, the Prophet is supposed to have conveyed to him a whole series of interpretations. More trustworthy are reports which state that Ibn 'Abbās asked for information from the Prophet's older Companions and also Jewish converts as well as people of the book religions (*ahl al-kitāb*). When warnings are issued against seeking information from Jews and Christians, this in itself indicates indirectly some of the various tendencies which were at work in the formation of the traditional exegesis. Regarding doubtful linguistic expressions, Ibn 'Abbās is supposed to have referred back to illustrative material from ancient Arabic poetry, thus opening up to the exegesis of the Qur'ān a methodological principle which was subsequently extended to other areas of the old language. It may be that reference to such illustrations (*shawāhid*, sing. *shāhid*) in order to explain word meanings actually does go back to Ibn 'Abbās or his pupils, for the introduction of extensive grammatical investigations into Qur'ānic exegesis is of an early origin; however, these investigations presuppose an extent of linguistic reflection that was hardly extant before the middle of the second century after the Hijra.

According to Muslim tradition, Ibn 'Abbās wrote his own commentary on the Qur'ān. While up to the present time, the correctness of this report has been doubted, recently a few indications to the contrary have been brought forward. In fact, Ibn 'Abbās probably aided his memory with extensive notes, which were then utilized by his pupils. Among the immediate pupils of Ibn 'Abbās, who in part wrote independent works and in part conveyed the material again to their pupils, were Sa'īd ibn Jubair (died 713), Mujāhid ibn Jabr (died 721), 'Ikrima (died 724), 'Aṭā' ibn Abī Rabāḥ (died 732), and Abū Ṣāliḥ Bādhām (died 719). Other exegetes of the first century of the Muslim era who stand in more or less direct relationship to the school of Ibn 'Abbās are Ḥasan al-Baṣrī (died 728), Qatāda ibn Di'āma (died 730 or later), and Muḥammad ibn Ka'b al-Quraẓī (died 735 or later), a man of Jewish origin. Striking is the fact that most of the exegetes of this and the following generations came from the slave class. Of the commentaries of the first century after the Hijra, which do not yet exhibit the unified character of the later works of exegesis, some survive in more recent versions, and others can be at least partly reconstructed on the basis of what has been handed down in the Tradition. Sunnite Islam has been the primary supporter of traditional Qur'ānic exegesis; however, the Shī'ites too have used in part the inherited material and, in particular, have also recognized Ibn 'Abbās as an authority on doctrine.

The exegetical traditions (*aḥādīth*) also found entrance into the canonical collections of the Tradition. Thus one finds, for instance, in the famous Tradition collection of al-Bukhārī (died 870) and in that of at-Tirmidhī (died 892) separate chapters on Qur'ānic interpretation, which of course do not nearly cover all of the material. Alongside the more or less compilatory Qur'ānic interpretation of the early commentaries, after the second century following the Hijra, purely philological works on the Qur'ān appear, which were subsequently continued at a later time. Examples of works of this kind, which have a certain usefulness even today, are the books *Gharīb al-qur'ān* ('Obscure Aspects of the Qur'ān'), and *Mushkil al-qur'ān* ('Doubtful Aspects of the Qur'ān') by Ibn Qutaiba (died 889).

Traditional exegesis found a high point, and at the same time a certain finality, in the activity of Abū Ja'far Muḥammad aṭ-Ṭabarī (died 923), a scholar of Persian ancestry whose strength lay above all in his industrious collecting. In addition to various theological and judicial works, Ṭabarī wrote an extensive history of the world and a voluminous commentary on the Qur'ān, which filled thirty volumes in its first edition of 1903. The value of Ṭabarī's commentary on the Qur'ān, which bears the title *Jāmi' al-bayān fī tafsīr al-qur'ān* ('Collection of Explanations for the Interpretation of the Qur'ān'), usually cited simply as *Tafsīr* or 'Commentary',[55] lies above all in his bringing together the entire breadth of the material of traditional exegesis extant in his time, and in so doing providing a valuable source for modern historical-critical research.

Ṭabarī seeks to cite the material of the standard authorities as fully as possible for every verse or verse segment of the Qur'ān and notes also even insignificant variants.[56] He meticulously reproduces the exact chain of authorities (*isnād*) and therefore many times places side by side the same content (*matn*) received through different chains of authorities. He openly expresses reservations concerning the validity of certain material and does not spare the pupils of Ibn 'Abbās. Ṭabarī also deals with the different variants, although he treats these in a special monograph, which unfortunately has not survived. To illustrate the text, Ṭabarī provides simplifying paraphrases and lexical references including numerous poems. There are also grammatical discussions which refer back to matters of Baṣran and Kūfan linguistics. Together with the compilation of the more or less dissimilar material of older exegesis, Ṭabarī often gives his own judgment on the validity or probability of an interpretation. The purpose, plan and presuppositions of the work are presented in a valuable introduction.

In his interpretation, Ṭabarī espouses the principle that above all the clear, immediately visible meaning should be definitive and that one may deviate from this only if convincing reasons can be shown.[57] Ṭabarī is averse to laborious justifications of unimportant details.[58] Thus, when he places himself consciously on the foundation of inherited concepts of doctrine and seeks to find a moderate middle view, this does not prevent him from occasionally deriving dogmatic, practical applications from the material or from arguing extensively against certain doctrinal views. In this sense, for example, he disagrees strongly with the metaphorical interpretation of the Mu'tazilites and their dogmatic conclusions or presuppositions. Since the size of Ṭabarī's Qur'ānic commentary placed limits on its distribution, a series of excerpts was later compiled, but other works were also incorporated with them.

If, in the first centuries after Ṭabarī, no significant commentary on the Qur'ān was written within Sunnite Islam, this in no way implies that stagnation occurred in Qur'ānic exegesis. Interpretation of the Qur'ān is not limited to the comprehensive works of the commentaries, but rather is to be found everywhere in theological, judicial, and other works. In this sense, the above-mentioned work by al-Ghazzālī on 'The Revival of the Religious Sciences' also contains a number of basic reflections concerning exegesis and a large number of individual interpretations. As a supplement to the systematic exegesis one must also consult introductions to the Qur'ān, works on 'the occasions of revelation' (*asbāb an-nuzūl*), legal decisions regarding Qur'ānic passages, and similar writings, since in later times these continued to be written. On the other hand, it is evident that more significant commentaries on the Qur'ān often mark the end or the high point of a theological development. To a certain extent this applies also to the commentary *Al-kashshāf 'an ḥaqā'iq ghawāmiḍ at-tanzīl* ('The Unveiler of the Realities of the Secrets of Revelation'), which the Persian-Arab scholar Abū l-Qāsim Maḥmūd ibn 'Umar az-Zamakhsharī (died 1144) completed in the year 1134. Zamakhsharī's commentary contains a quintessence of Mu'tazilite doctrine and, in this respect, stands much more intentionally on a specifically dogmatic foundation than does Tabarī's commentary. On the whole, Zamakhsharī's commentary is characterized more strongly by the personal view-point and talent of the author, who exhibits his perceptiveness and his brilliant knowledge of language in a number of grammatical, lexical, and philological writings, while bringing these to bear again and again in his commentary on the Qur'ān.

If Zamakhsharī's commentary has had considerably less influence than Ṭabarī's commentary, in spite of an enrichment in the linguistic-rhetorical sphere, this is due primarily to the fact that Zamakhsharī omits parts of the traditional material and only includes what he himself considers important; moreover, regarding the chain of authorities, he is satisfied with abbreviated references to origin or omits them altogether. Instead, he brings to the text the characteristic themes of Mu'tazilite theology, for example, the doctrine of the unity and justness of God, the rejection of anthropomorphic concepts, the recognition of the intellect as the source of understanding of faith, and the advancement of freedom of will. In this connection belongs also the rejection of unnatural, superstitious concepts. Through the pronounced dogmatization of the exegesis, Zamakhsharī's commentary loses some of its significance for historical-critical Qur'ānic research, however, it gains significance through its perceptive linguistic details.

For Zamakhsharī himself there is no doubt that his type of interpretation is rooted directly in the Qur'ān, even though it is stated in the revelation itself that certain verses of the Qur'ān are clearly and unambiguously formulated while others are ambiguous.[59] The existence of such ambiguous verses is of positive value to the extent that it offers an occasion for deeper reflection which may clarify these verses in the light of the unambiguous ones. Zamakhsharī sees the path to such a clarification in linguistic-rhetorical analysis, by means of which questionable passages can be viewed in the right light when specific uses of language are demonstrated in them. If in so doing it is shown that the revelation is clothed in a garment of pictures and metaphors, therein lies a proof of the incomparable nature and miraculous character of the diction of the Qur'ān. Without doubt this view contains a *petitio principii*; yet Zamakhsharī eliminated this for himself through his artful handling of the philological method.

Even as orthodox theologians of the Sunna have been unable to escape the original achievements represented by Zamakhsharī's Qur'ānic interpretation, so also in the Shī'ite realm, certain influences can be demonstrated. Orthodox Islam has 'thoroughly pillaged' Zamakhsharī's commentary, but has either opposed or avoided the dogmatic inferences of his work. Thus the Alexandrian legal scholar Aḥmad ibn Muḥammad ibn Manṣūr ibn al-Munayyir (died 1284) wrote polemical glosses in opposition to Zamakhsharī's commentary. Strongly dependent on Zamakhsharī but also drawn from other sources is the commentary *Anwār at-tanzīl wa-asrār at-ta'wīl* ('The Lights of Revelation and the Secrets of the Interpretation'), by 'Abd Allāh ibn 'Umar al-Baiḍāwī (died 1286 or later), who likewise came from Persia. Baiḍāwī condensed the commentary of Zamakhsharī in places, but on the other hand also expanded it with details from other sources and assimilated it to orthodox theology. Baiḍāwī's commentary has been considered the best by the Sunnite theologians, although in no area is it complete nor does it represent such an original achievement as Zamakhsharī's commentary.

The Persian-Arab theologian and religious philosopher Fakhr ad-Dīn ar-Rāzī (died 1209) also opposed Mu'tazilite interpretation of the Qur'ān in his unfinished monumental commentary *Mafātīḥ al-ghaib* ('The Keys to the Hidden'), which was expanded by his pupils. In this work, which likewise is linked to Zamakhsharī and which is also called simply *At-tafsīr al-kabīr* ('The Great Commentary') because of its volume, Rāzī reaches out widely and brings into consideration philosophical thought, along with material from all other possible areas. Compared with Baiḍāwī's commentary, Rāzī's work differs not only in volume but also in many independent suggestions for solutions embedded in painstaking arguments. Certainly from the Muslim side, the objection has been raised, and not entirely unjustly, that Rāzī goes far beyond the realm of actual exegesis and in many instances misses the purpose.

Although productive Sunnite exegesis of the Qur'ān reached a certain conclusion with Rāzī's commentary, among the later interpreters should be mentioned above all the Egyptian Jalāl ad-Dīn as-Suyūṭī (died 1505), who re-establishes ties with the older traditional exegesis in a comprehensive, monumental work, well known in its condensed version. Still widely used is the clearly arranged compendium which Suyūṭī's teacher Jalāl ad-Dīn al-Maḥallī (died 1459) began and Suyūṭī completed. This book, which contains an ongoing paraphrase of the text of the Qur'ān with linguistic explanations, material from the Tradition, and variants, is called, after its authors, *Tafsīr al-jalālain* ('Commentary of the Two Jalāls'). In the form of his work *Al-itqān fī 'ulūm at-tafsīr* ('The Perfection in the Sciences of Exegesis'), Suyūṭī created an introduction to Qur'ānic exegesis that is rich in material.

From the standpoint of historical-critical research, it must be said that although the material in the above-mentioned commentaries is still of value today, it requires critical evaluation. Since the commentaries, in the final analysis, all rest on the assumption of the perfection of the Qur'ān as divine speech, they are inclined to relate difficult or corrupted passages to contexts which are unambiguous in meaning and wherever possible to concrete 'occasions of revelation' (*asbāb an-nuzūl*). In so doing they overlook the fact that what is involved in many instances are repetitions or quite general statements. In contrast to the tendency to interpret too minutely, there is also the opposite tendency among some scholars, a group to which Zamakhsharī also belongs to a certain degree, although he brings to his work on the Qur'ān view-points of a later historical situation much more than many other interpreters.

Much more clearly and more immediately evident than in the works just discussed is the tendency in Shī'ite circles to read their own concepts of belief into the Qur'ān. If one considers especially the more extreme tendencies of the Imāmites and Ismā'īlites among the Shī'ites, they do in fact recognize in general the major part of the religious Tradition (*ḥadīth*), but sanction and supplement it by means of the doctrinal authority of the imāms, who are supposed to have inherited the 'genuine' Qur'ān edited by 'Alī. Thus, when exegetical Traditions arose which tended towards momentary concerns, Shī'ite exegesis bore a much stronger and more direct relationship to post-Qur'ānic events because of the historical ties of the imāms, than did Sunnite exegesis. Thus, whenever positive statements in the Qur'ān were indefinite (*mubham*) or general enough, they were interpreted as referring to 'Alī, the imāms, and their community; and negative statements were interpreted as referring to their opponents, as well as to the first three caliphs. Of course, it is a matter of considerable doubt whether the later Shī'ites in such cases have always rightfully claimed the authority of the imāms. Nevertheless, various imāms were active in a literary manner in the field of Qur'ānic exegesis, among whom was the fifth imām, Muḥammad al-Bāqir, 'The Researcher' (died 733 or somewhat later), who is credited with a Qur'ānic commentary of his own.

Shī'ite exegesis reached a relatively completed form in the third to the fourth centuries after the Hijra. To be mentioned here, first of all, in the Imāmite realm is the concise commentary *Tafsīr al-qur'ān* by 'Alī ibn Ibrāhīm al-Qummī (died 939), a work which has retained its significance up to the present time alongside the larger commentary *Majma' al-bayān li-'ulūm al-qur'ān* ('Collection of Explanations of the Qur'ānic Sciences') by Abū 'Alī al-Faḍl aṭ-Ṭabarsī (died 1153 or later). Moreover, the Shī'ites were frequently active later in the area of Qur'ānic exegesis, without of course altering in any basic way the orientation that they had adopted. An example of a later commentary that synthesizes the material of the Tradition of earlier times is the work *Aṣ-ṣāfī fī tafsīr al-qur'ān* ('The Pure in the Interpretation of the Qur'ān'), written by the Imāmite scholar Muḥammad Murtaḍā al-Kāshī (died around 1505).

It is understandable that Shī'ite exegetes choose from among the Qur'ānic variants those favourable for their theology. They go still further, however, and undertake changes and expansions of the 'Uthmānic text, which they claim to derive from the 'genuine' Qur'ān of the imāms. Shī'ite exegesis also differs from traditional Sunnite exegesis in that it favours allegorical interpretation and finds in certain circumstances a many-faceted meaning for Qur'ānic passages, with deeper and deeper significance. Here the Shī'ites come in contact with the mystics. In a certain sense, Shī'ite interpretation of the Qur'ān is typical of sectarian Qur'ānic interpretation on the whole, as for instance is seen among the Khārijites and others. Often it reveals features of a malicious factional fanaticism. Of course, when Western Qur'ānic scholars portray Shī'ite exegesis as a 'miserable web of lies and stupidities',[60] this is not entirely correct. For, in the first place, one cannot dismiss all Shī'ite interpreters as stupid, and, secondly, the Shī'ites felt themselves for the most part to be fully conscious of the truth when they sought to legitimatize their hope for a transformation of the prevailing conditions by using the Qur'ān as their basis. The fact that there were, indeed, differences of level is obvious when, for example, the fragmentary Ismā'īlite Qur'ānic commentary *Mizāj at-tasnīm*[61] ('The Diluted Water of Tasnīm') by the Yemenite 'Caller' (*dā'ī*) Ḍiyā' ad-Dīn Ismā'īl ibn Hibat Allāh (died 1760), with its esoteric language, is compared with the incomparably more valuable works of Kāshī.

If Shī'ite commentaries on the Qur'ān are only in exceptional cases of definite value for historical-critical Qur'ānic research, this is also true for the exegesis of the mystics. In addition to the material of the Tradition, which is recognized as the basis for the 'external interpretation' (*tafsīr*), at least in moderate circles of mysticism, an additional source was at their disposal in the form of intuition, or a similar capacity to grasp meaning, by means of which they could come to decisions concerning this material and place an 'inner interpretation' (*ta'wīl*) alongside the external. According to the mystics, the legitimacy for their kind of Qur'ānic exegesis is based on alleged statements of the Prophet or his Companions, although the religious Tradition offers on the whole only a few points of departure in this direction.

Regarding its age, the same thing can be said of mystical interpretation of the Qur'ān as of the other tendencies within Qur'ānic exegesis: it is as old as its intellectual foundations. The oldest completed exegetical work appears to originate in the third century after the Hijra. By this time, the foundations for an Islamic neo-Platonism had already been laid through translations, as we find later in a distinct form in the so-called Pure Brothers (*ikhwān aṣ-ṣafā'*) of Baṣra in their grandly planned encyclopedia (between 950 and 1000). Mysticism is indeed not to be equated with this neo-Platonism, but exhibits many parallels to it in its striving towards purification of the soul and immersion in God, as well as in its intellectual models. Even al-Ghazzālī put in a good word for the mystical interpretation of the Qur'ān, although he was against excessive allegorization and a complete break with positive religion. A striking appearance within Muslim mysticism is the Andalusian Muḥyī' ad-Dīn ibn al-'Arabī (died 1240), who was completely filled with his mission and imagined himself to be in direct contact with the Prophet and the angels, and even with God himself. The system of his esoteric mysticism, which was permeated with pantheistic features, was described by him primarily in the so-called 'Meccan Contributions' (*Al-futūḥāt al-makkiyya*) and in the work *Fuṣūṣ al-ḥikam* ('Ring-stones of Wisdom'). Here also he shows himself to be knowledgeable concerning philosophical thought. Characteristic of the Qur'ānic exegesis of mysticism, even if not typical in all details, is the Tafsīr attributed to Ibn al-'Arabī, but in reality probably originating from his follower 'Abd ar-Razzāq al-Kāshānī (or, 'al-Qāshānī'; died 1330 or later).

Ibn al-'Arabī and his followers are representatives of 'parallel exegesis'. They maintain the character of reality of the external meaning; yet at the same time they see 'allusions' (*ishārāt*) in this, which are important to understand. Since the external meaning is generally treated exhaustively in the traditional exegesis, not much of an effort is made towards an interpretation in this direction.

In uncovering the inner meaning, a distinction is made between actual allegorical interpretation (*ta'wīl*) and the 'uncovering of parallels' (*taṭbīq*). While real allegory aims at a directly implied inner meaning, as for example in the case of the Flood and Noah's Ark, where the sea is related to matter and the saving ship to divine law, this approach of using parallels sees actual events and lawful decisions as symbols for the spiritual world. For example, when the Ethiopian king, Abraha, in the sūra called 'The Elephant' (105), marches towards the holy place of Mecca with elephants in order to destroy it, to begin with, nothing more is meant by this other than a concrete historical event which has its own inherent meaning. One can, however, view the king, Abraha, as the symbol for the dark Ethiopian soul that wants to annihilate the sanctuary of the heart. Underlying this is the idea that sensual forms stand dependent upon a more general spiritual world into which one may 'cross over'.

On the whole Ibn al-'Arabī and his school are representatives of a moderate mysticism to the extent that they do not lose sight of the religious law in favour of a hazily defined piety. In fact, although they are acquainted with a type of letter and script symbolism, cabbalistic methods do not play the same role here as with other mystics or with many Shī'ites.

Although the mystics had at their disposal an additional source for exegesis in the form of intuition and the tradition which grew out of it in the course of time, Muslim philosophers also had such a source in Greek thought, which was being translated into Arabic, and in the resultant activation of the intellect (*'aql*). Of course, the Greek cultural heritage available to the Muslims was not uniform in itself but rather included the thought of various schools, whose significance was variously emphasized by different Muslim philosophers. As a consequence, the attitude towards the phenomenon and content of revelation varied. Although the philosophers showed little interest in a systematic interpretation of the Qur'ān, they could not ignore the central phenomenon of 'believing' and had to relate this to 'knowing'. Obviously, in so doing they made reference to Qur'ānic passages which served their purpose, and they interpreted more or less comprehensive parts of the revelation in this respect. In its extreme form this endeavour led to the conclusion, by Ibn Rushd (Averroes, died 1198), that philosophical thought contains the absolute truth and therefore also the absolute religion. Revealed religion is likewise a derivative of absolute religion, representing it in a historically-bound form appropriate to the general spiritual situation. Therefore there is no inner contradiction between revelation and science; on the contrary, a number of passages in the Qur'ān itself can be cited which encourage intellectual activity and, therefore, anticipate Muslim philosophy. Even if medieval Islam, which for scholastic philosophy meant practically nothing more than one intellectual movement among many, did not adopt these thoughts on a broad scale, still the modernists, when faced by the penetration of Western science, saw themselves encountering similar questions as the medieval philosophers faced.

Most significant, among the modernists, for Qur'ānic exegesis is Muḥammad 'Abduh, who was born in 1849 in a village in Lower Egypt and attended al-Azhar University in Cairo. In Cairo he came into contact with Jamāl ad-Dīn al-Afghānī, earned the teaching certificate at al-Azhar University, and was then active as a history teacher for a short time at the Dār al-'Ulūm, a normal school in Cairo. At the instigation of the British, he was forced to leave Egypt with Jamāl ad-Dīn and was able to return to al-Azhar University only after a long exile. When he died in 1905 he was Muftī of the Lands of the Nile. Muḥammad 'Abduh presented his Qur'ānic exegesis in the form of lectures at al-Azhar University and within the scope of legal opinions (*fatāwā*, sing. *fatwā*) which were published separately at first in the periodical, *Al-manār* ('The Lighthouse'), and later, with the author's approval, were compiled, revised from a literary view-point, and continued by Muḥammad 'Abduh's pupil, Muḥammad Rashīd Riḍā. The work thus created, *Tafsīr al-qur'ān al-ḥakīm* ('Commentary on the Wise Qur'ān'), which deals only with the first ten sūras of the Qur'ān and which soon found a wide distribution in the Islamic world, cannot deny its origin in the language of the lecture. In its diction it is rather verbose and exhibits a considerable amount of repetition, conditioned partly of course by its character as a compilation.

Although Muḥammad 'Abduh had the opportunity in Europe for direct contact with Western science, one has the impression that he often understood it differently from what was meant by its intellectual fathers. Muḥammad 'Abduh adheres to the doctrine of the uniqueness of the Qur'ān; he even tries to provide new proofs for the inimitability of the Qur'ān. Regarding the special significance of the Qur'ān for the understanding of history, Muḥammad 'Abduh maintained that even though, on the one hand, the Qur'ān reflects specific historical situations and contains statements which can be understood only within the context of such situations, on the other hand, it is a textbook for history, in which the thought is expressed for the first time that a regularity prevails in social development. In this sense Muḥammad 'Abduh seeks and finds absolute statements behind relative determinations. Thus, for example, polygamy is generally supposed to have been best suited to the social structure in the time of Muḥammad, in terms of the welfare of the whole and of the individual.[62] Muḥammad 'Abduh, however, maintains that the Qur'ān itself teaches in an unequivocal way that monogamy and also the moral equality of male and female are the 'final condition' to be striven for. This 'final condition' is then achieved through monogamy, when the greatest possible good for all is present and morality is not affected, in the sense of being socially weaker through extra-marital relationships and dangers.

For Muḥammad 'Abduh there is no contradiction between the doctrines of the intellect and the revelation of the Qur'ān. This applies also in regard to modern natural science. The Qur'ān, to be sure, is not a book that was revealed solely for the explanation of scientific facts; therefore, one should not be offended when, for the glorification of God, specific historically-conditioned images and expressions have been employed which do not correspond directly with modern natural science. Also, one cannot expect the Qur'ān to anticipate, in a constructive manner, the discoveries of modern technology. Yet in a direct manner the Qur'ān unambiguously encourages intellectual involvement with nature and in no way contains explicitly anti-intellectual or superstitious doctrines. This principle occasionally leads Muḥammad 'Abduh to offer baffling interpretations, which, of course, should not be overemphasized in relation to the total structure of his exposition. For instance, he draws the conclusion, from the ancient Arab view incorporated into the Qur'ān that the spirits or jinn cause sickness, that these beings are to be understood as the microscopic germs of modern medicine.

All in all, then, it follows that the modern interpretation of the Qur'ān, which found additional representatives after Muḥammad 'Abduh, is also the explication of a specific theology and world-view based on the Qur'ān, and not an historical-critical investigation of the Qur'ān. Also, it would be fundamentally unfair to expect a renunciation of faith to the point of an inner surrender. On the other hand, the time will come when Muslim theology will be forced to incorporate within itself not only the intellectual foundations of modern technology and civilization, but also the results of Western studies of the Qur'ān. These must eventually receive their place within the realm of Muslim orthodoxy. In the Christian realm, historical studies have also led to the contemplation of inherited religious beliefs, and here also men have found in the sacred scripture again and again whatever dogmas they have sought to find.

I

REVELATION

1. Methods of divine inspiration

Zamakhsharī on Sūra 42:51/50f.

> *It belongs not to any mortal that God should speak to him, except by inspiration* (waḥy), *or from behind a veil, or that He should send a messenger and he reveal whatsoever He will, by His leave; surely He is All-high, All-wise.*

It belongs not to any mortal: it does not fall to any man's lot *that God should speak to him, except* in three ways:

(1) With the help of suggestion, that is, inspiration (*ilhām*), and lowering into the heart, or visions, just as God inspired the mother of Moses[1] and commanded Abraham[2] through inspiration to sacrifice his son. From Mujāhid (it is related) that God inspired David by placing the Psalms in his heart....

(2) In such a way that God causes man to hear his words, which he creates within someone's body,[3] without the hearer seeing the one who speaks to him—since in his essence God is invisible. God's expression *from behind a veil* is a simile. That is, (he speaks to him) like a king who is hidden behind a veil when he converses with one of his eminent people, so that this person hears his voice but cannot see his figure. In the same manner God spoke with Moses[4] and speaks with the angels.

(3) In such a way that God sends an angel to man as a messenger to inspire him, just as the prophets were inspired, with the exception of Moses.

Some say: *by inspiration*, just as God inspired the messengers through the mediation of angels. *Or that He should send a messenger*, that is, a prophet, just as God spoke to the peoples of the prophets in their own languages....

It is related: The Jews said to the Prophet: 'If you are a prophet, can you not speak with God and see him like Moses did? We will not believe in you until you do this.' To this the Prophet answered: 'Moses did not see God.' Then the present verse came down.

From 'Ā'isha (is related): Whoever asserts that Muḥammad saw his Lord perpetrates an evil slander against God. Then she said: 'Have you not heard your Lord say...' and recited this verse.

Surely He is All-high above the qualities of his creatures and *All-wise*: he causes his acts to occur according to the requisites of wisdom and speaks sometimes indirectly and sometimes directly, (that is,) it might be through inspiration or through speech.

Baiḍāwī on Sūra 4:164/162

And messengers (rusul) *We have already told thee of before, and messengers We have not told thee of; and unto Moses God spoke directly.*

... This is the most direct form of inspiration, as Moses was unique among the messengers.[5] However, God granted (to the Prophet) Muḥammad priority, in that he gave to him something which counterbalanced (everything) that he had given to the (earlier) messengers.

Zamakhsharī on the same passage

... The supposition that the (word) 'speak' (*kallama*) here is derived from the word 'wound' (*kalm*), and that the meaning may thus be that God wounded Moses with nails of affliction and claws of temptation, belongs to the category of (heretical) innovations (*bida*') in the interpretation of this verse.

2. Gabriel as the mediator of revelation

Baiḍāwī on Sūra 2:97f./91f.

Say: 'Whoever is an enemy to Gabriel—he it was that brought down the Qur'ān[6] *upon thy heart by the leave of God, confirming what was before it, and for a guidance and good tidings to the believers.*

Whoever is an enemy to God and His angels and His messengers, and Gabriel, and Michael—surely God is an enemy to the unbelievers.'

(These verses) came down regarding (Rabbi) 'Abd Allāh ibn Ṣūriyā', who once asked the Messenger of God: 'Who usually brings down the revelation?' When the latter answered: 'Gabriel', the former replied: 'He is our enemy. He appeared hostile against us repeatedly, the worst time being when he sent down (the proclamation) to our prophet that Nebuchadnezzar would destroy Jerusalem.[7] Then we sent out someone to slay Nebuchadnezzar. When he found him in Babylon, Gabriel sent him away from Nebuchadnezzar saying: "If your God has commanded him to destroy you, he will give you no power over him. But if no such command exists, why do you seek to kill him?"'

Some say: One day 'Umar went to the synagogue of the Jews and asked them about Gabriel. They answered: 'He is our enemy who has given to Muḥammad information regarding our revealed knowledge which is kept secret. He makes use of every baseness and persecution. On the other hand, Michael retains it with fruitfulness and tranquillity.' When 'Umar then asked which positions they had with God, the Jews said: 'Gabriel stands on the right and Michael on the left side of God. Between them, however, enmity prevails.' Then 'Umar replied: 'If this is the case with them, as you say, then they are not enemies. You are indeed as disbelieving as the asses.[8] Whoever is an enemy of one of them is an enemy of God.' When 'Umar returned to Muḥammad he found that Gabriel had been there before him with the present revelation. Muḥammad said, however: 'God has agreed with you, 'Umar!' . . .

Upon thy heart: the heart is that which first receives the revelation and comprehends and preserves it. It would have been correct if Muḥammad had said 'upon my heart'. However, this wording came as the verbatim report of God's statement, as if it said: 'Say what I have stated!' . . .

3. The receiving of divine inspiration

Zamakhsharī on Sūra 75:16–19

Move not thy tongue with it to hasten it;

Ours it is to gather it, and to recite it.
So, when We recite it, follow thou its recitation.
Then Ours it is to explain it.

With it: that is, with the Qur'ān. As the Messenger of God received the revelation with immediate understanding, he attempted to snatch the recitation away from Gabriel and did not have patience until the latter had finished it. For he wanted to commit the revelation to memory quickly and he feared that some of it might slip away from him. Thereupon he was commanded to listen to Gabriel and devote his heart and hearing to him so that he could transmit his relevation to him completely. Then Muḥammad could devote himself to a thorough study until he was certain of it. The meaning is (therefore): Do not move your tongue with the recitation of the revelation so long as Gabriel is still reciting it!

To hasten it: so that you receive the Qur'ān quickly and it does not slip away from you. Now God established the prohibition against excessive haste when he said: *Ours it is to gather it, and to recite it* in your heart, and to confirm his recitation through your tongue.

So, when We recite it: Here God places Gabriel's recitation on the same level as his own. And the recitation (*al-qirā'a*) is the Qur'ān.

Follow thou its recitation: follow Gabriel in it and do not enter into competition with him! Have no fear that the recitation will not be preserved. We guarantee it.

Then Ours it is to explain it: when any of its meanings cause difficulties for you. It is as if Muḥammad was in too great a hurry with the memorization, as well as with the questions regarding the meaning, as is seen when someone shows much thirst for knowledge. Accordingly it is said (in the Qur'ān): 'And hasten not with the Qur'ān before its revelation is accomplished unto thee! And say: "O my Lord, increase me in knowledge."' (Sūra 20:114/113).

4. The occasion of the earliest proclamation

Zamakhsharī on Sūra 2:185/181

[*Prescribed for you is the Fast during*] *the month of Ramaḍān, wherein the Qur'ān was sent down to be a guidance to the people, and clear signs of the guidance and the salvation. So let those of you, who are present at the month, fast it; and if any of you be sick, or if he be on a journey, then a number of other days; God desires ease for you, and desires not hardship for you; and that you fulfil the number, and magnify God that He has guided you, and haply you will be thankful.*

(The word) *ramaḍān*[9] is the verbal noun (*maṣdar*) from *ramaḍa* (to burn); specifically, this word comes from *ramḍā'* (glowing ground). The word 'month' was then added and it became a proper name. . . .

If one now asks why the month of Ramaḍān was designated as the time of fasting, then I answer: The fast during this month is an old form of worship. The time of fasting was given this name to some extent because one 'becomes inflamed' by the heat of hunger and the suffering of austerity during this month. Likewise, this month has also been designated as *nātiq* (agitated), since it agitates the men, that is, it afflicts them in a burdensome manner because of its severity. Some say: The names of the months are understood to have been taken from the old language; and the months were named according to the times in which they fell. Thus, this month fell during the days of burning heat. . . .

Wherein the Qur'ān was sent down: . . . The meaning of these words is: wherein it began to be sent down. This occurred during the Night of Destiny (*lailat al-qadr*[10]). Some say that it may have been sent down as a whole to the lowest heaven (on this night) and then piece by piece to the earth. Others say (that the meaning is): '(the month of Ramaḍān) on account of which the Qur'ān was sent down', yet God's word reads: 'Prescribed for you is the Fast, even as it was prescribed for certain days for those who were before you—perhaps you will be godfearing' (Sūra 2:183f./179f.). . . . From the Prophet (the following) is related: The sheets (*ṣuḥuf*) of Abraham came down in the first night of Ramaḍān; the Torah[11] had been sent down after a lapse of six nights, the Gospel after a lapse of thirteen, and the Qur'ān after a lapse of twenty-four (nights of Ramaḍān). . . .

Zamakhsharī on Sūra 44:2/1–5/4

By the clear Book (al-kitāb al-mubīn).
We have sent it down in a blessed night.

We have warned (man thereby).
In this night[12] *every wise bidding is determined*
as a bidding from Us.

... *The clear Book* is the Qur'ān and the *blessed night* is the Night of Destiny (*lailat al-qadr*). Some say that it refers to the middle night of (the month) Sha'bān[13] and that it has four names: blessed night (*lailat mubāraka*), the night of innocence (*lailat al-barā'a*), the night of contract (*lailat aṣ-ṣakk*), and the night of mercy (*lailat ar-raḥma*). Others say that between it and the Night of Destiny lie forty nights. Concerning its designation as the 'night of innocence' and the 'night of contract', some say: When the agent collects the land tax he writes out a receipt for the people concerned. It is the same with God, who issues to his believing servants in this night the document of innocence.

(Further) it is said that this night may be distinguished in particular through five characteristics:

(1) In it every wise concern and the purity of worship are separated out (*tafrīq*). The Messenger of God has said: Whoever prays one hundred *raka'āt* (sing. *rak'a*)[14] in this night, God will send to him one hundred angels—thirty to announce paradise to him, thirty to protect him from the punishment of the fire, thirty to keep the accidents of this world, and ten the cunning of Satan, far from him.

(2) Mercy comes down in this night. The Prophet has said: God shows mercy to my (religious) community (*umma*) in this night in ways as numerous as the sheep of the Banū Kalb[15] have hair.

(3) Forgiveness occurs in this night. The Prophet has said: In this night God forgives all Muslims with the exception of the soothsayer (*kāhin*), the sorcerer (*sāḥir*), the one who is quarrelsome, the one who drinks (intoxicating beverages), the one who is disobedient to his parents, and the one who is unchaste.

(4) In this night the Messenger of God received the complete measure of his intercession (*shafā'a*). That is, in the night of the 13th of Sha'bān he prayed for his (religious) community and was given one-third of his intercession. Then, on the night of the 14th he prayed and received (altogether) two-thirds of his intercession. Finally, on the night of the 15th he prayed and (therewith) received all of his intercession, (for all of his community) except those who flee from God like obstinate camels (who bolt and run away).

(5) On the basis of the custom of God (which regulates the occurrence of natural phenomena), in this night the water of the well of Zamzam (in Mecca) used to increase noticeably.

Most Traditions say (however) that the 'blessed night' is the Night of Destiny, for God's word says: 'Behold, We sent it (that is, the Qur'ān) on the Night of Destiny' (Sūra 97:1). Moreover, his words *In this night every wise bidding is determined* correspond with his words: 'In it the angels and the Spirit descend, by the leave of their Lord, upon every command' (Sūra 97:4). Finally, this also corresponds with his words: 'The month of Ramaḍān, wherein the Qur'ān was sent down' (Sūra 2:185/181[16]). According to most Traditions the Night of Destiny falls during the month of Ramaḍān.

If one asks what the sending down of the Qur'ān in this night means, then I answer: It is said that God sent it down in its entirety from the seventh heaven[17] to the lowest heaven. Then he commanded excellent writers to transcribe it in the Night of Destiny. Gabriel (then) sent it down piece by piece to the Messenger of God....

(The words) *every wise bidding is determined* mean: Every wise bidding is discharged and fixed in writing, that is, the means of sustenance for God's servants, the times of their deaths, and also all their affairs from this night on until the future life. Some have said that the copying of these things from the well-preserved (heavenly) tablet (*lauḥ maḥfūẓ*[18]) began in the Night of Innocence and was completed in the Night of Destiny. The copy containing the means of sustenance will be handed over by Michael, and that with the wars will be handed over by Gabriel, along with the copy with the earthquakes, flashes of lightning, and the sinking in (of the earth). The copy with the deeds (of men) will be handed over by Ismā'īl to the lord of the lowest heaven, one of the mighty angels. And that copy with the accidents is preserved by the Angel of Death.

5. *The celestial original text*

Zamakhsharī on Sūra 43:2/1–4/3

By the clear Book,
behold, We have made it an Arabic Qur'ān.
Perhaps you will understand!
And behold, it[19] *is with Us in the* umm al-kitāb,
sublime indeed, wise.

By the clear Book (*al-kitāb mubīn*): I swear by the clear Book, that is, by the Qur'ān. God has placed his words *We have made it an Arabic Qur'ān* as the final clause of the oath (as is shown by the contents). This is a beautiful and unique oath because both the vow and the concern which is being sworn by the oath go well together and are both derived from the same area (*wādī*). . . .

Clear (*mubīn*): clear for those to whom the Book was sent down, since it is (composed) in their language and style. Some say (also that it may mean): evident to those who reflect upon it. Others say that *mubīn* refers to that which distinguishes (*abāna*[20]) the paths of true guidance from those of error, and that which separates out (*abāna*) what the community (*umma*) needs in the religious areas (*abwāb*). . . .

Perhaps (*la'alla*): (This word) conveys the meaning of a wish, because there is a correlation between the significance of this term and that of hoping.[21] (Consequently) it means: We have created the Book in Arabic and not in other languages because we had the wish that the Arabs would understand it and not be able to say: 'If only the verses (*āyāt*) of the Book had been set forth clearly!' . . .

The original text is the tablet[22] corresponding to the words of God: 'No, it is a glorious Qur'ān, in a well-preserved tablet' (Sūra 85:21f.). This writing is designated *umm al-kitāb* (mother of the book[23]) because it represents the original (*aṣl*) in which the (individual) books are preserved. They are taken from it for copying. It is of elevated rank among the books, for it is contrasted from them as a matchless miracle (*mu'jiz*[24]). . . .

6. *Concerning the concept* Qur'ān

Baiḍāwī on Sūra 12:1–3

Alif Lam Ra
These are the signs of the clear Book.
We have sent it down as an Arabic Qur'ān;
perhaps you will understand.
We will relate to thee the fairest of stories in that we have
revealed to thee this Qur'ān, though before it thou wast one of
the heedless.

These are the signs (or 'verses', āyāt) of the clear Book: (the word) 'these' (*tilka*) is a demonstrative pronoun referring to the (following) verses of the sūra. By the 'book' here is meant the sūra itself. The meaning is (therefore): These verses constitute the verses of the sūra which presents itself clearly as inimitability (*iʿjāz*); or, as that of which the meanings are clear; or, as that which makes clear (*bayyana*) to anyone who reflects upon it that it comes from God; or, that which makes clear to the Jews what they have asked about. It is related that the learned men among the Jews said to the leaders of the polytheists: 'Ask Muḥammad why the family of Jacob moved from Syria to Egypt, and (ask him) about the story of Joseph!' Thereupon this sūra was sent down....[25]

As an Arabic Qur'ān: This part (of the whole revelation) is designated here as *qur'ān*. In origin this word is a generic noun which is applicable to the whole (of the class) as well as to a part of it. It then became predominant as a proper name referring to the whole....

Perhaps you will understand: This is the reason why God sent down the Book in this (Arabic) form. The meaning is (therefore): We have sent it down to you as something that is composed in your own language or can be recited in your own language, so that you will be able to understand it and grasp its meanings; or, that you will employ your intellect and (through it) discover that the account, out of the mouth of a man like this who could not produce a (comparable) account (previously),[26] is a matchless miracle (*muʿjiz*) which one can conceive only as having been revealed.

We will relate to thee the fairest of stories: (We will relate) in the best manner, since the account is given in the finest linguistic form; or, (we will relate) the best account (regarding its content), since it contains marvellous things, wisdom, signs (*āyāt*), and admonitions....

Though before it thou wast one of the heedless of this account, since it had never come to your mind, nor had you ever heard of it. It is for this reason that the account must have been inspired.

7. *The faithful rendering of the revelation*

Zamakhsharī on Sūra 22:52/51

We have never sent any messenger or prophet before thee, but that Satan cast into his fancy, when he was fancying; but God annuls what Satan casts, then God confirms His signs—surely God is All-knowing, All-wise.

We have never sent any messenger or prophet: (This) is a clear proof that a distinction exists between a messenger (*rasūl*) and a prophet (*nabī*). (It is related) from the Prophet that he was asked about the prophets, whereupon he said: '(There are) one hundred and twenty-four thousand.' When he was then asked how many messengers there were among these, he answered: 'The great host of three hundred and thirteen.'[27] The distinction between the two is that a messenger is one of the prophets to whom, together with the verification miracle (*mu'jiza*), the Book is sent down. A prophet, on the other hand, who is not a messenger, is one to whom no book is sent down, but who was commanded only to restrain people on the basis of the earlier revealed law (*sharī'a*).

The occasion of the sending down of the present verse is the following: As the members of the tribe of the Messenger of God turned away from him and took their stand against him, and as his relatives also opposed him and refused to be guided by what he brought to them, then, as a result of the extreme exasperation concerning their estrangement and as a result of the eager desire and longing that they be converted to Islam, the Messenger of God sheltered the wish that nothing would come down to him that could make them shy away. Perhaps he should have been able to use that for the purpose of converting thcm and causing them to be dissuaded from their error and obstinacy. Now this wish continued in him until the sūra called 'The Star' (that is, Sūra 53) came down. At that time he found himself with this wish in his heart regarding the members of his tribe. Then he began to recite, and when he came to God's words 'and Manāt, the third, the other' (Sūra 53:20), Satan substituted something in accordance with the wish which the Messenger of God had sheltered, that is, he whispered something to him which would enable the Messenger to announce his wish. In an inadvertent and misleading manner, his tongue hurried on ahead of him, so that he said: 'These (goddesses[28] are the) exalted cranes. Their intercession (with God) is to be hoped for.' . . . Yet, the Messenger of God was not clear at this point until the protection (of God) (*'iṣma*) reached him and he then became attentive again.

Some say that Gabriel drew his attention to it, or that Satan himself spoke those words and brought them to the people's hearing. As soon as the Messenger of God prostrated (for prayer) at the end of the sūra, all who were present did it with him and felt pleased (that is, the unbelievers felt pleased that their goddesses had been accepted as intercessors with God). That the possibility to do this would be given to Satan was a temptation and God's test through which the 'hypocrites' (*munāfiqūn*) should increase in grievance and injury, but the believers should increase in enlightenment and assurance.

The meaning (of this verse) is: The messengers and prophets before you were subject to the same custom. If they wished for certain things like you did, God placed Satan in the way as an obstacle to introduce something into their wishes just as he did with you. God wished thereby to test those who were around the prophets. It is incumbent upon God according to his will to put his servants to the test through (various) kinds of trials and temptations, in order to multiply the reward for those who are steadfast and to increase the punishment for those who waver.

Some say that (the word) 'to wish' (*tamannā*) here has the meaning 'to recite' (*qara'a*) and cite (the following verse as an example):

> He recited (*tamannā*) the Book of God at the beginning of the
> night, just like David conveniently recited (*tamannā*) the Psalms.

Also, (the expression) 'his wish' (*umnīyatuhu*) is synonymous with 'his recitation' (*qirā'atuhu*).

Others say that (the expression) 'these exalted cranes' refers to the angels. That is, they are the ones who intercede with God, and not the idols (*aṣnām*). . . .

But God annuls what Satan casts: that is, God causes it to disappear and destroys it.

8. Clarity and ambiguity in the revelation

Zamakhsharī on Sūra 3:7/5

> *It is He who sent down upon thee the Book* (al-kitāb), *wherein are clear verses that are the* umm al-kitāb, *and others that are ambiguous. As for those in whose hearts is swerving, they follow the ambiguous part, desiring dissension, and desiring its interpretation. But none knows its interpretation, except God and those firmly rooted in knowledge. They say: 'We believe in it; all is from our Lord'; yet none remembers, but men of understanding.*

Clear verses (*āyāt muḥkamāt*): those whose diction and meaning are clear to the extent that they are preserved from the possibility of various interpretations and from ambiguity.[29] *And others that are ambiguous* (*mutashābihāt*): those (verses) which are ambiguous in that they allow various interpretations.

That are the umm al-kitāb: that is, the origin (*aṣl*) of the book, since the ambiguous (verses) are to be traced back to it and must be reconciled with it.[30] Examples[31] of it are the following: 'The vision reaches Him not, but He reaches the vision; He is the All-subtle, the All-aware' (Sūra 6:103).[32] 'Upon that day faces shall be radiant, gazing upon their Lord' (Sūra 75:22f.).[33] 'And whenever they commit an indecency they say: "We found our fathers practising it, and God has commanded us to do it." Say: "God does not command indecency! What, do you say concerning God such things as you know not?"' (Sūra 7:28/27).[34] 'And when We desire to destroy a city, We command its men who live at ease, and they commit ungodliness therein. Then the word is realized against it, and We destroy it utterly' (Sūra 17:16/17). If one then asks whether the (meaning of the) entire Qur'ān might be (clearly) determined, (I answer that) men would (then) depend on it since it would be so easily accessible, and (in this manner) turn away from what they lack—research and meditation through reflection and inference. If they did that, then they would neglect the way by which alone one can reach the knowledge of God and his unity (*tauḥīd*). (Further grounds are the following): In the ambiguous verses lie a trial and a separation between those who stand firm in the truth and those who waver regarding it. And great advantages, including the noble sciences and the profit of higher orders, are given by God, when the scholars stimulate each other and develop their natural abilities, arriving at the meanings of the ambiguous verses and reconciling these with the (clearly) determined verses. Further, if the believer is firmly convinced that no disagreement or contradiction can exist in God's words (that is, the Qur'ān), and then he notices something that in outward appearance seems to be a contradiction, and he then zealously seeks some means by which he can bring it into harmony, treating it according to a uniform principle, and he reflects upon it, coming to an insight about himself and other things and being inspired by God, and (in this manner) he acquires a clear perception of the harmony which exists between the ambiguous verses and the (clearly) determined verses, then, his certainty regarding the contents of his conviction and the intensity of his certitude increase.

As for those in whose hearts is swerving: These are the people who introduce (heretical) innovations (*bida*ʿ, sing. *bidʿa*).

They follow the ambiguous part: They confine themselves to the ambiguous verses, which (on the one hand) allow the point of view of the (heretical) innovations without harmonizing them with the (clearly) determined verses. However (on the other hand), (these verses) also allow an interpretation which agrees with the views of the orthodox (*ahl al-ḥaqq*).

Desiring dissension: seeking to lead the people into error and divert them from their religion.

And desiring its interpretation: and seeking the interpretation they wanted it to have.

And none knows its interpretation, except God and those firmly rooted in knowledge: Only God and his servants who have a firmly-rooted knowledge, that is, those who are firm in knowledge and thereby 'bite with the sharp molar', come to the correct interpretation, according to which one must necessarily explain it. Some people place a pause after *except God* and begin a new sentence with *and those firmly rooted in knowledge ... say*. They interpret the ambiguous verses as those concerning which God reserves to himself alone the knowledge of their meaning and the cognizance of the wisdom present in them, as is the case with the exact number of the executioners of hell and similar questions.[35] The first (interpretation regarding where the sentence should end) is correct. A new statement begins with *they say*, setting forth the situation of those who have a firmly-rooted knowledge, namely, in the following sense: These who know the meaning say *we believe in it*, that is, in the ambiguous verses.[36]

All is from our Lord: that is, every ambiguous verse and every (clearly) determined verse is from him. Or, not only the ambiguous verses in the Book but also the (clearly) determined verses are from God, the Wise One, in whose words there is no contradiction and in whose Book there is no discrepancy. ...

9. The abrogation of revelations

Zamakhsharī on Sūra 2:106/100

And for whatever verse We abrogate or cast into oblivion,

We bring a better (verse) or one which is equal to it. Knowest thou not that God is powerful over everything?

(As the occasion of the revelation of this verse) the following is related: The unbelievers had challenged the cancelling of verses and said: 'Look at Muḥammad, how he commands his companions to do something, and then forbids it to them and commands the opposite. He says something today and retracts it tomorrow.' Thereupon this verse came down.

Instead of *whatever verse We abrogate (nansakh)*, some read: whatever verse we allow (or cause) to be abrogated (*nunsikh*). . . .

Or cast into oblivion (nansa'hā): Some read: or cause to be cast into oblivion (*nunsihā*[37] or *nunassihā*). Others read this as if addressed specifically to the Messenger of God: or when you forget it (*tansahā*). Still others read: or when you are caused to forget it (*tunsahā*). 'Abd Allāh (ibn 'Abbās) read: when we cause you to forget (*nunsika*) or to abrogate it (*nansakhhā*). And Ḥudhaifa read: when we abrogate (*nansakh*) a verse or cause you to forget it (*nunsikahā*).

To abrogate a verse means that God removes (*azāla*) it by putting another in its place. To cause a verse to be abrogated means that God gives the command that it be abrogated; that is, he commands Gabriel to set forth the verse as abrogated by announcing its cancellation. Deferring a verse means that God sets it aside (with the proclamation) and causes it to disappear without a substitute. To cause a verse to be cast into oblivion means that it no longer is preserved in the heart. The following is the meaning: Every verse is made to vanish whenever the well-being (*maṣlaḥa*) (of the community) requires that it be eliminated—either on the basis of the wording or the virtue of what is right, or on the basis of both of these reasons together, either with or without a substitute.

We bring a verse which is *better* for the servants (of God), that is, a verse through which one gains a greater benefit, *or one which is equal to it* in this respect.

God is powerful over everything: he is able to produce what is good, but also something which is even better or something which is equal in its goodness to the first.

Baiḍāwī on the same passage

. . . This verse proves the possibility of abrogation and of the postponement of revelation, since it concerns the rule (*aṣl*) that (the Arabic word) *in* ('if') (as the particle of the real conditional sentence), in addition to the contents of the verse, refers to the (entire) range of possible things. It is true that the introduction of regulations and the sending down of verses for the benefit of the servants (of God) and the perfecting of their souls result from divine goodness and mercy. However, regarding different ages and persons there are distinctions in this, just as there are different means of livelihood. What can be of use in one age can be harmful in another.

Those who refuse any abrogation which does not have (an equal) substitute, or one that is more important, use the present verse as an argument for rejecting the abrogation of (any part of) the Book (of God) by means of (statements in) the *sunna*, since that which abrogates is what is brought as a substitute, and this is not the purpose of the *sunna*. This stands on weak grounds, however, since sometimes what is lacking in a certain regulation, or in one that is more important, is more useful (*aṣlaḥ*) (than the existing one), and the abrogation also can be made discernible from another quarter. Also, the *sunna* is indeed something which God has brought. Since here the speech is among the best or most important, it is not meant in any way other than what is provided in its external wording.

The Mu'tazilites based on (the doctrine of abrogation) their view that the Qur'ān originated (in time, and thus has not existed from eternity), since the properties of change and diversity are connected with it as necessary properties (implied in its essence). To this I reply that both of these properties belong among the non-essential (linguistic-material) aspects, to which is attached the meaning (*ma'nā*) (of the Qur'ān) which exists in itself from eternity.

10. Revelation, divination, and poetry

Baiḍāwī on Sūra 69:40–43

It is the speech of a noble messenger.
It is not the speech of a poet
(little do you believe)
nor the speech of a soothsayer
(little do you remember).
A sending down from the Lord
of all Being.

. . . The Qur'ān *is the speech of a noble messenger*, who delivers it from God. Since the 'messenger' does not speak for himself . . . either Muḥammad or Gabriel is referred to here.

Unlike the denial of the soothsayer character (of the Qur'ān) based on the warning nature of the utterances, the denial of the poetic character (of the Qur'ān) is clear to all except those who stubbornly deny the facts, for no kind of similarity exists between the Qur'ān and poetry.[38] The difference between the Qur'ān and soothsaying exists on other grounds, for to recognize them is based on the fact that one permits himself to be admonished through the circumstances of the Messenger and the meaning of the Qur'ān which are incompatible with the way of the soothsayers and the meaning of their utterances. . . .

Zamakhsharī on Sūra 36:69f.

We have not taught Muḥammad[39] *poetry; it is not seemly for him. It*[40] *is only a remembrance and a clear Qur'ān,*
that he may warn whosoever is living, and that the word may be realized against the unbelievers.

Some took the Messenger of God to be a poet, and indeed it is related that (the Meccan) 'Uqba ibn Abī Mu'aiṭ was one who did this. Thereupon it was said (by God): *We have not taught him poetry*; that is, while teaching him the Qur'ān, we have not taught him poetry. This is to be understood in the sense that the Qur'ān is neither poetry nor does it have anything to do with it, but on the contrary is far removed. Poetry consists of statements that convey meaning through metre and (poetical) rhyme (*muqaffā*). Where, however, are metre and (poetical) rhyme (in the Qur'ān)? And to what extent are the themes (*ma'ānī*) to which the poets devote themselves the themes of the Qur'ān? How far removed, furthermore, is the structure (*naẓm*) of the poet's assertions from the structure and style of the Qur'ān? Thus, close investigation shows that the only relationship between the Qur'ān and poetry is that both are written in the Arabic language.

It is not seemly for him: He is not successful in the art of poetry, (a skill) that would be unattainable (for him even) if he aspired to it. That is, we have created him in such a way that even if he wanted to compose poetry he would not be able to do so and would not succeed in it. Also, we have made him to be an uneducated man (*ummī*) who has not been introduced to the art of writing and thus has not mastered it, so that (in this manner) the evidence (for his prophetic mission) becomes stronger and the suspicion (against it) may be invalidated more easily.[41]

From al-Khalīl (is related) that poetry was dearer to the Messenger of God than many (other) ways of speaking; yet the art of poetry was not given to him. Now one can ask about the (following) lines (in the *rajaz* metre[42]):

> I am the Prophet. That is no lie.
> I am the son of 'Abd al-Muṭṭalib.

and

> You (my soul) are nothing but a finger bleeding.
> What you suffered happened for the sake of God.

To this I answer: Here are nothing more than examples of one of his manners of expression, as he was in the habit of uttering hastily without artistic skill and without any formal display. Although (these examples) correspond (with poetry) since they happen to be metrical, the agreement with poetry is unintentional and unnoticed by him, just like numerous formulations of men in their speech, letters, and discussions occur in metrical form which no one designates as poetry and by which neither the speaker nor the hearer comes to the opinion that he is dealing with poetry. If one examines every utterance according to this kind of criterion, one will find that what is created in this manner is not admirable (at all). For this reason al-Khalīl did not (even) regard the *rajaz* hemistich as poetry.

And since God did not wish that the Qur'ān become poetry in any sense, he said: *It is only a remembrance and a clear Qur'ān*. By this the following is meant: It is only a remembrance of God by which both men and jinn[43] are warned, just as God says: 'It is only a reminder to all beings' (Sūra 12:104 and 81:27). And it is only the Qur'ān from a heavenly book which one recites in the prayer niche and reads out in the places of worship, whereby through recitation and appropriate actions one gains success in both worlds (this world and the next). How great then is the distance between the Qur'ān and poetry, which is provoked here by the satans!

That he (or, it) may warn: that is, (either) the Qur'ān or the Messenger of God. . . .

Whosoever is living: that is, those who are sensible and those who meditate,[44] since those who are inattentive are like the dead. Or, those one may know to be believing and thus through faith will be alive.

And that the word may be realized: and that the word of judgment may be inevitable.[45]

Against the unbelievers: against those who do not meditate and of whom one cannot anticipate that they will believe.

11. The first proclamation

Zamakhsharī on Sūra 74:1–5

O thou shrouded in thy mantle,
arise, and warn!
Thy Lord magnify,
thy robes purify,
and defilement flee!

O thou shrouded in thy mantle (muddaththir)[46]: O you who wear a mantle (*dithār*). This is worn over the undergarment which comes in direct contact with the body. To this refers the saying of the Prophet: 'The "helpers" (*anṣār*) are the undergarment and the (other) men the *dithār*.'

Some assert that this was the first sūra to be sent down.[47] Jābir ibn 'Abd Allāh related (the following account) from the Messenger of God: I was on Mount al-Ḥirā' (near Mecca) when someone called out to me: 'Muḥammad! You are the Messenger of God.' I looked to the right and to the left, but saw nothing. Then I looked up above me and there I saw something. In the Tradition according to 'Ā'isha it is said (by the Prophet): I glanced up above me and there I saw someone sitting on a throne between heaven and earth—meaning that it was the angel (Gabriel) who had called to him. I was frightened and returned to Khadīja and called out: 'Dress me in a *dithār*, dress me in a *dithār*!' Then Gabriel came and said: 'O thou shrouded in thy *dithār*!'

From az-Zuhrī (is related): The first sūra to come down is 'Recite in the name of thy Lord' down to the words of God 'what he had not known' (Sūra 96:1–5). (After the sending down of this sūra) the Messenger of God became sad (because a cessation had occurred in the proclamation[48]) and began to climb to the tops of the mountains. Then Gabriel came to him and said: 'You are the Prophet of God.' And then Muḥammad returned to Khadīja and called out: 'Dress me in a *dithār* and pour cold water over me!' Thereupon came down (the sūra which begins): 'O thou shrouded in thy *dithār*!'

Others say that the Prophet heard certain things from the (members of the tribe) Quraish which displeased him, and that this caused him to grieve. Afterwards he was wrapped in his robe reflecting on what grieved him, as grieving people were accustomed to do. Then he was commanded (through the present sūra) to warn his countrymen unremittingly (of the punishment of God), even when they had insulted him and had caused him injury. . . .

Thy robes purify: This is a command to keep the clothes free from all impurity, since the cleanliness (*ṭahāra*) of the clothes is a necessary condition for the (ritual) prayer (*ṣalāt*) which otherwise is not valid. Besides prayer, cleanliness is the fairest and most desirable state, and it is detestable when a good believer is burdened with what is repugnant. Some say that what is involved here is a command to shorten the robes and to wear them differently from the Arabs, who kept their robes long and wore trains (which dragged in the dirt); however, one could not be certain that dirtiness would thereby be prevented.

Others say that what is involved here is a command to keep the soul pure from unclean acts and objectionable habits. One says 'so and so has clean robes, pockets, trains, and sleeves' when he wants to represent someone as being completely free from faults and weaknesses of character. (In the opposite manner one says) of pernicious people 'so and so has dirty robes'. Since the robe covers the man and wraps around him, one can use it metonymically for him. . . .

12. The essential and the non-essential in revelation

Zamakhsharī on Sūra 80:24–32

Let man consider his nourishment.
We poured out the rains abundantly,
then We split the earth in fissures
and therein made the grains to grow,

and vines and reeds,
and olives and palms,
and dense-tree'd gardens,
and fruits and herbage (abb),
an enjoyment for you and your flocks.

... *Then We split the earth in fissures*: Here is a reference to the splitting of the earth by the plants as they spring up, but possibly also a reference to its splitting by ploughing with oxen. God mentions the splitting himself in such a manner as one attributes an act to its cause. ...

From Abū Bakr, the eminently veracious (*aṣ-ṣiddīq*), (is related) that when asked about the meaning of *abb*[49], he said: 'Which heaven would cover me and which earth would support me if I were to say that there is something in the Book of God that I know not?'

From 'Umar (is related) that he once recited this verse and said: 'We all know that. But what is *abb*?' Then he threw away a stick which he had in his hand, and said: 'By the eternal God! That is artificiality. What does it amount to for you, son of the mother of 'Umar, if you do not know what *abb* is?' And then he added: 'Obey what is clear to you in this Book and leave aside what is not clear!'

One may now say: This appears to forbid inquiry into the meaning of the contents of the Qur'ān and examination of its obscure passages. To this I answer: 'Umar did not mean this. But the people (at that time) had turned their primary concern to doing things, while to them the pursuit of scholarliness, which does not serve practical matters, was considered artificiality. 'Umar meant that this verse was produced because man took for granted the favour of sustenance; and here he is summoned to thankfulness. 'Umar knew from the context of this verse that *abb* is something that man plants for his necessities of life or for his grazing animals. (What he meant is:) One should reflect primarily upon those blessings of God listed here which are clear and not obscure, since they awaken thankfulness to God in stronger measure. And one will not be dissuaded from this through the question of the meaning of *abb* and the knowledge of certain plants which bear this name. One is to be satisfied (for the present) with the knowledge that is adequate, until these words are made clear at a later time. Then, 'Umar recommended to men that they observe this rule also with (other) similar obscure passages of the Qur'ān.

Ṭabarī on Sūra 12:20

Then they [50] *sold him for a paltry price, a handful of counted dirhams; for they set small store by him.*

. . . By the phrase a *handful of counted dirhams* God means that they sold him for (a number of) dirhams which were insufficient, inadequate, and not weighed, because *they set small store by him.* Some say that the term 'counted' indicates that the number was fewer than forty, since at that time any number of dirhams fewer than forty was not weighed because the smallest and most insignificant weight was the *uqiyya*[51] which amounted to forty dirhams. Others say that God indicates with his word 'counted' simply that it was only a few dirhams for which they sold him.

Some commentators say that it may have been twenty dirhams. . . . Others say that it may have been twenty-two, so that each of the eleven brothers of Joseph received two. . . .

At any rate, it is correct to say the following: God has declared that they sold him for 'counted' rather than 'weighed' dirhams, without specifying the amount according to weight and number. There occurs in addition to this neither an indication in a book (of God) nor an account from the Messenger. Possibly it was twenty or twenty-two or forty dirhams, or (it could have been) more or fewer. However many it may have been, it was in any case 'counted' and not 'weighed' dirhams. If one knew the amount of their weight, this would bring no advantage for religion, and if he did not know it, this would bring no harm. Man's duty (*farḍ*) is to believe in the external wording (*ẓāhir*) of the revelation; he is not required to know anything which goes beyond this.

13. The Qur'ān in the lives of the believers

Ghazzālī on the excellence of the Qur'ān[52]

. . . The Prophet has said: There is no intercessor (*shāfi'*) who enjoys such excellent esteem with God as the Qur'ān, neither a prophet nor an angel nor anything else. . . . He also said: The most excellent worship for my (religious) community (*umma*) is recitation of the Qur'ān. Further: God recited sūras Ṭā Hā (Sūra 20) and Yā Sīn (Sūra 36) a thousand years before he began the creation. And when the angels heard the recitation (*qur'ān*), they exclaimed: 'Blessed be a community to which this will be sent down, and blessed be the hearts (*ajwāf*) which will preserve it, and blessed be the tongues which will pronounce it!' Also the Prophet said: The best among you are those who learn and teach the Qur'ān. And: God has said: 'To whomever recitation of the Qur'ān occupies to the extent that he forgets to call upon me and to make requests of me, to him will I grant the most excellent reward for those who are thankful.' And: The people who occupy themselves with the Qur'ān (*ahl al-qur'ān*) constitute the family and intimate friends of God. . . .

Ibn Mas'ūd said: If you want knowledge, then disseminate the Qur'ān, for in it lies the knowledge of the forefathers and the descendants! And further: None of you will be questioned about himself without reference to (his relation to) the Qur'ān. Whoever loves and admires the Qur'ān loves God and his Messenger; whoever abhors the Qur'ān abhors God and his Messenger.

'Amr ibn al-'Āṣ has said: Every verse of the Qur'ān is a step into paradise and a light in your homes. He also said: Little by little prophecy will penetrate into whoever recites the Qur'ān, except that a (direct, divine) revelation will not be granted to him.

Abū Huraira has said: A house in which the Qur'ān is recited becomes rich with its people. Good increases in it and the angels are present in it, while the satans abandon it. But a house in which the Book of God is not recited falls into distress with its people. Good decreases and the angels abandon it, while the satans are present in it.

Aḥmad ibn Ḥanbal has said: I saw God in my sleep and said to him: 'Lord! What is the best way to draw near for those who wish to draw near to you?' God answered: 'Through my words (in the Qur'ān), Aḥmad.' Then I asked: 'Lord! With or without understanding?', and he said: 'With and without understanding'. . . .

14. The sciences of revelation

Ghazzālī on the sciences as collective duty[53]

. . . The sciences of revelation (*'ulūm shar'iyya*) . . . are all praiseworthy; however, one sometimes confuses them with sciences which, although considered to be sciences of revelation, are (in reality) blameworthy.[54] Consequently one must classify these sciences as praiseworthy or blameworthy. The praiseworthy sciences have roots (*uṣūl*), branches (*furū'*), suppositions (*muqaddimāt*), and completions (*mutammimāt*). They comprise, therefore, four kinds.

The 'roots',[55] of which there are four, constitute the first kind: the Book of God, the *sunna* of his Messenger, the consensus of the (religious) community (*ijmā' al-umma*), and the Traditions (*āthār*) concerning the Companions of the Prophet. The consensus (of the community) is a 'root' because it furnishes indications of the *sunna*. As a 'root' it is ranked third (in relation to the Qur'ān which is ranked first and the *sunna* which is ranked second as roots of the sciences of revelation). The same is true for the Traditions (concerning the Companions of the Prophet) which likewise provide indications of the *sunna*. The Companions witnessed the inspiration and sending down (of the Qur'ān) and were able to comprehend much through a combination of circumstances which others were unable to observe. Sometimes the explicit statements (of revelation) do not contain something that one can comprehend through a combination of circumstances. For this reason the men of learning found it beneficial to follow the example of the Companions of the Prophet and to be guided by the Traditions regarding them. . . .

The 'branches' constitute the second kind. This group deals with that which one comprehends on the basis of the 'roots' mentioned above—and indeed which cannot be gleaned from the external wording alone—through which the mind is awakened and understanding is thus expanded, so that one comprehends other meanings which are beyond the external wording. Thus one comprehends from the words of the Prophet: 'The judge may not judge in anger' that he (also) should not judge when hungry, needing to urinate, or in the pains of sickness. The 'branches' comprise two sub-types, the first of which deals with the requisites of the present world. This subtype is contained in the books of law (*fiqh*) and is entrusted to the lawyers, who are thus the men of learning responsible for the present world. The second sub-type deals with the requisites of the hereafter, thus the knowledge of the circumstances of the heart, its praiseworthy and blameworthy characteristics, that which is pleasing to God, and that which is abhorrent to him. That sub-type is contained in the second half of the present work (on 'The Revival of the Religious Sciences'). . . .

The 'suppositions' constitute the third kind. They are tools such as lexicography and grammar, which are naturally one tool for gaining knowledge of the Book of God and the *sunna* of his Prophet. In themselves lexicography and grammar do not belong to the sciences of revelation; however, one must become engrossed in them for the sake of revelation because the latter appears in the Arabic language. Since no revelation comes forth without language, the mastering of the language concerned becomes necessary as a tool. Among the tools (of this kind) belong also the skill of writing; however, this is not unconditionally required since the Messenger of God was illiterate (*ummī*).[56] If a man were able to retain in his memory everything that he hears, then the skill of writing would be unnecessary. Yet, since people are not able to do this, in most cases the skill of writing is essential.

The 'completions' (*mutammimāt*), that is, in relation to the study of the Qur'ān, constitute the fourth kind. This group contains the following divisions: (1) that which is connected with the external wording, such as the study of the (various) readings and of phonetics; (2) that which is connected with the meaning of the contents, such as (traditional) exegesis (*tafsīr*), where one must also rely upon tradition (*naql*) since the language alone does not yield the meaning; and (3) that which is connected with the 'decisions' of the Qur'ān, such as the knowledge of the abrogating and abrogated (verses), the general and the particular, the definite and the probable, as well as the kind and manner, in the same way that one makes one decision in relation to others. This is the science which has been designated as 'roots of law'. It extends also to the *sunna*.

The 'completions' relating to the Traditions and accounts consist of: (1) the study of the authorities, including their names and relationships (with one another), as well as the names and characteristics of the Companions of the Prophet; (2) the study of the reliability of the transmitters; (3) the study of the circumstances under which the transmitters lived, in order to be able to distinguish between those who are unreliable (*ḍa'īf*) and those who are reliable (*qawī*); and (4) the study of the life spans of the transmitters, through which that which is transmitted with defective chains of authorities (*asānīd*, sing. *isnād*)[57] can be distinguished from that which exhibits unbroken chains. The same designation also refers to other aspects connected with these.

These are the sciences of revelation and they are all praiseworthy. Moreover, they belong (not among the duties of individuals, but) among the collective duties (about which enough is done when a sufficient number of believers are concerned about them).

II

MUḤAMMAD

1. Muḥammad's proclamation

Zamakhsharī on Sūra 61:6

And when Jesus son of Mary said: 'Children of Israel, I am indeed the messenger of God to you, confirming the Torah which was before me,[1] *and giving good tidings of a messenger who shall come after me, whose name shall be Aḥmad.'*[2] *Then, when he brought them the clear signs, they said: 'This is a manifest sorcery.'*

Some maintain that Jesus said 'Children of Israel' (*yā banī isrā'īl*), and not 'fellow tribesmen' (*yā qaum*) as Moses had done, because Jesus had no relatives among them through whom they would be his fellow tribesmen[3]. . . .

According to Ka'b (al-Aḥbār, it is related) that the disciples of Jesus asked: 'Oh spirit (*rūḥ*) of God, will there be another (religious) community (*umma*) after us?', and that Jesus then said: 'Yes, the community of Aḥmad. It will consist of people who are wise, knowing, devout, and pious, as if in religious knowledge (*fiqh*) they were prophets. They will be satisfied with modest sustenance from God, and he will be pleased with modest conduct on their part'. . . .

Baiḍāwī on the same passage

. . . *And giving good tidings of a messenger (rasūl) who shall come after me, whose name shall be Aḥmad*: that is, Muḥammad. The meaning is: My religion subsists in holding on firmly to the books of God and his prophets. Accordingly, Jesus mentions (as a part of the collective books of God and all the prophets only) the first of the well-known books, concerning which the (earlier) prophets gave their decision, and only that prophet who (as the last) constitutes the seal of those who are sent (by God). . . .

2. *Muḥammad's human nature*

Baiḍāwī on Sūra 3:144/138

Muḥammad is only a messenger; messengers have passed away before him. Why, if he should die or is slain, will you turn about on your heels? If any man should turn about on his heels, he will not harm God in any way; and God will recompense the thankful.

Muḥammad is only a messenger; messengers have passed away before him: he will pass away as they did, through a natural or violent death.

Why, if he should die or is slain, will you turn about on your heels? Here it is denied that the believers will desert and turn away from their religion simply because the Messenger of God passes through a natural or violent death, since they know that the messengers before him passed away and their religion endured as something to which its adherents held fast. . . .

(As the occasion for the proclamation of the present verse) the following is related: 'Abd Allāh ibn Qumai'a al-Ḥārithī threw stones at the Messenger of God, breaking his teeth and making his face bloody.[4] Muṣ'ab ibn 'Umair, the standard-bearer (of the Prophet), protected him until Ibn Qumai'a slew Muṣ'ab. But Ibn Qumai'a thought he had slain the Prophet, so he said: 'I have killed Muḥammad!' Then someone cried out: 'Indeed, Muḥammad has been slain!' Then as the men began to retreat, the Messenger of God called out: 'To me, servants of God!' Thirty of his followers closed in around him and protected him until they drove away the polytheists, and the others had scattered. (Meanwhile) one of those protecting the Prophet (became frightened and) said: 'Oh, that ('Abd Allāh) Ibn Ubayy would seek protection for us from Abū Sufyān!'[5] And certain (other) 'hypocrites' (*munāfiqūn*) (who took Muḥammad for dead) said: 'If he had (really) been a prophet, then he could not have been killed. So turn back to your (heathen) brothers and to your (old) religion!' Thereupon, Anas ibn an-Naḍr, the uncle of Anas ibn Mālik, said: 'People, if Muḥammad has been killed, surely his Lord is alive and will never die. What do you want to do with your lives after he is no longer here? (Be prepared to die) and fight for that for which he fought (surrendering his life)!' Then he added: 'Oh, God, I ask for your forgiveness for what they have said; I have nothing to do with it.' He then drew his sword and fought on until he was killed. Thereupon the (present) verse came down.

If any man should turn about on his heels through his apostasy, *he will not harm God in any way* but only himself. *And God will recompense* for the benefit of Islam *the thankful* who hold fast to it like Anas and people like him.

Zamakhsharī on Sūra 7:188

Say: 'I have no power over benefit or harm to myself, except as God wills. If I had knowledge of the unseen I would have acquired much good, and evil would not have touched me. I am only a warner and a bearer of good tidings to a people who believe.'

Say: I have no power over benefit or harm to myself: Here is declared the (human) servant nature (of Muḥammad) and his lack of knowledge of the unseen, which belongs specifically to the (divine) nature of the master alone. The meaning is: I am a feeble servant who (alone) can neither provide profit nor prevent harm, just as is the case with those in bondage and those servants (in the position of slaves).

Except as God, my Lord, *wills* to provide profit for me and to prevent harm from me. *If I had knowledge of the unseen*: that is, if my situation were other than it (now) is, so that *I would have acquired much good*, obtaining abundant profit, and were I able to avoid evil and whatever is harmful so that I would not have to suffer, and in battle were not sometimes the victor and sometimes the vanquished, and in trading were not sometimes the gainer and sometimes the loser, and in planning were not sometimes on the mark and sometimes going astray.

I am only a servant who has been sent as *a warner and a bearer of good tidings*. It is not for me to know the unseen.

To a people who believe: It is possible that this passage refers not only to (the word) 'warner' but also to (the expression) 'bearer of good tidings', since warning and bearing good tidings both bring benefit to the believers. However, the passage may refer only to (the expression) 'bearer of good tidings', so that (the word) 'warner' would then be independent (and supplementary). Therefore: I am nothing other than a warner to the unbelievers and a bearer of good tidings to people who believe.

Zamakhsharī on Sūra 29:50/49

The unbelievers[6] *say: 'Why have no signs been sent down upon Muḥammad*[7] *from his Lord?' Say: 'The signs are only with God, and I am only a plain warner.'*

In this verse some read 'why have no signs', while others read 'why has no sign'. The unbelievers mean: Why has no (miraculous) sign been sent down upon Muḥammad, like the she-camel which was given to Ṣāliḥ as a sign, the table which was sent down to Jesus[8], and others like these?

The signs are only with God: He sends down among them only what he wishes, and if he had wished to send down the sign which they demand then he would have done so.

I am only a plain warner: I am commissioned to warn and to make this warning clear through the sign (that is, the Qur'ān) which has been given to me. It is not for me to make a choice from among God's signs, so that I could say: 'Send down to me one of this kind and not one of that kind!' Besides, I know that each sign has a lasting purpose, and each sign is as good as that of anyone else in this regard.

Baiḍāwī on Sūra 25:7/8

The unbelievers[9] *also say: 'What ails this messenger that he eats food and goes in the markets? Why has an angel not been sent down to him, to be a warner with him?'*

What ails this messenger (rasūl): what ails this one who claims to be a messenger. In this (expression) lies contempt and scorn.

That he eats food as we do *and goes in the markets* to seek his sustenance as we do. The meaning is: If what he asserts is correct, then why is it that he is not in a different state from us? The unbelievers said this because they were perplexed and were limited to their view of the physically perceptible indications (of his nature). (In fact) the messengers are not distinguished from other men by physical signs, but by their spiritual condition, as God has shown in his words: 'Say: "I am only a mortal like you; it is revealed to me that your God is One God"' (Sūra 18:110). . . .

3. A temptation of Muḥammad

Zamakhsharī on Sūra 17:73f./75f.

Indeed the unbelievers[10] *were near to seducing thee from that which We revealed to thee, that thou mightest forge against Us another than the Qur'ān*[11], *and then they would surely have taken thee as a friend;*
and had We not confirmed thee, surely thou wert near to inclining unto them a very little.

(As the occasion for the proclamation of this passage) the following is related: The (members of the tribe) Thaqīf[12] said to the Prophet: 'We will not join your cause unless you grant to us conditions which we can extol to (other) Arabs, namely, that the tithe not be demanded from us, that we not be expelled (from our hereditary habitats), that we not be required to throw ourselves down in prayer, that (in spite of the prohibition against usury) we be paid all interest on money borrowed from us but that all interest be exempted for those to whom we are indebted, that you permit us to continue to manage the shrine of (the goddess) al-Lāt[13] for one more year and that after the year we not be required to destroy it with our own hands, and that you assume protection against those who break into our valley Wajj to take away the (sacred) trees. If the (other) Arabs ask you why you have made these (concessions), then say: "God has commanded me to do it."' Now they brought their document and Muḥammad ordered to be written: 'In the name of God, the Merciful, the Compassionate. This is a writing from Muḥammad, the Messenger of God, to (the tribe) Thaqīf. The members of this tribe are not required to pay the tithe and will not be expelled.' (As the scribe reached this point) they said: '(Now continue:) "And they are not required to prostrate themselves (at prayer)."' But the Messenger of God remained silent (and did not continue to dictate), so they said to the scribe: 'Write: "And they are not required to prostrate themselves (at prayer)!"' At that, the scribe looked at the Messenger of God, and 'Umar ibn Khaṭṭāb rose up drawing his sword and said: 'Men of (the tribe) Thaqīf you have set the heart of our Prophet on fire!' But they replied: 'We are not speaking with you, but with Muḥammad.' Thereupon the present verses came down.

(Also) it is related that the (unbelieving members of the tribe) Quraish said to Muḥammad: 'Change a verse of mercy into a verse of punishment and a verse of punishment into a verse of mercy in order that we may believe in you!' Thereupon the present verses came down.

Indeed they were near to seducing thee: ... The meaning is: Those who were involved with the affair had almost deluded you, that is, through misleading infatuation.

From that which We for our part as command and prohibition as well as promise and warning *revealed to thee, that thou mightest forge against Us another*: so that you would say something that we have not said in a manner that will be falsely judged as against us. What is meant is the change of promise which the (members of the tribe) Quraish had demanded of Muḥammad, and also the imperious proposal of the (tribe) Thaqīf that Muḥammad should ascribe something to God which had not been sent down upon him.

And then, that is, if you had complied with their wish, *they would surely have taken thee as a friend*, and you would have become their intimate friend (*walī*) and would have lost the relationship of confidence with me.

And had We not confirmed thee: had not our strengthening and protection ('*iṣma*) been with you.

Surely thou wert near to inclining unto them: you had almost inclined towards their deception and cunning. Here God gives to the Prophet encouragement and gracious strengthening, wherein lies an act of mercy for the believers. ...

4. The night journey and the ascension

Zamakhsharī on Sūra 17:1

Glory be to Him who carried His servant by night from the holy mosque to the farthest mosque[14] *the precincts of which We have blessed, that We might show him some of Our signs. He*[15] *is the One who hears, the One who sees.*

... *Who carried (asrā*[16]*) His servant by night (lailan)*: ... One may ask: Since the (word) *asrā* in itself already means 'to undertake a night journey', then what does the stipulation 'by night' add to the meaning of the statement? To this I reply: With the expression 'by night'[17] ... God wishes to indicate the duration of the night journey as short, saying that within a (single) night he and his servant accomplished the journey from Mecca to the Syrian lands (*ash-sha'm*[18]) which (usually) required forty nights. ...

There is disagreement regarding the place from which the night journey originated. Some say that it was the holy mosque (of Mecca) (*al-masjid*[19] *al-ḥarām*) itself. This is likely since it is mentioned in the following account from the Prophet: While I was between being asleep and awake in the apartments near the Ka'ba (*al-bait*) at the holy mosque, Gabriel came to me with the (steed) Burāq.[20] Others say (however) that the journey of Muḥammad originated from the dwelling of (his cousin) Umm Hāni', the daughter of Abū Ṭālib. In this case the expression 'holy mosque' would indicate the holy precinct (of Mecca) (*al-ḥaram*), since this area includes the mosque and can thus be referred to by this designation. According to Ibn 'Abbās the entire sacred precinct is a mosque.

(Furthermore) the following is related: After the evening prayer Muḥammad slept in the dwelling of Umm Hāni', when he was taken on the night journey (to Jerusalem) and returned in the same night. Afterwards he related the story to Umm Hāni', saying: 'The prophets have appeared to me and I have performed the prayer with them.' As he now rose to go to the mosque, Umm Hāni clung to his robe, and he said: 'What do you want?' She answered: 'I fear that your fellow tribesmen will accuse you of falsehood if you relate that to them.' To this he replied: 'What, would they accuse me of lying?', and he went away. Then when Abū Jahl sat down next to him and the Messenger of God related the story of the night journey to him, Abū Jahl called out: 'Men of the (tribe of) Banū Ka'b ibn Lu'ayy, come here!' Then Muḥammad related the account to them. While some gave their approval to him, others placed their hands on their heads with astonishment and disapproval. Some people who had believed in the Prophet previously now turned away from him. Some men, however, ran to Abū Bakr, who (after hearing their account) said: 'If Muḥammad said this then it is the truth.' When the men then asked: 'Do you then believe (*ṣaddaqa*) that he did this?', he answered: 'I believe him in matters even more unlikely than this.' For this reason Abū Bakr is called 'the eminently veracious' (*aṣ-ṣiddīq*).

Among those present, however, were some who had previously travelled to that place and they challenged Muḥammad to give a description of it. Jerusalem (*bait al-muqaddas*) stood clearly before his eyes, so he looked over it immediately and began to describe it to them. They said: 'The description is accurate', and then they added: 'Tell us about our caravans (which are returning from Jerusalem)!' So he told them the number of their camels and their condition and then said: 'They will arrive at sunrise on such and such a day, with a grey camel leading them.' On that day the Meccans went (out from their city) and ran quickly to (the passageway) ath-Thaniyya. Then one of them said: 'By God, the sun is just coming up!' And another said: 'By God, here comes the caravan with a grey camel at the head, just as Muḥammad said.' (In spite of this) they did not believe (Muḥammad's account of his night journey to Jerusalem), but said: 'This is nothing but manifest magic (*siḥr mubīn*).'

In the same night (in which the journey to Jerusalem occurred) Muḥammad was (also) raised up to heaven; that is, the ascension[21] took its departure from Jerusalem. Muḥammad told the (members of the tribe) Quraish also of the wonderful things which he had seen in heaven, that he met the prophets there and went as far as the house visited (by the pilgrims) (*al-bait al-ma'mūr*[22]) and the Zizyphus tree at the far end of heaven (*sidrat al-muntahā*[23]).

There is (also) disagreement concerning the date of the night journey. While some say that it occurred one year before the emigration (to Medina), according to Anas (ibn Mālik) and al-Ḥasan (al-Baṣrī) it took place (even) before the mission (of Muḥammad as a prophet). (Furthermore) there is disagreement concerning whether the night journey occurred (while Muḥammad was) in the state of being awake or asleep. The following is (related) from 'Ā'isha: 'By God, the body of the Messenger of God was not missed (during the night journey); rather, the ascension to heaven occurred with his spirit (*rūḥ*).' According to Mu'āwiya (also) it took place only with the spirit. On the other hand, according to al-Ḥasan (al-Baṣrī) it was a vision which Muḥammad had in his sleep; yet most Traditions stand in opposition to this contention.

The farthest mosque:[24] Jerusalem. At that time no mosque existed farther away (from Mecca) than the one at Jerusalem.

The precincts of which We have blessed: God means the blessing of religion and of the present world, for Jerusalem had been since the time of Moses the place of worship of the prophets and the place to which (divine) inspiration was restricted (before the time of Muḥammad), and it is surrounded with flowing rivers and fruit-bearing trees. . . .

He is the One who hears the speech of Muḥammad, *the One who sees* his deeds and the one who knows of his purity and uprightness. . . .

5. *Accusations against Muḥammad*

Zamakhsharī on Sūra 16:103/105

And We know very well that the unbelievers[25] *say: 'Only a mortal* (bashar) *is teaching him.'*[26] *The speech of him at whom they hint is foreign, while this is clear Arabic speech.*

The man referred to by the unbelievers was a servant (*ghulām*) of Ḥuwaiṭib ibn 'Abd al-'Uzzā. This servant had embraced Islam and was an excellent Muslim. He was called 'Ā'ish or Yā'ish and he possessed books. Some say (however) that the reference is to Jabr, a Byzantine servant (*ghulām*) of 'Āmir ibn al-Haḍramī. Others say the reference is to two slaves, Jabr and Yasār, who manufactured swords in Mecca and used to read (*qara'a*) the Torah and the Gospel. When the Messenger of God passed by them, he stopped to listen to what they read. From this the unbelievers asserted that these two taught him (what he later proclaimed as revelation). When this was said to one of them, he said: 'No, Muḥammad teaches me!' (Finally, still) others say that the reference is to (the Persian) Salmān al-Fārisī. . . .

The speech of him at whom they hint (yulḥidūna, sing. perf.: *alḥada)*: One says (in Arabic) *alḥada l-qabra* . . . when someone deviates from a straight line and digs to one side when digging up a grave.[27] This word is used regarding any deviation from a straight line. Thus one says: 'He deviates from the straight line in his assertion (*qaul*)'; and, 'So-and-so deviates from the straight line in his religion (*dīn*).' The (word) *mulḥid* (heretic, unbeliever) refers to this because the *mulḥid* deviates from all religion in his beliefs, and in renouncing one religion does not turn his belief to another. (In the present case) the meaning is: The speech of him at whom they bend their assertion, deviating from the straight line, *is foreign* (non-Arabic), unclear speech.

While this Qur'ān (on the contrary) *is clear Arabic speech*, which possesses clarity and purity (*faṣāḥa*) and (in this manner) disproves the assertion of the unbelievers and destroys their slander. . . .

6. God's comfort and support for Muḥammad

Zamakhsharī on Sūra 93:6–8

Did He not find thee an orphan, and shelter thee?
Did He not find thee erring, and guide thee?
Did He not find thee needy, and suffice thee?

Here God enumerates for his Prophet the mercies and benefits that he had granted to him, and reminds him that he did not allow any failure since the beginning of his shaping and growth. God wishes to prepare him for what he has in mind for him (for later). From the preceding demonstrations of mercy, Muḥammad should be able to consider what he (still) has to wait for from God's goodness, so that he should prepare for the best result as well as an increase of good and authority, rather than becoming faint-hearted and impatient.

Did He not find thee an orphan: Here the expression 'find' has the sense of knowing (about Muhammad's situation). . . . The meaning is: Were you not an orphan? Muḥammad's father died three months before Muḥammad was born, and his mother died when he was eight years old. Then God appointed Muḥammad's paternal uncle Abū Ṭālib as his guardian and awakened in him a feeling of affection for Muḥammad, so that Abū Ṭālib brought him up well. . . .

Did He not find thee erring: The meaning is that (at that time) Muḥammad was found erring regarding knowledge of the revealed laws (*sharā'i'*, sing. *sharī'a*), which can be perceived only through being instructed (*sam'*[28]). Thus God says: 'Thou knewest not what the (revealed) Book was, nor belief; but We made it a light, whereby We guide whom We will of Our servants. And thou, surely thou shalt guide unto a straight path' (Sūra 42:52). However, some say that in his youth Muḥammad once lost his way on a mountain path near Mecca and that Abū Jahl brought him back to (his grandfather) 'Abd al-Muṭṭalib. Others say that (the wet nurse) Ḥalīma led Muḥammad astray outside the gates of Mecca as soon as she had weaned him, and wanted to bring him back to 'Abd al-Muṭṭalib. Still others say that Muhammad got lost once on the way to Syria when Abū Ṭālib took him along on a journey.

And guide thee: and introduce to you the Qur'ān and the revealed laws. Or: and see to it that you no longer stray away from the right path from your grandfather and your paternal uncle. If one asserts that for forty years Muḥammad lived just like his fellow tribesmen, and if this is meant in the sense that like them he lacked learning, which can be gained only through being instructed (*sam'*), then this is fine; however, if, one means it in the sense that he lived according to the religion and the unbelief of his fellow tribesmen, then God forbid! For the prophets must remain free (*ma'ṣūm*) from shameful sins, both serious and mild, before and after the commencement of their prophethood, and how then can there be unbelief and ignorance of the (divine) creator? (The answer to this is given in the words of God:) 'It is not ours to associate anything with God (as a partner in his divinity)' (Sūra 12:38). In the eyes of the unbelievers it would be a sufficient defect in the Prophet if he had lived in unbelief before the commencement of his prophethood. . . .

And suffice thee: and make you rich either through the wealth of (your wife) Khadīja or through the booty which God furnished for you. (In the latter sense) the Prophet said: 'My livelihood is placed under the shadow of my lance.' However, some say (that it means): God has granted you contentment and has made your heart rich.

Zamakhsharī on Sūra 2:119/113

We have sent thee with the truth, to bear good tidings and warning. Thou shalt not be questioned (lā tus'alu) *concerning the inhabitants of hell.*

We have sent thee: in order to proclaim good news and to warn, but not to force people to believe. The purpose here is to comfort the Messenger of God and take away his sorrow. He was grieved and depressed because of the persistence and tenacity of his compatriots in their unbelief.

And we will not ask you *concerning the inhabitants of hell* (in order to receive from you an account on this point), why they have not believed after you have exerted yourself again and again summoning them (to belief). To this refers God's words: 'Whether We show thee a part of what We promise them or call thee to Us, it is thine only to deliver the message; and the reckoning is Ours' (Sūra 13:40).

Some read in the sense of a prohibition: And you are not to ask (*lā tas'al*) about the inhabitants of hell. It is related that Muḥammad once said: 'If I only knew the fate of my parents!' Then he was forbidden to ask about the circumstances (*aḥwāl*) of unbelievers and to grieve over the enemies of God. Others say that this prohibition indicates that the punishment which comes upon the unbelievers is especially severe. This is like asking: 'How is it with such-and-such a person?', when inquiring about someone who has fallen into misfortune, and then receiving the answer: 'You had rather not ask about him!' When through such a prohibition (the punishment or the misfortune of the one concerned) is represented as especially severe, then the above is fundamentally the case, because the one questioned must be afraid of it, bringing to the relatives the dreadful condition of the one concerned. Thus, do not question him and trouble him with something that (only) agonizes! Or (the following reason is submitted): You who ask are not able to bear hearing the report you seek, for this causes torment and grief to the listener; so (rather) do not ask. . . .

Baiḍāwī on Sūra 48:1–3

Surely We have given thee a manifest victory,
that God may forgive thee thy former and thy latter sins, and complete His blessing upon thee, and guide thee on a straight path,
and that God may help thee with mighty help.

Surely We have given (fataḥnā) thee a manifest victory (fatḥ mubīn): Either this is a promise that Muḥammad will conquer (*fataḥa*) Mecca,[29] this promise being given in the form of the perfect tense (with the content of the promise thus being represented as something already accomplished, although Mecca had not yet been conquered at the time of the sending down of this revelation), thus indicating that the conquest was already a certainty, or it is a promise of what happened to Muḥammad in that year (in which this revelation came down), like the conquest of Khaibar and Fadak.[30] Or, it is a report of the agreement of al-Ḥudaibiya (which had just been accomplished). In this case the term 'victory' (and not simply 'agreement') is used because this agreement occurred when Muḥammad had already subdued the polytheists to the extent that they had asked for an agreement; and because of it the conquest of Mecca was made possible. Through it the Messenger of God won time (to occupy himself) with the remaining Arabs. He could attack them, conquering villages and causing numerous men to enter into Islam. Also, at al-Ḥudaibiya an important sign (*āya*) appeared to Muḥammad: The water there had completely dried up, and when he rinsed out his mouth (with water) and spat it out at this spot, the water (of al-Ḥudaibiya) flowed so abundantly that all his companions could drink from it.

Or, this is a reference to the victory of the Byzantines who defeated the Persians in that year (in which this revelation came down[31]). One knows indeed from the sūra called 'The Byzantines' (Sūra 30) that this was a victory for the Messenger of God (who had predicted the success of the Byzantines and had represented it as a joyous event for the believers).

Some say (also) that the (word) *fataḥa* ('to grant a victory') here has the meaning of *qaḍā* ('to determine'). (In this case) the verse means: We have determined for you that you shall soon enter Mecca (as a conquerer).

That God may forgive thee: This is a reason for the victory (which was granted to Muḥammad as pardon and reward for his zeal). That is, the occasion given here for the victory is that Muḥammad had fought against the unbelievers and had taken the trouble to elevate the religion, to eliminate idolatry, (to begin) to perfect the imperfect souls so they might come step by step to voluntary perfection, and to liberate the weak from the hands of tyrants.

Thy former and thy latter sins: everything blameworthy that has proceeded from you.

And complete His blessing upon thee: by elevating the religion and now also by linking the rule (of the country) with the prophethood.

And guide thee on a straight path: by establishing the mission, and with the appointment of rules of conduct for the guidance (of the community). . . .

7. *Muḥammad's personal situation*

Zamakhsharī on Sūra 33:40

Muḥammad is not the father of (any) one of your men, but the Messenger of God, and the Seal of the Prophets; God has knowledge of everything.

Muḥammad is not the father of (any) one of your men: that is, he is not actually the father of (any) one of your men, so that between him and you exist the same marriage prohibitions and marriage relationships as between a father and his (male) offspring.

But (he is) the Messenger of God: ... Every messenger is the father of his (religious) community (*umma*) in so far as they are obliged to respect and honour him, and he is obliged to provide for them and give them advice. On the other hand, regarding the other regulations existing between fathers and sons, he is not the father of his community. Zaid (ibn Ḥāritha, whom Muḥammad had adopted as a son) is (also) one of your men who are not actually his offspring; thus, the same lawful regulation applies to him as to you, since adoption and the acceptance of a child are nothing but instances in the realm of special relations and the choice of a companion (and establish no relationship of paternity).

And the Seal of the Prophets (khātam an-nabiyyīn): ... That is, if he had received a male offspring who had reached the age of adulthood, then the latter (also) would have become a prophet and Muḥammad would not be the Seal of the Prophets. Thus it is related that Muḥammad said after the death of (his son) Ibrāhīm[32]: 'Had he lived (longer) he would have become a prophet.'

If one now asks whether Muḥammad was not the (actual) father of aṭ-Ṭāhir, aṭ-Ṭayyib, al-Qāsim, and Ibrāhīm, then I answer: They do not fall under the denial (of fatherhood) in God's words: 'Muḥammad is not the father of (any) one of your men' for two reasons: first, these sons did not reach the age of adulthood; and second, with the word 'men' God was referring to those being addressed and not to these (sons of Muḥammad), who would be Muḥammad's 'men' and not those of the hearers.

If one asks (further) whether Muḥammad was not the father of (his grandsons) al-Ḥasan and al-Ḥusain, then I answer: Certainly, but they were not men at that time, and they too would be Muḥammad's 'men' and not those of the hearers. Moreover, there is a further reason: The text refers to a (direct) offspring of Muḥammad and not to his grandchild, as follows from God's words 'and the Seal of the Prophets', since al-Ḥasan lived past the age of forty and al-Ḥusain lived past the age of fifty (without either becoming a prophet and thus forming the Seal of the Prophets). . . .

If one (finally) asks how Muḥammad (as the Seal of the Prophets) can be the last prophet when Jesus will come down at the end of time (as a sign that the hour of judgment has come),[33] then I reply: That Muḥammad is the last of the prophets means that after him no one else will be active as a prophet; and Jesus was active as a prophet before Muḥammad. And when Jesus comes down he will do this because he devotes himself to the law (*sharī'a*) of Muḥammad and performs his prayer according to Muḥammad's direction of prayer (*qibla*) (facing Mecca), as if he were a member of his community.

Zamakhsharī on Sūra 33:37

When thou saidst to him whom God had blessed and thou hadst favoured: 'Keep thy wife to thyself and fear God', and thou wast concealing within thyself what God should reveal, fearing other men; and God has better right for thee to fear Him. So when Zaid had accomplished what he would of her, then We gave her in marriage to thee, so that there should not be any fault in the believers, concerning the wives of their adopted sons, when they have accomplished what they would of them; and God's commandment must be performed.

To him whom God had blessed (an'ama): through Islam, which represents the greatest blessing, and through the support (*taufīq*[34]) which God grants to you, as you had thereby liberated him (from slavery), had grown fond of him and (through the adoption as a son) had established an especially intimate relationship with him.[35]

And thou hadst favoured (an'amta): through every act by which God grants (*waffaqa*) his assistance to you. Thus, Zaid ibn Ḥāritha lived not only under the mercy (*ni'ma*) of God but also within the special favour (*ni'ma*) of the Messenger of God.

Keep thy wife to thyself: that is, Zainab bint Jaḥsh. After having given her to Zaid ibn Ḥāritha as a wife, the Messenger of God once caught sight of her, and she made an impression of him. At this sight he said: 'Praise be to God who changes the heart!' Previously his soul had turned away from her so that he had not desired her (as a wife). If he had desired her at that time, he would have asked for her hand in marriage. Now Zainab heard of this praise and mentioned it to (her husband) Zaid, who understood and to whom God gave antipathy against her and aversion to intimacy with her. So Zaid said to the Messenger of God: 'I might divorce my wife', to which the latter replied: 'What is it? Has something filled you with mistrust against her?' Zaid answered: 'By God, no! I have observed only good in her; yet her noble rank places her too high above me and causes me to feel hurt.' Thereupon the Messenger of God said: 'Keep thy wife to thyself and fear God.' But Zaid (nevertheless) separated from her, and as soon as the waiting period (during which the wife may enter into no new marriage[36]) had elapsed, the Messenger of God said (to Zaid): 'I have no one whom I trust more than you; therefore, seek the hand of Zainab for me!'

Zaid reported: I went forth and there I suddenly found her just as she was leavening some dough. As soon as I saw her she made such an impression on me, since I knew that the Messenger of God had been speaking of her. So I turned my back to her and said: 'Zainab, be happy, for the Messenger of God asks for your hand in marriage.' Then she was pleased and said: 'I do nothing without first seeking advice from my Lord God.' Then she set off for her mosque and (the following portion of) the Qur'ān came down: *We gave her in marriage to thee*. Then the Messenger of God took her as a wife and consummated the marriage with her. He had given none of his wives such a feast as he gave to her.[37] He had sheep slaughtered and supplied the men with bread and meat until the light of day spread forth.

If one now asks what God meant with his words *and fear God*, I answer that he meant: And fear God and do not set her free! God wished thereby to forbid Zaid from holding his wife in too high a position and untouched, for it would have been most appropriate if he had not separated from her. Some say (however) that God meant: And fear God and do not blame her for her high position and the offence she thus inflicts upon her husband!

One may ask what the Prophet kept secret within himself. To this I answer: the fact that he was devoted to her in his heart. Others say: the wish that Zaid might separate from her. Still others say: his knowledge that Zaid would separate from her and that he would marry her, for God had already given this knowledge to him. From 'Ā'isha is (the following related): If the Messenger of God kept to himself something of the revelation which God had given to him then it would be this verse (which was embarrassing for him).

(Further) one may ask what the Prophet should have said when Zaid informed him that he wanted to separate from Zainab, since it would have been objectionable if he had said: 'Do it, for I want to marry her!' To this I reply: It may perhaps be God's will that in this case he keep silent or say to Zaid: 'You know your situation best.' In this manner he would not have contradicted his secret which he (later) indicated had been revealed. God wishes from his prophets that the external and the internal be the same, that they show firmness in their calling, that the situations into which they fall are proper, and that they remain on a determined path. Thus, there is a Tradition according to which the Messenger of God wished to have 'Abd Allāh ibn Abī-Sarḥ put to death, a design that 'Uthmān opposed through intercession. In this Tradition it is said that 'Umar said to Muḥammad: 'My eye is set right on you; if you give me a (secret) sign, I will put him to death.' Then the Messenger of God answered: 'The prophets give no secret signs; with them the external and the internal are one and the same.'

(Also) one may ask how God could blame the Prophet for keeping something secret when the Prophet considered its open announcement to be objectionable. But did the Prophet not consider the open announcement of the affair objectionable only because this affair was itself objectionable and indeed was opposed by men who witnessed something which they viewed as scandalous according to their understanding and their custom? And why did God not reprove the Prophet for the affair itself and command him to suppress his desire, and refuse to himself the feeling of inclination for Zainab and the retention of this wife? Why did God not protect (*'aṣama*) his Prophet from this association with something objectionable and the gossip which affected him (at that time)?

To this I answer: There are many situations in which a person exercises caution and in which he feels uneasy even though these matters are completely legal (*mubāḥ*) and are absolutely allowed (*ḥalāl*), and concerning which before God there is neither rumour nor reproach! Frequently, participation in such lawful matters becomes a stairway for the attainment of duties (*wājibāt*) which have a great influence in the religion and result in a significant reward. If a person were to exercise no caution here, then many people would give a free course to their tongues regarding the matter (and would put all sorts of rumours into circulation), except, of course, those people who have preserved not only excellent knowledge, religion, and insight into the real nature (of the matter) but also the kernel as well as the external appearance of the affair. Are the people then not like those who (once) ate in the apartments of the Prophet and who (after the meal) stubbornly remained seated, without making a move from their places because they sought sociability through conversation? At this their remaining seated annoyed the Messenger of God and their conversation made him uneasy, but his sense of shame prevented him from ordering them to rise from the table. Finally (the following verse) came down: 'O believers, enter not the apartments of the Prophet for a meal unless you have been given permission, and wait not until meal-time. But come when you are invited, and disperse when you have had the meal, not lingering for idle talk. For that is hurtful to the Prophet, and he is shy before you. But God is not shy before the truth!' (Sūra 33:53).

Had the Messenger of God (in this case) expressed his secret thoughts openly and commanded the people to go their way, then he would have caused them grief and this would have resulted in some gossip. The wish of the Prophet regarding marriage with Zainab involves the same kind of situation. When the heart of a man aspires to something desirable like a wife or something else, then this can be considered as objectionable neither against reason nor against divine law (*shar'*[38]), since such an aspiration is not the work of the man and does not persist through his free choice (*ikhtiyār*). If one (then) receives what is legal in a lawful way, then nothing of impropriety lies therein. This is true also for the courtship (by the Prophet) of Zainab and his marriage with her, since Zaid was not asked to renounce her and no request was put to him. More significant than (an act like) putting on a garment, it is incumbent upon the Prophet to assist Zaid in his separation from her, especially since it was quite certainly known to him that Zaid's soul was no longer in any way filled with affection for Zainab but was alienated from her, while the soul of the Messenger of God was devoted to her. Moreover, the people did not consider it as offensive, since a man had renounced all claim to his wife for the benefit of his friend, and they did not hold it objectionable that the other married her after such a renunciation. When the 'emigrants' (*muhājirūn*) arrived in Medina, the 'helpers' (*anṣār*) shared everything with them, even to the extent that a man who had two wives renounced one of them, and the 'emigrant' (to whom he surrendered her) married her.

It is now therefore as follows: The affair (of the courtship and marriage with Zainab) was legal in all points and contained nothing that was objectionable in any way, nor anything disgraceful, nor any wrong to Zaid or anyone (else). On the contrary, it brought (numerous) benefits (*maṣāliḥ*) with it, not the least of which is the fact that the daughter of the paternal aunt of the Messenger of God (that is, Zainab) was (in this way) preserved from the destiny of being without a man and (thus) from perishing, and that she attained a high position and became one of the 'mothers of the Muslims'.[39] Also, this led to the general benefit mentioned by God when he said: *so that there should not be any fault in the believers, concerning the wives of their adopted sons, when they have accomplished what they would of them.* (Since this was the case and Muḥammad's inclination for Zainab was not blameworthy as such) then the appropriateness (of the situation) lay in the fact that God rebuked his Messenger for exercising secrecy and going so far as to say (to Zaid): 'Keep thy wife to thyself and fear God!' and that God sanctioned no other conduct by his Messenger than that in which there was conformity between the internal and the external and steadfastness in matters of truth, so that the believers could take him as an example and thus must perceive no shame in him, when they were confronted with the truth. (This was appropriate) also since it was bitter (for the Prophet). . . .

Zamakhsharī on Sūra 33:50/49–52

O Prophet, We have made lawful for thee thy wives to whom thou hast given their dowries, and those whom thy right hand owns (as slaves), whom God has given to thee as spoils of war, and the daughters of thy paternal uncles and paternal aunts, thy maternal uncles and maternal aunts, who have emigrated with thee, and any woman believer, if she give herself to the Prophet and if the Prophet desire to take her in marriage. This is a special

exception for thee and not for the believers, so that no fault may be found in thee. We know what We have imposed upon the believers concerning their wives and what their right hands own (as slaves). God is All-compassionate, All-forgiving.
Thou mayest put off whom thou wilt of them, and whom thou wilt thou mayest take to thee; and if thou seekest any thou hast set aside there is no fault in thee. So it is likelier they will be comforted, and not sorrow, and every one of them will be well-pleased with what thou givest her. God knows what is in your hearts; God is All-knowing, All-clement.
Thereafter women are not lawful to thee, nor art thou permitted to take other wives[40] *in exchange for them, even though their beauty please thee, except what thy right hand owns (as slaves); God keeps watch over everything.*

Their dowries: their bridegroom's gift (*mahr*) to the bride on the day after marriage. This bridegroom's gift is a payment for the (surrender of the) vulva. One could either pay the bridegroom's gift at once (as soon as the marriage settlement is concluded) or the amount could be arranged and stipulated in the marriage settlement (and paid later). One may now ask: Why does God say: Those *to whom thou has given their dowries* as well as those *whom God has given to thee (mimmā afā'a llāhu 'alaika') as spoils of war* and those *who have emigrated with thee*? Wherein lies the advantage of these (restricting) specifications? To this I answer: God has chosen for his Messenger the most excellent and most appropriate and has recommended to him the best and the purest, just as he also granted others to him (in addition to the particular ones which are specified here) and has also distinguished him through other signs. Reference to the bridegroom's gift in the marriage settlement is more appropriate and more excellent than omitting the reference, although the marriage settlement is possible (also without this). (In the latter case) the man has the right to touch the woman and the duty to pay to her the 'appropriate bridegroom's gift' (*mahr al-mithl*[41]) when he cohabits with her. On the other hand, 'compensation' (*mut'a*) is to be paid if he does not cohabit with her (and withdraws from the marriage). Immediate payment of the bridegroom's gift (as soon as the marriage settlement is concluded) is now more excellent than a reference to it (in the marriage settlement) and deferment of payment. Immediate payment was the custom and practice among the ancestors, and nothing different from this was known then.

The same is true of the female slave, when she has been captured by the one who possesses her, in which case the sword and lance are the suitors of the betrothed, and she belongs among the booty which God has granted (to the believers) when in the 'sphere of war' (*dār al-ḥarb*[42]), allowing (for marriage) sooner and better than one who is acquired through importation and purchase. . . . Also the female relatives who emigrated with the Messenger of God were in a similar position and were not forbidden to him (for reasons of too close a blood relationship or relationship by marriage), but were more excellent (for marriage) than those who had not emigrated with him. From Umm Hāni', the daughter of Abū Ṭālib (and cousin of Muḥammad on his father's side), (the following account) is related: The Messenger of God asked for my hand in marriage, but I excused myself regarding his proposal and he accepted the excuse, whereupon God sent down the present verse. Now I was no longer allowed to him (for marriage) since I did not emigrate with him but had been an unbeliever up to the time of the surrender of Mecca.

And any woman believer, if she give herself to the Prophet and if the Prophet desire to take her in marriage: We have allowed to you such of the believing women who desire to give themselves to you, without requiring a bridegroom's gift—should this case ever occur. For this reason (because it is undecided whether this case occurs), (the word) 'woman' appears without the definite article. There is no agreement that this (actually) ever happened. According to Ibn 'Abbās, the Messenger of God did not receive a single wife (who gave herself to him) as a gift. (On the other hand) some say that he had four wives who had given themselves to him, namely, Maimūna bint al-Ḥārith, Zainab bint Khuzaima, the 'mother of the poor among the "helpers" (*anṣār*)', as well as Umm Sharīk bint Jābir and Khaula bint Ḥakīm. . . .

So that no fault may be found in thee: so that you may not be hampered (by any fault) in your religion, since we have especially distinguished you through the purification (of your humble way of acting) and through the selection of what is more appropriate and excellent; and (that no fault may be found in thee) in your secular life (*fī dunyāka*) because we have allowed to you (in spite of the alleged restrictions based upon principle all) categories of wives whom one may marry (that is, non-relatives, slaves, paternal as well as maternal female cousins), and have added to this those who give themselves to you. . . .

God is All-compassionate towards him who falls into oppression, provided that he becomes converted, and *All-forgiving* since he is generous concerning his servants.

The following is related: When the 'mothers of the believers'[43] (once) were jealous of each other and wished (each for herself) for an increase in their allowances and for this reason caused the anger of the Messenger of God, he held himself aloof from them for an entire month. Then the (so-called) *takhyīr* came down (that is, the verse: 'Thy Lord creates whatever He wills and chooses (*ikhtāra*); they have not the choice (*al-khiyara*)', Sūra 28:68), and they became apprehensive that the Prophet would divorce them. So they said: 'Messenger of God, make the decision yourself concerning us, and rule according to your wish!' From 'Ā'isha is related that she said to the Prophet: 'Messenger of God, I see that your Lord is in a hurry whenever your inclination for affection (*hawāka*) is concerned.'

Thou mayest put off whom thou wilt of them, and whom thou wilt thou mayest take to thee: . . . That is: You may refrain from sexual intercourse with whomever you please and cohabit with whomever you please among them. Or, you may divorce whomever you please and retain whomever you please. Or, you are not required to grant a share (of sexual intercourse) to any unless you so desire, and you may grant a share to whomever you please. Or, you may discontinue marriage with women of your (religious) community (*umma*) from whom you wish to separate, and you may enter into marriage with whomever you wish. (Finally) from al-Ḥasan (al-Baṣrī) (is related): When the Prophet sought marriage with a woman, no one else could ask to marry her until the Prophet released her.

Thus, an extensive pattern is suggested here, of which the following is to be kept in mind: The Prophet may divorce (a woman) or keep (her). If he keeps (her) he may practise or refrain from sexual intercourse (with her) and grant to her a share (of sexual intercourse) or not. If he divorces or separates (from her) he may leave the divorced woman alone without wishing to take her (back) or he may wish to take her again.

It is related that the Prophet (refrained from sexual intercourse and) put off temporarily the following wives: Sauda, Juwairiya,

Ṣafiyya, Maimūna, and Umm Ḥabība. In so doing he used to grant them a share (of sexual intercourse) according to his wish. Among the wives whom the Prophet preferred to take to himself belong 'Ā'isha, Ḥafṣa, Umm Salama, and Zainab (bint Jaḥsh). Thus, he used to put five off temporarily in order to take four to himself. (On the other hand) it is related that, disregarding divorce and the selection concerned with it, the Prophet treated (all his wives) the same, with the exception of Sauda, who relinquished the night belonging to her to 'Ā'isha and said (to the Prophet): 'Do not divorce me but let me remain in the company of your wives!' ...

God knows what is in your hearts: Herein lies a threat against the wives of the Prophet who are not satisfied with what God has decreed in this respect, but who have entrusted themselves to the will of his Messenger. (At the same time, herein lies) an inducement for the submission of their hearts, for a peaceful settlement among themselves, and for a common effort towards the contentment and happiness of the Messenger of God. ...

Thereafter: after the nine (wives which you have[44]). That is, nine is the right number of wives for the Messenger of God, just as four is the right number for his community. He is not allowed to exceed this number.

Nor art thou permitted to take other wives in exchange for them: ... (According to this revelation) the Prophet is restricted to his nine wives (named above), whom he left behind (as widows) at his death. ...

III

SALVATION HISTORY

1. Religious communities and prophets

Ṭabarī on Sūra 2:213/209

The people were a single community; then God sent forth the prophets as messengers of good tidings and as warners. And He sent down with them the Book with the truth, that He might decide between the people concerning their differences. But those to whom it had been given disagreed concerning it, after clear signs had come to them, being insolent one to another. Then, by His leave, God guided those who believed to the truth concerning the matters about which the people[1] *disagreed; and God guides whomever He wills to a straight path.*

The people were a single community (umma wāḥida) . . . : The commentators (*ahl at-ta'wīl*) disagree regarding the meaning of (the word) *umma*[2] in this passage and regarding the people whom God characterizes as a single *umma*. Some (commentators) maintain that the people referred to are the ten generations between Adam and Noah, all of whom followed a law of truth (*sharī'a min al-ḥaqq*), after which the people came to disagree. To be cited (as authorities) for this view are (the following):

Muhammad ibn Bashshār has related to us the following statement of Ibn 'Abbās on the basis of (a chain of authorities including) Abū Dāwūd (aṭ-Ṭayālisī), Hammām ibn Munabbih, and 'Ikrima: Between Noah and Adam lay ten generations which followed a law of truth. The people later came to disagree and God sent the prophets forth as messengers of good tidings and as warners. Ibn 'Abbās says that 'Abd Allāh (ibn Mas'ūd) is reported to have read (the present verse): 'The people were a single *umma*, but later came to disagree;[3] then God sent. . . .'

Al-Ḥasan ibn Yaḥyā has related to us . . . the following statement of Qatāda concerning the words of God 'the people were a single *umma*': They all found themselves on the path of right guidance, but then came to disagree. Then God caused the prophets to appear as messengers of good tidings and as warners. The first prophet to appear was Noah.

Thus, the interpretation (*ta'wīl*) of (the word) *umma*, according to the report (*qaul*) of Ibn 'Abbās which is related above, is 'religion' (*dīn*), as (the poet) an-Nābigha adh-Dhubyānī says:

> I swear it, and leave behind
> no suspicion in your soul.
> Can a man with *umma* then go astray?

What is meant is a man with religion. According to the meaning contained in the statements of these authorities, the (present) verse is to be interpreted as follows: The people were one *umma* which was unified by a single creed (*milla*) and a single religion (*dīn*), but then came to disagree. Then God caused the prophets to appear as messengers of good tidings and as warners.

The original meaning of *umma* was a 'community' (*jamā'a*) which was unified by a single religion. One then spoke of 'the *umma*' instead of 'the religion' because the latter indicated the former. In this sense God says: 'If God had willed, He would have made you one *umma*' (Sūra 5:48/53; 16:93/95), that is, adherents of a single religion and a single creed. Thus, in his interpretation of God's words 'the people were a single *umma*', Ibn 'Abbās followed the view that they were adherents of a single religion, but then came to disagree.

Other (exegetes) maintain (however) that the interpretation is (as follows): Adam was in reality a model (*imām*) for his children; then God caused the prophets to appear among his descendants. These commentators interpret (the word) *umma* in such a way that obedience to God as well as the demand to acknowledge his unity and to follow his command (therefore, a manner of action as was characteristic of Adam) are also contained in the meaning of this term. To support this view they refer to the words of God: 'Surely, Abraham was an *umma* obedient to (the one) God, a man of pure faith (*ḥanīf*) and no idolater' (Sūra 16:120/121[4]), since here with the word *umma* God means a model (*imām*) by which one is led to virtue and which one follows. To be cited (as authorities) for this view are (the following):

Muḥammad ibn 'Amr has related to us ... the following statement of Mujāhid: By God's words 'the people were a single *umma*', Adam is meant. ...

Al-Qāsim has related to us ... the following statement of Mujāhid: By God's words 'the people were a single *umma*', Adam is meant. Between Adam and Noah there were ten prophets; then God sent forth the (other) prophets as messengers of good tidings and as warners. Adam was a single *umma*.

Those who advocate this view thus consider it permissible to refer to an individual with the designation for a community (*jamā'a*) because the various virtues found dispersed among members of the community come together in that individual whom God designates as *umma*. Thus one says: 'So and so constitutes an *umma*', when he assumes the position of such a person.[5]

It is (also) possible that God so designated Adam because the latter brought together various people in the virtues to which he called them. Since Adam now constituted the occasion for the coming together of his descendants, who were grouped together until they (later) came to disagree, God designated him as an *umma*.

Other (exegetes) say that the meaning may be as follows: In those days the people were a single *umma* with a single religion (*dīn*) when God caused the children of Adam to come forth from the loin of the latter and presented them to him. To be cited (as authorities) for this view are (the following):

'Ammār has related to us ... the following statement of Ubayy ibn Ka'b concerning the words of God 'the people were a single *umma*': When the people were presented to Adam, they were a single *umma*. At that time God created them so that they found themselves in the state of submission to God (*islām*). They devoted humble adoration to him and were a single *umma* and were altogether people submitted to God (*muslimūn*). Then after (the death of) Adam they came to disagree. Ubayy read (the text of the Qur'ān as follows): 'The people were a single *umma*, but later came to disagree; then God sent the prophets as messengers of good tidings and as warners.' (According to Ubayy) God first sent forth the messengers and sent down the books on account of the disunity of the people. ...

Interpreting the verse according to this view is in accordance with the interpretation (*ta'wīl*) of those who maintained with Ibn 'Abbās that between Adam and Noah the people followed a single religion—this view is explained above. However, the time during which the people constituted a single *umma* according to this view is not the same as that suggested by Ibn 'Abbās.

In opposition to these views, other (exegetes) say that God's words 'the people were a single *umma*' mean nothing more than that they followed a single religion and that God then sent the prophets (without signifying anything further). To be cited (as authorities) for this view are (the following):

Muḥammad ibn Sa'd has related to us ... from Ibn 'Abbās (the following interpretation of) the words of God 'the people were a single *umma*': They constituted a single religion and then God sent the prophets as messengers of good tidings and as warners.

(Aṭ-Ṭabarī concludes that) among the interpretations of this verse one comes closest to what is correct if one says that God proclaims the following to his servants: The people were a single *umma* (in the sense of a community) with a single religion (*dīn*) and a single creed (*milla*). ... The religion which they followed was the religion of truth. ... Later they became at variance in their religion; then, on account of the disunity in their religion, God sent the prophets as messengers of good tidings and as warners, and he sent down with them on each occasion the Book in order to decide between the people concerning their disagreement. God did this out of mercy towards his creatures and in order to be just with them (when he later calls them to account).

It is possible that the period during which the people were a single *umma* lasted from the time of Adam to the time of Noah, as 'Ikrima relates from Ibn 'Abbās and as Qatāda maintains. It is (however also) possible that this was the case (only) at that time when God presented his creatures to Adam. (Finally) it is (also) possible that this was at another time. There exists no hint in the Book of God and no report through which a trustworthy argument might be produced to show that this period was that of the Fall. On the contrary, it is impossible to say regarding it other than what God has said: that the people were a single *umma* and that after they came to disagree he sent among them the prophets and messengers. In this matter, ignorance of the time in question produces just as little harm to us as knowledge of it produces benefit for us, since it does not represent an act of obedience to God.

This may therefore remain undecided, but it should be noted that in every case the Qur'ān clearly shows that those whom God proclaims to have been a single *umma* were so designated on the basis of their belief and their religion of truth and that there was with them no unbelief and no idolatry. God has said in the sūra in which Jonah is mentioned: 'The people were (originally) only one *umma*; then they fell into disagreement. Had it not been for a word from thy Lord that preceded, a decision would already have been given between them concerning their differences' (Sūra 10:19/20). Thus, God has pronounced a threat against disunity and not against harmony and the existence of a single *umma*. If the people were in agreement in unbelief before disunity entered and if they became at variance later, then such disunity would have originated only under the assumption that some of these people turned (from unbelief) to belief. In this case, however, it would have been more appropriate to divine wisdom for a promise to be pronounced rather than a threat, since it then would have been the case that some of these people would have turned to obedience to God. It is unthinkable that God would pronounce a threat if such a condition for repentance and conversion existed, or that he would neglect to do so if all (people) were in agreement in unbelief and idolatry.

Indeed (aṭ-Ṭabarī concludes), God's words *then God sent forth the prophets as messengers of good tidings and as warners* mean that he sent messengers to those who obeyed him, bringing good tidings concerning abundant reward and precious return (to God). With the expression *as warners* God means that the prophets should warn the disobedient and the unbelievers about severe punishment, harmful revenge, and their eternal stay in the hell-fire.

And He sent down with them the Book with the truth, that He might decide between the people concerning their differences: by which God means that the Book (*al-kitāb*), that is, the Torah (*at-taurāt*), should decide between the people concerning that about which they disagreed. God has assigned the decision to the Book and has established it and not the prophets and messengers as that which decides between the people, since whenever one of the prophets or messengers had to bring down a decision, he did this on the basis of the indications which are given in the Book which is sent down by God. Thus the Book was the deciding factor between the people on the basis of its indications of that which (at that time) had qualified as an indication of the right decision, since the verdict between the people was also set down from the other side (that is, from the prophets).

The discussion of the interpretation (*ta'wīl*) of God's words *But those to whom it had been given disagreed concerning it, after clear signs had come to them, being insolent one to another.* His words *disagreed concerning it* mean that they disagreed concerning the Book which God had sent down, that is, the Torah. (His words) *those to whom it had been given* mean the Jews of the Children of Israel.[6] They are the ones who had been given the Torah and its knowledge. ... (His words) *after clear signs had come to them* mean: after they had received the arguments and the proofs (*adilla*) of God indicating that the Book, concerning which they disagreed in their decisions, had come from God and that it constituted the truth, concerning which they were not to disagree and which must not be disobeyed. Thus, God proclaims that the Jews of the Children of Israel disobeyed the Book, the Torah, and disagreed concerning it in spite of the knowledge that it contains. Thereby they deliberately disobeyed God since they violated his command and the decision of his Book.

Thus God proclaims that this (disunity) occurred through mutual rebellion among themselves, when they sinned intentionally and committed disobedience by disobeying God's command. ...

God's words *But those to whom it had been given disagreed concerning it, after clear signs had come to them, being insolent one to another* mean: Those who disagreed among the Jews of the Children of Israel disagreed concerning my Book, which I sent down to them by my prophets, not because they had not known it; on the contrary, they came to disagree regarding it only after knowing it, for they disobeyed the decision of the Book, when its arguments had already been presented thoroughly. (This disunity originated) out of rebellion among themselves because some of them desired mastery over the others and regarded them with scorn. ...

The discussion of the interpretation (*ta'wīl*) of God's words *Then, by His leave, God guided those who believed to the truth concerning the matters about which the people disagreed; and God guides whomever He wills to a straight path.* God's words *Then ... God guided those who believed to the truth* mean that God has granted success to those who are believing, that is, those who support belief in (the one) God and his Messenger, Muḥammad, and who put their trust in the latter and are convinced that his message, concerning which those to whom the Book had been given previously disagreed, comes from God. The disunity in which God left these people alone, while rightly guiding and helping to the truth those who believe in Muḥammad, concerns (Friday as) the 'day of gathering' (for worship). Although this day had been enjoined upon them as a duty just as it has been upon us, they deviated from it and changed (their day of worship) to the Sabbath. The Prophet has said: Although we are the last, we surpass (the others in following God's commands), even though the Book was given to them before it was given to us and we thus possessed it after they did. God has rightly guided us to this day, concerning which they have disagreed. The Jews have taken the following day and the Christians have taken the day after that (as the day of worship). . . .

Concerning the matters about which the people disagreed, Ibn Zaid is reported to have said, according to Yūnus ibn 'Abd al-A'lā, that God's words 'then God guided those who believed to the truth' mean (that he led the believers) to Islam. The people disagreed concerning prayer. Some prayed facing towards the East while others faced towards Jerusalem (*bait al-muqaddas*). Then God led us to the (right) direction of prayer (*qibla*) towards Mecca.[7] (Also) the people disagreed concerning fasting. Some fasted at certain times of the day while others fasted at certain times of the night. Then God led us to the (right) times of fasting.[8] (Also) the people disagreed concerning the 'day of gathering' (for worship). While the Jews chose the Sabbath, the Christians took Sunday; then God led us to the (right) 'day of gathering' (on Friday). (Also) the people disagreed concerning Abraham. The Jews considered him to be a Jew and the Christians considered him to be a Christian. Then God freed him from such a suspicion and showed him to be a *ḥanīf* who was surrendered to God (*ḥanīfan musliman*[9]), who also was not to be classed among the heathen as some maintained, who claimed that he had been one of the unbelievers. (Finally) the people (also) disagreed concerning Jesus. The Jews considered him to be the victim of a falsehood while the Christians considered him to be a god (*rabb*). Thereupon God led us to the truth concerning him. God says all of this (with his words): *Then . . . God guided those who believed to the truth concerning the matters about which the people disagreed.*

(Aṭ-Ṭabarī concludes that) when God by his goodness leads to the truth those who believe in Muḥammad and his message, concerning which these groups of the Children of Israel who had possessed the Book previously disagreed, then this guidance lies in his assisting them to (return to) the truth, according to which the people lived before the disunity that God depicts in this verse existed. For those people were a single *umma*, namely the religion (*dīn*) of Abraham, the *ḥanīf* who was surrendered to God and the friend of the compassionate.[10] Those who believe have been made 'an *umma* standing in the middle' so that they may be 'witnesses among the nations'—so your Lord describes them (in Sūra 2:143/137).[11]

2. *Abraham the* ḥanīf

Baiḍāwī on Sūra 3:65/58–68/61

People of the Book! Why do you dispute concerning Abraham?
The Torah and the Gospel were not sent down until after him.
What, have you no reason?
Ha, you are the ones who (like to) dispute regarding what you
know. But why do you dispute regarding a matter about which
you know nothing? God knows, but you know not.
No! Abraham in truth was neither a Jew nor a Christian, but a
ḥanīf *surrendered to God* (ḥanīfan musliman). *Certainly he was*
never one of the idolaters!
Surely the people standing closest to Abraham are those who
followed him and this Prophet, and those who believe; and God
is the Protector of the believers.

People of the Book! Why do you dispute concerning Abraham?[12] . . . : There was a quarrel between the Jews and the Christians concerning Abraham, as each party maintained that he belonged to them. When they brought this dispute before the Messenger of God, the (present) verse came down. The meaning is the following: Judaism and Christianity were instituted when the Torah came down to Moses and the Gospel came down to Jesus. Now Abraham lived a thousand years before Moses and two thousand years before Jesus. How then could he have belonged to either of these religions?

What, have you no reason?: for you maintain what is absurd.

Ha, you are the ones who (like to) dispute regarding what you know . . . : . . . Your folly lies in that you have argued stubbornly about things concerning which you have knowledge, that is, on the basis of what you have found in the Torah and the Gospel, or what you claim to be contained in these books. But why do you dispute (now) concerning something about which you have no knowledge and that is not contained in your books, namely, the religion of Abraham? . . .

God knows: that concerning which you dispute. . . .

Abraham in truth was neither a Jew nor a Christian, but a ḥanīf, one who had kept away from false doctrine, *surrendered to God* (*muslim*), one who was led by God. This does not mean that Abraham belonged to the creed (*milla*) of Islam. If this were the claim, then the same refutation would apply in this case.

Certainly he was never one of the idolaters: Here is indicated indirectly that the Jews and Christians (in reality) are polytheists, since they associate Ezra and Christ with God (as divine beings)[13]. . . .

3. *Abraham and the holy place at Mecca*

Baiḍāwī on Sūra 2:125/119

And when We appointed the House to be a place of visitation for the people, and a sanctuary. And (We said): 'Take to yourselves Abraham's station for a place of prayer.' And We made covenant with Abraham and Ishmael (with the words): 'Purify My House for those who shall go around it and those who cleave to it, to those who bow and prostrate themselves.'

And when We appointed the House (*al-bait*): that is, the Ka'ba, which is often called (simply) 'the house', just as (in Arabic) the Pleiades are often called (simply) 'the constellation' (*an-najm*).

To be a place of visitation (*mathābatan*) *for the people*: to be a place to which eminent visitors and the like return (*yathūbu*). Or: to be a place of reward (*thawāb*), in that the people who visit there will receive (heavenly) reward, if they go to this place as pilgrims (*bi-l-ḥajj wa-l-i'timār*). Some read (instead): 'to be places of visitation (*mathābātin*)', since the verse deals with a place for each individual (visitor).

And a sanctuary: and a place of safety where the people who stay there are not exposed to any danger, as God says: 'Have they not seen that We have appointed a sacred sanctuary in the district of Mecca, while all about them the people are snatched away (by force)? What, do they believe in vanity, and do they disbelieve in God's blessing?' (Sūra 29:67) Or: (a place of safety, in the sense) that the people who undertake the pilgrimage to that place are safe from the punishment of the hereafter, since the pilgrimage eradicates previous (sins). Or: (a place of safety) at which a criminal who seeks refuge there is not called to account until he leaves this place. This is the teaching of Abū Ḥanīfa.

And (We said): take (wa-ttakhidhū) to yourselves Abraham's station for a place of prayer: ... The station of Abraham (*maqām ibrāhīm*) is the stone on which his footprint is found and the place at which he stood when he arose to summon the people to the pilgrimage or for the erection of the House (that is, the Ka'ba). It is the spot which (still) today is called the 'station of Abraham'.

It is reported that Muḥammad seized the hand of 'Umar and said: 'This is the station of Abraham.' Then 'Umar asked: 'Do we not want to make it a place of prayer?', to which the Prophet answered: 'That has not been commanded to me.' However, no sooner had the sun set than the (present) verse came down.

Some say (also) that it was here that the command came to do two prostrations (*rak'ān*, sing. *rak'a*) in the circumambulation (*ṭawāf*) (of the Ka'ba), since Jābir has related that when the Prophet had completed his circumambulation he proceeded to the station of Abraham where he performed (*khalfahū*) two prostrations and recited: 'Take to yourselves Abraham's station for a place of prayer.' ... Others say that the station of Abraham is the entire sacred area (*ḥaram*). (Still) others say that it consists of the stations of the pilgrimage. If these were made into a place of prayer, then this would mean that the people would call (to God) and come near him at these places.

Nāfi' and Ibn 'Āmir read the past tense (or perfect) form *wa-ttakhadhū* (instead of *wa-ttakhidhū*) and connected the sentence to the (previous one): 'And when We appointed the House. ...' That is: (And when We appointed the House to be a place of visitation for the people, and a sanctuary) and (when) the people took the so-called station of Abraham, that is the Ka'ba, as the orientation point for the direction of prayer (*qibla*).

And We made covenant with Abraham and Ishmael (with the words): Purify My House: We commanded them to purify (the house). ... The meaning of these words is: Purify it of the idols, the impurities, and whatever is not worthy of it! Or, make it free for those who make the circumambulation around this House and give themselves to worship, (that is) for those who visit there or devote themselves to worship there! ...

4. *Noah and the flood*[14]

Zamakhsharī on Sūra 11:36/38–39/41

And it was revealed to Noah, saying: 'None of thy people shall believe but he who has already believed; so be thou not distressed
by what they may be doing.
Make thou the Ark under Our eyes, and as We reveal; and do not speak to Me concerning those who have done evil; they shall
(without doubt) be drowned.'
So he was making the Ark; and whenever the chiefs of his people passed by him they scoffed at him. He said: 'You may scoff at us, but we surely will scoff at you, just as you scoff
(at us).
And you shall know to whom will come a chastisement degrading
him, and upon whom shall alight a lasting chastisement.'

None of thy people shall believe: Here hope is terminated for Noah that his (unbelieving) countrymen would believe, (and he is informed here) that this is now unthinkable and no expectation should be retained regarding it.

But he who has already believed: except those among whom Noah found that his expectation regarding belief had already been realized. ...

So be thou not distressed (fa-lā tabta'is): Do not grieve like a poor sorrowful person. (The poet Ḥassān ibn Thābit) has said:

Take what God apportions (to you) without
being troubled about it (*ghaira mubta'is*)!
Remain noble and of good courage!

The meaning is: Do not grieve over the slander, abuse, and enmity which they have brought against you! The time has come when you shall be avenged towards them.

The meaning of the statement *make thou the Ark under Our eyes* is: And construct the Ark, protected (by us)! Properly it means: (And construct it) covered by our eyes! It is as if God had eyes just like Noah had which protected him from deviating from the correct way of constructing the Ark, and which prevented his enemies from interfering with his work.

And as We reveal: ... According to Ibn 'Abbās, Noah did not know how to build the Ark. So God revealed to him that it should be built in the shape of a bird's breast (*ju'ju' aṭ-ṭā'ir*).

And do not speak to Me concerning those who have done evil: And do not call to me on behalf of your fellow tribesmen, attempting to spare them the punishment through your intercession!

They shall (without doubt) be drowned: They are condemned to the drowning. This is an inevitable matter and is determined by the decree of God. The writing reed (with which this decree has been written down) has already dried up so that one can no longer repeal it. (Thus the case here is) as in God's words: 'Abraham, turn away from this; thy Lord's command has surely come, and there is coming upon them a chastisement not to be turned back!' (Sūra 11:76/78). ...

They scoffed at him and his shipbuilding. Noah built the Ark in a pathless desert which was a long distance from water, and (indeed) at a time when the water was already rising enormously. The unbelievers laughed and said: 'Noah, you have changed from a prophet into a carpenter!'

But we surely will scoff at you, just as you scoff (at us): that is, we shall mock you just as you (mock us), since the drowning comes to you in this world and the burning (of hell-fire) comes to you in the next world. Others say (that the meaning is): While you regard us as stupid for building the Ark, we regard you as stupid for being in the state of unbelief and abandoned to the anger and punishment of God. You must be regarded as much more stupid than we are. Or: since you regard us as stupid, then we regard you as stupid (precisely) because you regard (others) as stupid, for you could do this only because you do not know the true state of affairs, and you rely only on external appearance, as is usually the case with the ignorant (*al-jahala*) who are far from the facts (*al-ḥaqā'iq*).

The following is also related: Noah prepared the Ark for two years. It was three hundred yards (*dhirā'*) long, fifty yards wide, and towered up to a height of thirty yards. It was made of teak wood and had three rooms inside. Into the lower one Noah placed the wild and carnivorous animals, as well as the reptiles (having selected one pair of each kind), and in the middle one (he placed) the riding and pasture animals (which he had selected in the same manner). He (himself) and his companions stayed in the upper room along with the necessary provisions. (Moreover) Noah took the body of Adam with him and laid it crosswise between the men and the women. According to al-Ḥasan (al-Baṣrī) the Ark was a thousand two hundred yards long and six hundred yards wide.

It is reported (concerning Jesus) that, when the disciples said to him: 'Send to us just one man who was a witness of the Ark and could tell us about it!', he (continued) walking along with them until he came to a pile of dirt; then he took a handful of it and said: 'Do you know who this is?' They replied: 'God and his messenger know very well.' Then Jesus said: 'This is Ka'b ibn Ḥam (the grandson of Noah).' As he said this he struck the pile with his staff and added: 'Rise up, as God wills!' And behold, Ka'b ibn Ḥam arose and shook the dust from his head. He was an old man; yet when Jesus asked him if he had died as an old man, he answered: 'I died as a young man; but (when you just awakened me) I thought the Hour (of judgment) had come[15] and thus I have grown old.' Then Jesus said: 'Tell us about the Ark of Noah!', and he answered: 'It was a thousand yards long and six hundred yards wide. It had three decks: one for the riding animals and the wild animals, one for the people, and one for the birds.' At this point Jesus said: 'Return now, if God wills, to the condition you were in (until now)!' Then he returned to dirt. . . .

Zamakhsharī on Sūra 11:42f./44f.

So it ran with them amid waves like mountains; and Noah called to his son who was standing apart: 'Embark with us, my son, and be thou not with the unbelievers!'

He said: 'I will take refuge in a mountain that will protect me from the water.' Noah said: 'Today there is no protector from God's command but for him on whom He has mercy.' And the waves came between them, and he was among the drowned.

. . . Some say the name of Noah's son was Canaan, and others say the name was Yām.[16] 'Alī read 'their son' (*ibnahā*) (instead of 'his son'), in which case the pronoun refers also to Noah's wife ... thus supporting the view of al-Ḥasan (al-Baṣrī). Qatāda says: I asked al-Ḥasan (about Noah's unbelieving son) and received the following answer: 'He was certainly not his son.' To this I objected to al-Ḥasan: 'God (himself) reports (in Noah's words): 'My son is of my family (*min ahlī*) (Sūra 11:45/47). But you say that he cannot be Noah's son, while among the People of the Book there is no disagreement that he was Noah's son.' To this al-Ḥasan replied: 'Who then will receive his religion from the People of the Book?' Al-Ḥasan draws his conclusion from the fact that the text states 'of my family' rather than 'of me (*minnī*)'. This son can thus be attributed to his mother in two ways: Either he was a stepson of Noah (belonging to his wife by an earlier marriage), as 'Umar ibn Abī Salama was for the Messenger of God (through his marriage with Umm Salama); or he was an illegitimate child, though this would have been a blemish from which the prophets have been kept free (*'uṣima*). ...

5. *Joseph and his brothers*

Baiḍāwī on Sūra 12:4ff.[17]

(Remember) when Joseph said to his father: 'Father, I saw
eleven stars and the sun and the moon; I saw them bowing down
before me.'
His father[18] *said: 'My (little) son, relate not thy vision to thy*
brothers, lest they devise against thee some guile. Surely Satan is
to man a manifest enemy.
So will thy Lord choose thee, and teach thee the interpretation of
tales, and perfect His blessing upon thee and upon the family of
Jacob, as He perfected it formerly on thy fathers Abraham and
Isaac. Surely thy Lord is All-knowing, All-wise.'
In Joseph and his brothers were signs for those who ask
questions.

... *I saw*: as a vision (*ru'yā*) and not with the eyes (*ru'ya*). (That a vision is intended here) is clear from God's words: 'Relate not thy vision!' (verse 5) and 'This is the interpretation of my vision of long ago' (verse 100/101).

Eleven stars and the sun and the moon. From Jābir it is related that a Jew came to the Messenger of God and said: 'Muḥammad, tell me about the stars which Joseph saw.' The Prophet was silent (at first); then Gabriel came down and gave him the information about it, whereupon the Prophet said to the Jew: 'If I tell you (about it), will you profess Islam?' When the Jew consented, the Prophet said: '(The stars were) Jaryān, aṭ-Ṭāriq, adh-Dhayyāl, Qābis, 'Amūdān, al-Falīq, al-Muṣabbiḥ, aḍ-Ḍarūḥ, al-Far', Waththāb, and Dhū l-Katifain. Joseph saw them and the sun and the moon descending from heaven and they bowed down before him.' Then the Jew said: 'Yes, indeed, these are the names.'

... *My (little) son*: The diminutive form of 'son' appears here either as a sign of affection or as an indication of Joseph's youth, for he was twelve years old. ...

Relate not thy vision to thy brothers, lest they devise against thee some guile: lest they contrive some trick in order to destroy you. Jacob understood from Joseph's vision that God was choosing him to be a messenger and was raising him up over his brothers; thus, he feared that they would envy and hate Joseph. A vision (*ru'yā*) is like a visible sight (*ru'ya*) except that the former refers especially to what appears in sleep. ... A vision is the impression (*inṭibā'*) of an image (*ṣūra*) which is communicated from the realm of imagination (*mutakhayyila*) to the realm of sense-perception (*ḥiss mushtarak*) (which involves the individual senses).[19] A genuine vision occurs only through the contact of the soul with the supernatural world (*malakūt*) on account of the relationship between the two which exists when the soul is freed to any extent from the control of the body. At that time it is capable of shaping (*taṣawwara*) an image according to its capacity, based on concepts (*ma'ānī*) which are given to it from the supernatural world. Then the imagination tunes in upon this concept through a related (sensory) image which transmits it to the common sense-perception where it (finally) becomes perceptible. When this image is so closely related to the concept (from the supernatural world) that the only distinction lies in the universal character (*kulliyya*) (of the concept) and the particular character (*ghuz'iyya*) (of the image), then the vision requires no interpretation. Otherwise, such an interpretation would be needed. ...

Surely Satan is to man a manifest enemy: He clearly demonstrated enmity (against mankind) through what he did to Adam and Eve.[20] Thus, he would spare no pains in deluding Joseph's brothers and stirring up envy among them, inciting them to the use of treachery.

So: that is, just as God chose you through this vision, which indicates high standing as well as power and perfection of the soul, *will thy Lord choose thee* for prophethood and rulership, or (simply) for great things. . . .

And teach thee the interpretation of tales (aḥādīth): the interpretation of the vision. If the vision is true, it is based upon narratives of the angel; but if it is false, it is based upon narratives of the (human) soul and of Satan.[21] Or, (it may mean) the interpretation of the obscure matters in God's books, the practices (*sunan*) of the prophets, and the sayings of wise men. It is a plural form of *ḥadīth*. . . .

And perfect His blessing upon thee: by bestowing prophethood upon you, or by granting to you the blessing of the next world as well as the blessing of this world.

And upon the family of Jacob: by which God means either the other sons of Jacob, in which case Jacob may have inferred their prophethood from the light of the stars; or alternatively, God may mean the descendants of Jacob.

As He perfected it formerly on thy fathers: by appointing them as messengers. Some say (that God perfected his blessing) on Abraham by taking him as a 'friend' (*khalīl*)[22] and by saving him from the fire (into which the unbelievers had cast him),[23] and (he perfected it) on Isaac by delivering him from the sacrifice and by ransoming him with a great victim (for the sacrifice)[24]. . . .

In Joseph and his brothers: that is, in the story about them.

Were signs: meaning either evidences of God's power and wisdom, or indications of your (Muḥammad's) prophethood (since this story of Joseph and his brothers could have become known only through revelation).

For those who ask questions: for those who ask about the story of Joseph and his brothers.[25] And by 'his brothers' are meant the ten[26] half-brothers, who included Judah, Reuben, Simeon, Levi, Zebulon, Issachar, and Dinah, who were born to Jacob by his cousin Leah, whom he married first. After her death he married her sister Rachel who bore him Benjamin and Joseph. Others say that Jacob was married to Leah and Rachel at the same time, since this was not prohibited at that time (that is, having sisters as wives).[27] (Also among the so-called half-brothers) were four others: Dan, Naphthali, Gad, and Asher, who were born by two concubines, named Zilphah and Bilhah.

(*Contents of verses 8–14*: The brothers now decide to kill Joseph or to expel him, and they agree to cast him into a well so that some traveller will find him and take him away. They persuade Jacob to let Joseph go with them on the following day, and Jacob gives his consent, but at the same time reminds them of the dangers which are a threat from the wolves.)

> *15. Thus they went with him and agreed to put him in the bottom of the well. And We revealed to him: 'Thou shalt tell them of this deed of theirs when they are unaware.'*

And agreed to put him in the bottom of the well: and resolved to cast him into the well, that is, the well of Jerusalem (*bait al-muqaddas*), or a well in the land of Jordan, or one between Egypt and Midian, or one that is three leagues[28] from Jacob's home. The main clause (to which the present is a subordinate clause) is omitted, but would read something like: 'They harmed him in various ways.' Thus it is related that when they came to the desert with him, they began to harm and to beat him until they almost killed him. Then when he cried and called out for help, Judah said: 'Did you not agree with me that you would not kill him?' So they took him to the well and cast him down into it. Then, since he clung to the rim of the well, they bound his hands. And they tore his shirt from his body so they could smear it with blood and thus deceive his father. Joseph implored: 'Brothers, give my shirt back to me so I can cover myself in it!' But they answered: 'Call on the eleven stars and the sun and the moon to clothe you and befriend you!' Then, when he was half-way down, they let him fall. There was water in the well and he sank down (into it) until he reached safety on a rock that was there. On this rock he stood weeping until Gabriel came to him with a revelation, as is stated in God's words: *And We revealed to him*. (At that time) Joseph was seventeen years old, or, others say he was just reaching puberty and had already received revelations as a child, like John (the Baptist) and Jesus.[29] The following story is also related: When Abraham was cast into the fire, his clothes had been stripped off him, and Gabriel brought him a shirt made of paradise silk and clothed him in it. (Later) Abraham handed this shirt on to Isaac, and Isaac gave it to Jacob, who put it in an amulet which he hung on Joseph. Gabriel then took the shirt (in the well) and clothed Joseph in it.

Thou shalt tell them of this deed of theirs: You will report to them what they have done to you.

When they are unaware: that you are Joseph. For you will receive a high position and be elevated far above their expectations. Also, a long time will have passed during which one's appearance and form change. The expression here is a play on words, referring to what he said to them (later) in Egypt when they came to him to buy grain, and he recognized them while they took him to be a stranger. God gave Joseph the good news concerning the outcome of his affair in order to comfort him and calm his heart. Others say that (the words) 'when they are unaware' are closely connected with 'and We revealed to him'; this would mean: 'We comforted him with a revelation although they were unaware of it.'

(*Contents of verses 16–20*: The brothers bring the bloody shirt to their father and report that Joseph must have been eaten by a wolf. Meanwhile, some travellers find Joseph and sell him 'for a paltry price, a handful of counted dirhams'.)

> *21. He who bought him, being of Egypt, said to his wife: 'Give him goodly lodging for it may be that he will profit us, or we may take him for our son.' So We established Joseph in the land, that We might teach him the interpretation of tales. God prevails in His affairs, but most men know not.*

He who bought him, being of Egypt, said: This was the 'Azīz[30] who was in charge of the storehouses of Egypt, and his name was Qiṭfīr or Iṭfīr.[31] The king of Egypt at that time was Rayyān ibn al-Walīd, the Amalekite, who believed in Joseph and died during Joseph's lifetime. Other say (however) that Rayyān ibn al-Walīd was the Pharaoh of Moses and he lived four hundred years, for (in the Qur'ān) God says (concerning the Pharaoh at the time of Moses): 'Joseph brought you the clear signs before' (Sūra 40:34/36). The commonly accepted view is that the Pharaoh of Moses was a descendant of the Pharaoh of Joseph and that the verse (just mentioned) is to be understood as a situation where descendants are addressed in the circumstances of their ancestors. It is related that the 'Azīz bought Joseph when the latter was seventeen years old, that he stayed in his house for thirteen years, that Rayyān made Joseph his vizier at the age of thirty-three, and that Joseph died at the age of one hundred and twenty. ...

To his wife: Rā'īl or Zulaikhā. ...

Or We may take him for our son: ... The 'Azīz was childless (and thus spoke of adopting Joseph) and, because of his knowledge of men, had perceived that Joseph was a person of integrity. In this regard it is said that three people are famed as the best judges of men: the 'Azīz of Egypt, Shu'aib's daughter[32] who said: 'Father, hire Moses!' (Sūra 28:26), and Abū Bakr, when he appointed 'Umar to be his successor as caliph.

So We established Joseph in the land: just as we firmly established the love for Joseph in the heart of the 'Azīz; or, as we established Joseph in the house of the 'Azīz; or, as we delivered Joseph and made the 'Azīz favour him, thus making a place for him in the land.

That We might teach him the interpretation of tales. (This statement is) connected with something not directly spoken, the meaning of which may be: (We gave Joseph power in the land) so that he might administer with justice and we might teach him. That is, we delivered him and gave him power so he would exercise justice and direct the affairs of men and know the meaning of the books and decrees of God in order to implement them. Or, he should know the interpretation of dreams which foretell future events, in order to prepare for these events and work for their implementation before they occur, just as he did through the years (of plenty and drought).

God prevails in His affairs. Nothing can turn God back and nothing can oppose him in what he wills. Or (the meaning may be): (And God prevails) in Joseph's affairs, for his brothers willed one thing and God willed something else, and only what God willed occurred. . . .

(*Contents of verses 22–53*: Joseph lives in the house of the 'Azīz, whose wife begins to attempt to snare him. Even though Joseph withstands the temptation with the help of God, he is still put in prison where he interprets dreams for two servants who are his fellow-prisoners. Both interpretations, that is, that one prisoner will be crucified and the other set free, come true. Joseph remains in the prison for several more years; meanwhile, the king of Egypt has a dream in which he sees seven fat cows which are eaten by seven lean ones, and seven green ears of grain along with seven that are withered. When the nobles of the court are unable to interpret this dream, the former fellow-prisoner remembers Joseph, who then interprets the dream correctly and is freed from prison by the king, after the king obtained clarification regarding Joseph's relationship with the wife of the 'Azīz, thus learning of Joseph's innocence.)

54–5. The king said: 'Bring him to me! I would attach him to my person.' Then, when he had spoken with him, he said: 'Today thou art established firmly in our favour and in our trust.' Joseph[33] said: 'Set me over the land's storehouses; I am a knowledgeable guardian.'

. . . *Then, when he had spoken with him*: that is, after they had brought him (to the king) and the king had spoken with him and had observed his integrity and wisdom.

He said: Today thou art established firmly in our favour: you have power and authority, *and in our trust*: and in all matters (you are) granted our trust. It is related that when Joseph came out of prison he washed and purified himself and put on new clothes, and when he entered the king's presence, he said: 'God, I ask you for a little of his goodness and I take refuge in your strength and power from his evil.' Then he greeted him in the Hebrew language and invoked blessings on the king, who asked: 'What language is this?', and he answered: 'The language of my forefathers.' Now the king was fully conversant in seventy languages, and he spoke to Joseph in all of them. When Joseph answered the king in each language, the king was amazed and said: 'I now desire to hear my vision from you.' Joseph related the dream to him and described the cows and the ears of grain, including the precise details, just as the king had seen them. Then the king placed Joseph on the throne and entrusted his rule (*amr*) to him. Others say that Qiṭfīr died at that time and the king placed Joseph in his position and gave him Rāʿīl as a wife, and that Joseph found her to be a virgin and Ephraim and Manasseh were born to him by her.

Joseph said: Set me over the land's storehouses: make me the head (*wallā*) of their transactions. The 'land' was Egypt.

I am a guardian (ḥafīẓ) of them from those who have no right to them, *knowledgeable* in methods of managing them. Perhaps Joseph, when he perceived that the king was indeed going to appoint him to rule, wanted to choose an area of activity in which widespread benefits and significant results would be produced. This passage shows that one may strive for the position of a leader (*walī*), indicate one's readiness for it, and accept the appointment by an unbeliever, so long as it is known that it would be impossible to establish justice and rule over the people without such assistance. (However) according to Mujāhid (it is related that) the king became a Muslim (*aslama*) through the aid of Joseph.

(Verses 56–7 state that Joseph's proposal was accepted and he was put in charge of the storehouses in Egypt.)

> *58–60. And the brothers of Joseph came and entered unto him,*
> *and he knew them but they knew him not.*
> *When he had equipped them with their provisions, he said: 'Bring me a certain brother of yours from your father. Do you not see*
> *that I fill up the measure and am the best of hosts?*
> *But if you do not bring him to me, there shall be no (more) provisions for you from me, nor shall you come near me*
> *(again).'*

And the brothers of Joseph came. It is related that when the king had made Joseph his vizier, Joseph brought justice (to the land), striving to increase the harvest and control the produce until the (seven) lean years finally came and famine was widespread throughout Egypt, Syria, and the neighbouring regions. The people then came to Joseph and he sold the produce of the harvest, at first for money (literally, 'dirhams and dinars') until the people had none left, and then for ornaments and jewels, then for animals, then for property and estates, and finally for the people's freedom until he had enslaved them all. Then Joseph reported the matter to the king, who said: 'Do whatever you think is best!' So Joseph set the people free and returned their property to them. Canaan was afflicted with the same misfortune as the other countries, so Jacob sent his sons, except for Benjamin, to Joseph to purchase provisions.

And entered unto him, and he knew them but they knew him not. That is, Joseph recognized them but they did not recognize him, because of the length of time that had passed, and their having parted from him when he was young, and their forgetting him and supposing him to be dead, and the difference between the state in which they now saw him and his state when they parted from him, and because they did not observe his outward appearance carefully on account of their awe and reverence (for him).

When he had equipped them with their provisions: assembled their supplies for them and had their camels loaded with what they had come for. . . .

He said: Bring me a certain brother of yours from your father. It is related that when they went in to Joseph, he said: 'Who are you and what is your business? Perhaps you are spies!' But they answered: 'God forbid! We are (all) sons of a single father, who is an old man and one of the prophets. His name is Jacob.' Joseph asked: 'How many are you?' They answered: 'We were twelve, but one of us went into the desert and perished.' Joseph then asked: 'How many of you are here?' They said: 'Ten.' He asked: 'And where is the eleventh?' They said: 'With our father who finds consolation in him for the (son) who perished.' He asked: 'Who can bear witness on your account?' They said: 'There is no one here who knows us and can testify on our behalf.' Then Joseph said: 'Then leave one of you with me as a hostage and bring your brother to me from your father so I can believe you.' So they cast lots and the lot fell on Simeon. Others say that Joseph was giving a load (of provisions) to each of them and they asked for an extra load for a brother of theirs born to their father. So Joseph gave this (extra load) to them but stipulated that they must bring this other brother to him so he could verify their truthfulness. . . .

But if you do not bring him to me, there shall be no (more) provisions for you from me, nor shall you come near me (again). That is, you can neither come into my presence nor enter my territories. This is either a negative command or (simply) a negative statement. . . .

(*Contents of verses 61–9*: Joseph had the goods placed again in their packs, but they did not observe this until they returned home. Before the next trip, Jacob got from them the promise to take good care of Benjamin. When they came to Joseph with him, Joseph made known his secret to him.)

> *70. Then, when he had equipped them with their provisions, he put his drinking-cup into the saddlebag of his (younger) brother (Benjamin). Then a herald proclaimed: 'Ho, cameleers, you are thieves!'*

. . . *Into the saddlebag of his (younger) brother (Benjamin)*: Some say that the drinking-cup was used as a vessel for measuring (the grain). Others say that it was used for watering the animals and for measuring (the grain). According to some, it was made of silver; according to others, it was made of gold. . . .

Ho, cameleers, you are thieves. Possibly the one who called out did not say this at Joseph's command (since a false accusation is not appropriate to a prophet); or, inserting the drinking-cup and calling out about it could have been done with the consent of Benjamin. Others say that the meaning may be: 'You have stolen Joseph from his father' or 'Are you thieves?' ...

(*Contents of verses 71–97/98*: The younger brother is then detained after the goblet is found among his possessions, and the other brothers return to Jacob without him. Jacob now mourns for two sons and, growing blind in his grief, he sends the brothers back to Egypt in search of both of them. Finally, Joseph allows his brothers to recognize him and he invites them and their parents to move to Egypt. The brothers return to Jacob with Joseph's robe, which restores Jacob's power of sight when it is laid against his face, and they ask for his forgiveness.)

> *98/99. Jacob*[34] *said: 'Surely I will ask my Lord to forgive you. He is the All-forgiving, the All-compassionate.'*

Jacob postponed this prayer for forgiveness until the (next) morning or the (next) evening prayer, or until the (next) Friday evening, because he wanted to seek a time when the prayer would receive a favourable hearing. Or (he postponed it), because he wanted to receive the sanction of Joseph (for such intercession) for them; or, because he wanted to know that Joseph had (for his part) forgiven them, since the forgiveness of the wronged person is a prerequisite for (divine) forgiveness. This interpretation is supported by the following tradition: When Jacob stood facing in the direction of prayer (*qibla*) and interceding (with God), Joseph stood behind him saying 'Amen'; and behind the two stood the brothers, humble and submissive. Finally Gabriel came down and said: 'God has answered your prayer for your sons and has sealed the covenant for their prophethood after your death.' If this is correct, then it is an indication that they (in fact) did become prophets and that (the sins) which they committed occurred before their elevation to prophethood.

(*Contents of verses 99f./100f.*: Joseph's parents and brothers now all move to Egypt and he thanks God, who has now fulfilled the vision of the stars.)

> *101/102. 'O my Lord, Thou hast given me to rule, and Thou hast taught me the interpretation of tales. O Thou, the Originator of the heavens and the earth, Thou art my Protector in this world*

and the next. O receive me to Thee in true submission, and join me with the righteous.'

. . . *And join me with the righteous*: (meaning those who are righteous) among Joseph's ancestors, or all of those who are righteous in rank and honour. It is related that Jacob stayed with Joseph for twenty-four years and then died. He had ordered that he be buried in Syria (*ash-sha'm*[35]) beside his father; so Joseph took him and buried him there. Joseph then returned (to Egypt) and survived his father by twenty-three years, after which his soul began to yearn for the eternal kingdom (of God), and he desired death; thus God took him to himself, righteous and pure. The Egyptians disputed among themselves regarding where they should bury him, until they were on the verge of fighting. Then they decided to place him in a marble sarcophagus and bury him in the Nile so the water would flow over him and reach (all) Egypt, and they would (all) have their share of him. Later Moses transferred Joseph to the burial place of his forefathers. Joseph lived one hundred and twenty years and was the father of Rā'īl, Ephraim, and Manasseh. The later was the ancestor of Joshua ibn Nūn[36] and Raḥma,[37] the wife of Job.

102/103. This[38] *is of the tidings of the Unseen that We reveal to thee. Thou wast not with (the brothers of Joseph*[39]*) when they agreed upon their plan, devising. Yet, be thou ever so eager, the most part of men believe not.*

This: referring to what has been related (in the foregoing verses of the sūra) of the story of Joseph. The one addressed is the Messenger (Muḥammad). . . .

Thou wast not with (the brothers of Joseph) when they agreed upon their plan, devising. . . . The meaning is that this story is a hidden matter which you could come to know only through revelation, since you were not present with Joseph's brothers when they decided on the plan to cast him into the bottom of the well, and when they were devising plots against him and his father so the latter would send Joseph with them. It is well known, and cannot be denied by those who call you a liar, that you never met anyone who had heard of this story so that you could have heard it from him. But this (last) part (of the chain of thought) is omitted (in this verse), since it is superfluous, having been mentioned in another story (in the Qur'ān), that is, in God's words: 'This is of the tidings of the Unseen, which We reveal to thee; thou didst not know it, neither thy people, before this' (Sūra 11:49/51). . . .

6. The temptation of Solomon

Zamakhsharī on Sūra 38:34f./33f.

Certainly We tried Solomon, and We placed upon his throne a mere body; then he repented.
He said: 'My Lord, forgive me and give me a kingdom such as may not befall anyone after me; surely Thou art the All-giver.'

Some say that after twenty years (of rule) Solomon[40] was subjected to a test and he reigned after that for twenty more years. The testing of Solomon proceeded as follows: When a son was born to Solomon, the satans (who were made subservient to Solomon) said: 'If this son continues to live, we will not be able to escape forced labour; thus, we should kill him or cause him to sink into madness.' Solomon learned of their plan, however, and caused his son to rise up into the clouds (so that he was hidden). Then he was completely surprised when God set a dead body on the throne (in his place), and he became aware of the sin he had (committed in that he had) not trusted in his Lord in this affair. He asked for forgiveness and turned in repentance to God.

The following account is related from the Prophet: Solomon (once) said: 'Tonight I shall visit seventy wives and each shall bear a knight who shall fight for God.' But he failed to add: 'If God wills.' Then he visited the wives, but only one became pregnant and she brought a monster into the world. By him in whose hand my soul lies, had he added 'if God wills', then all the knights (would have been born and) would have fought for God. God's words *certainly We tried Solomon* refer to this.

Such reports and similar ones are not to be rejected. On the other hand, regarding the (following) stories about the signet-ring, the satans, and the worship of idols in Solomon's house, God knows best whether they are true. It is related that Solomon received news of Sidon, a coastal city, and (he learned) that a powerful king ruled there, against whom one is powerless because (this king) is protected by the sea. Then Solomon set out on the wind until he came down on Sidon with his hosts of jinn and men, and he killed the king of this city. Now, Solomon found here a daughter of the king named Jarāda who was the most beautiful to behold among all of mankind, and he selected her for himself. She declared herself to be surrendered to God (*aslamat*), and Solomon loved her. But the tears that she shed out of grief for her father would not be dried up; so Solomon commanded the satans to make an image (*ṣūra*) of her father and to clothe it according to his style. Jarāda and her maids then went to this image in the mornings and evenings in order to worship it; as was customary in her father's kingdom. When (the vizier) Āṣaf reported this to Solomon, Solomon had the image destroyed and he punished the woman. Then he went out (of his palace) to a deserted place to be in solitude, and ashes were spread out before him. Then he sat down, humbly doing penance before God.

(Another account of idolatry in the house of Solomon reads as follows:) Solomon had a slave named Amīna, who became a mother (*umm walad*) through him. (Once) when he went for purification or to cohabit with one of his wives, he deposited with Amīna his signet-ring in which his power lay. He left it with her for one whole day; then the satan who lives in the sea came to her. This satan, whose name was Ṣakhr and who had proved to be indispensable to Solomon in the task of building the Temple (*bait al-muqaddas*), came to her in the form (*ṣūra*) of Solomon, and said: 'Amīna, (give me) my signet-ring!' Then he put the ring on (his finger) and sat down on Solomon's throne. (This ring) placed under his command the birds, the jinn, and men. Also, he transformed the outward appearance of Solomon so that when the later came to Amīna to fetch the signet-ring, she took him for a stranger and drove him away. Then he realized that he had fallen into a state of sin, and he wandered among the houses as a beggar. Whenever he said: 'I am Solomon', people threw dirt at him and insulted him. Then he went to the fishermen whom he assisted by hauling the fish. For this they gave him two fish per day, and he remained in this situation for forty days, that is, for as long as idolatry was practised in his house. However, Āṣaf and the (other) great men of Israel did not acknowledge the sovereignty of the satan (who had taken over Solomon's throne). Now, when Āṣaf questioned the wives of Solomon regarding (the impostor), they answered: 'He exempts none when one of us bleeds and does not purify herself from uncleanness.' On the other hand, others say that the rule of the satan included everyone, and not just the wives. (At the end of the period of testing Solomon) the satan dashed away and threw the ring into the sea. A fish swallowed it and came into the hands of Solomon, who split open the belly of the fish and saw the ring there. When he put the ring on (his finger) and knelt down to worship, his power returned to him. Then he drilled a hole in a stone boulder for Ṣakhr and put him in it and closed the whole with another boulder. Next, he had the two boulders bound together firmly with iron and lead, and he cast him (with the boulders) into the sea.

Others say that when Solomon was put to a test, the ring fell from his hand again and again and would not cling (to his finger) any longer. Then Āṣaf said: 'You must undergo a test on account of your transgression, as the signet-ring no longer wants to remain still on your hand.' At this, Solomon turned to God in repentance.

The pious scholars reject such (interpretations) and say that these belong to the false stories of the Jews. The satans are not capable of such acts. That God would give to them power over his servants so that they could change the laws (for the community), and that he would give to them power over the wives of the prophets so that they could commit adultery with them, is a detestable idea. The religious laws might differ concerning the use of statues (*tamāthīl*), for God said (in the Qur'ān): 'The jinn made for Solomon whatever he wished—palaces, statues, . . .' (Sūra 34:13/12). However, one cannot believe that God would permit his prophet to bow down before an idol (*ṣūra*). Should something take place (in Solomon's kingdom of which he is) unaware, then certainly it is not to be charged against him.

7. *The judgment upon the tribes of Thamūd and 'Ād*[41]

Jalāl ad-Dīn al-Maḥallī on Sūra 69:4–10

The Thamūd and the 'Ād declared (the threat of) the pounder
to be a lie.
Then the Thamūd were destroyed by the screamer;
and the 'Ād were destroyed by a clamorous, violent wind
that God[42] *compelled against them seven nights and eight days,*

uninterruptedly, so thou mightest see the people laid prostrate
in it as if they were the stumps of fallen-down palm trees.
Now dost thou see any remnant of them?
Pharaoh likewise, and those with him, and the subverted cities—
they committed error,
and they rebelled against the messenger of their Lord, and He
seized them with a surpassing grip.

The Thamūd and the ʿĀd declared (the threat of) the pounder (al-qāriʿa[43]*) to be a lie*: that is, the resurrection, since it pounds upon the hearts with its terror.

Then the Thamūd were destroyed by the screamer: by screams that exceeded the bounds in their strength.[44]

And the ʿĀd were destroyed by a clamorous wind: with a deafening noise; *violent*: one which proved strong and powerful to the ʿĀd over against their strength and power.

That God compelled: that he sent out with force *against them seven nights and eight days*: beginning on the morning of Wednesday, the 22nd day of Shawwāl[45] and lasting until the end of winter.

Uninterruptedly: in continuous succession. Here is a comparison with the continuous act of his which opens (*ḥasama*) (a diseased place on the body) in order to sear it again and again until it is cured (*inḥasama*).

So thou mightest see the people laid prostrate: stretched out on the ground and destroyed, *as if they were the stumps*: trunks *of fallen-down palm trees*: (palm trees which had) fallen down and were no longer producing.

Now dost thou see any remnant (*min bāqiya*) *of them*: (The word) *bāqiya* (which is feminine in Arabic) is either an attribute to an understood *nafs* (soul), or the feminine ending serves as an (indication of) exaggeration, in which case it would mean that there is nothing left remaining (to see).

Pharaoh likewise, and those with him (*qibalahū*): his attendants. Some read *qablahū*, thus designating the unbelieving communities which lived 'before him'.

And the subverted cities: meaning the inhabitants of these cities, that is, the places of the fellow tribesmen of Lot.[46]

They committed error: with sinful deeds.

And they rebelled against the messenger of their Lord: that is, against Lot, as well as others.

And He seized them with a surpassing grip: the strength of which surpassed all others.

8. Alexander the Great

Baiḍāwī on Sūra 18:83/82

> *They will question thee concerning Dhū l-Qarnain. Say: 'I will recite to you some of his story.'*

Reference here is to the Greek (*rūmī*) Alexander, king of Persia and Greece (*rūm*).[47] He is also designated as king of the East and the West, and for this reason has been given the name 'the one with the two horns (*dhū l-qarnain*)'.[48] Or (he is so called), because he roamed all over the two horns of the earth, namely the East and the West; or, because two generations (*qarnān*) of men passed away during his lifetime; or, because he had two 'horns', that is, two braids of hair; or, because his crown had two horns. Since one who is brave is called a 'ram', it is (also) possible that this nickname was given to Alexander on account of his bravery, because he battered his enemies like a ram. There is disagreement as to whether Alexander was a prophet; it is, however, agreed that he was believing and just.[49]

Those who raise the question (in this verse) are either the Jews, who advance this question in order to put Muḥammad to a test, or the unbelievers of Mecca. . . .

9. The announcement of the birth of Jesus

Zamakhsharī on Sūra 19:16–22

> *And mention in the Book Mary when she withdrew from her people to an eastern place,*
> *and she took a veil apart from them; then We sent unto her*
> *Our spirit* (rūḥ) *that presented himself to her a man without fault.*
> *She said: 'I take refuge in the All-merciful from thee! If thou fearest God, . . .'*
> *He said: 'I am but a messenger come from thy Lord, to give thee (news of) a boy most pure.'*

She said: 'How shall I have a son whom no mortal has touched, neither have I been unchaste?'
He said: 'Even so thy Lord has said: "Easy is that for Me;
and that We may appoint him a sign unto men and a mercy from Us; it is a thing decreed."'
So she conceived him,[50] *and withdrew with him to a distant place.*

... *When she withdrew from her people to an eastern place* (*makān sharqī*). ... Some say that Mary settled in an eastern place (*mashraqa*) when she wanted to purify herself from menstruation, and that she concealed herself behind a wall, or perhaps something (else) that would keep her out of view. The place where she (usually) stayed was the mosque (*masjid*). As soon as she received her menses, she went to the home of her maternal aunt; then, when she was again in the state of purity, she returned to the mosque. Now when she was at the place at which she customarily purified herself, the angel came to her as a young, smooth-faced man with pure countenance, curly hair, and a well-built body, without exhibiting a single blemish in his human appearance (*ṣūra*). ... He presented himself to her in the form of a man in order that she might have confidence in what he was to say and not flee from him. Had he appeared to her in the form of an angel, she would have fled from him and would not have been able to hear what he had to say. If Mary now sought refuge with God from this charming, towering, and handsome figure, then this shows that she was modest and pious. Through the appearance of the angel in this manner, Mary had undergone a test and her modesty was made certain.

Others say that Mary lived at the home of Zachariah, the husband of her sister, where she resided in a niche (*miḥrāb*) all her own. When Zachariah went away he usually locked her door. As she now wished to find a place of her own on the mount (Zion) in order to delouse her hair, the roof over her broke open and she climbed out and settled down at the sunny place[51] behind the mount (Zion). Then the angel came to her. (Still) others say that the angel appeared before her in the form of one of her contemporaries named Joseph, who belonged among the servants of Jerusalem (*bait al-maqaddas*).

Some say that the Christians adopted the practice of facing towards the east when praying because Mary retreated to an eastern place. The spirit is Gabriel, because the religion lives through him and his inspiration. Or, God has designated Gabriel as his spirit (*rūḥ*) in a metaphorical sense, because he loves him and regards him as his companion, as one says to his friend: 'You are my spirit.' ...

To give thee (news of) a boy most pure: to cause a son to be given to you through a breath under your chemise. ...

Whom no mortal has touched: Here God uses the term 'touch' to refer to legal sexual intercourse, since the former (term) is a metonymical expression (*kināya*) for the latter, just as in God's words: 'O believers, when you marry believing women and then divorce them before you touch them' (Sūra 33:49/48) and 'or (if) you have touched women' (Sūra 4:43/46; 5:6/9). One would refer to prostitution in other ways (than with the expression 'touch'), such as: 'he committed sin with her', 'he practised unchastity with her', or something similar. Prostitution is not esteemed such that one would think of it with (such) metonyms and elements of refined speech. ...

So she conceived him: According to Ibn 'Abbās, Mary found comfort in the words of the angel, and thus the latter approached near to her and breathed under her chemise so that the breath reached into her womb and she became pregnant. Some say that the pregnancy lasted for six months. According to 'Aṭā', Abū l-'Āliya, and aḍ-Ḍaḥḥāk it lasted seven months. Others say that it lasted eight months and that besides Jesus no child capable of living ever came into the world after (a pregnancy of only) eight months. Still others say that it lasted three hours. Some maintain that Mary was pregnant with Jesus for (only) one hour, that he was formed in one hour, and that she brought him into the world in one hour at sunset. According to Ibn 'Abbās the pregnancy lasted for (only) one hour. (Also) Mary is said to have brought (*nabadhat*) Jesus into the world as soon as she became pregnant with him.

Some maintain that she became pregnant with him at the age of thirteen. It is also said that this occurred when she was ten years old, after she had had the menses for two months previously. (Moreover) some say that every (newborn) infant cries and that Jesus is the only one who did not do this.

And withdrew with him: that is, she secluded herself while she was carrying him in her body. ...

To a distant place: to a place behind the mountain (Zion), which was far away from her relatives. Others say (that she moved away) to the other end of the country (*dār*). (Furthermore) it is reported that she was engaged to one named Joseph, a son of a paternal uncle. When people began to say that she became pregnant through prostitution, Joseph feared that the king would kill her, so he fled with her. On the way he became convinced that he should kill her. But Gabriel then came and said: 'The pregnancy was brought about by the Holy Spirit. So do not kill her!' So Joseph did no harm to her.

10. Jesus' verification miracle

Ṭabarī on Sūra 5:114f.

Said Jesus son of Mary: 'O God, our Lord, send down upon us a table out of heaven which will be for us a festival, the first and last of us and a sign from Thee. And provide for us, for Thou art the best of providers.'

God said: 'Verily I do send it down on you. Whoever among you hereafter disbelieves, verily I will chastise him with a chastisement wherewith I chastise no other being.'[52]

Said Jesus son of Mary . . . : Here God states that his prophet Jesus fulfilled the request of his people when they asked him to request from his Lord a table which should come down upon them from heaven.

The exegetes (*ahl at-ta'wīl*) disagree concerning the interpretation (*ta'wīl*) of God's words: *which will be for us a festival* (*'īd*). Some maintain that the meaning is: (Send down upon us a table) so that we will take the day on which it comes down as a feast day (*'īd*), which we and our descendants will hold in high respect. . . . Others maintain that the meaning is: (Send down upon us a table) from which we shall all eat together. . . . (Still) others say that when God speaks (here) of an *'īd*, it is meant (not in the sense of a festival, but) in the sense of a benefit which God grants to us, as well as an argument and proof.

(Aṭ-Ṭabarī concludes that) among these interpretations, that which comes nearest to being correct is the one which embraces the following meaning: (Send down upon us a table) which will be a festival (*'īd*) for us, in that we will pray and worship our Lord on the day when it comes down, just as the people used to do on their feast days. Thus, the meaning which we affirm corresponds to the usual meaning that people associate with (the word) *'īd* in their speech, and not with the interpretation that accepts as the meaning: a benefit for us from God. The meaning contained in the 'speech of God' (*kalām Allāh*) is to be interpreted as lying closer to the usual manner of speaking of the one who makes the request, than to something inaccessible and unknown to him.

Regarding God's words *the first and last of us*, the interpretation that comes closest to being correct is the one that adopts the meaning: for those of us who are living today and for those who will come after us. This is based on the same (linguistic) argument we cited for God's words 'that shall be for us an *'īd*', since the meaning adopted (in each case) is the predominant one.

God's words *and a sign* (*āya*) *from Thee* mean: and an indication or argument from you, Lord, for your servants, which affirms that you are the only God and that I speak the truth when I present myself in the role of your messenger to them. . . .

The exegetes disagree concerning whether or not the table was (actually) sent down (out of heaven) and concerning what was on it. Some say that it was sent down with fish and (other) food and that the people ate from it. Then, after its descent (the table) was lifted up because of (certain) innovations they introduced in their relationship to God. . . . Other exegetes maintain that it came down with fruit from paradise. . . . (Still) others say that on it lay every (kind of) food except meat. . . . Other interpreters maintain that God did not send down a table to the Children of Israel. Those who advocate this view disagree further among themselves. Many say that this may be only a simile that God has offered to his creatures in order thereby to prohibit them from demanding (divine) signs from the prophets of God. . . . Others maintain that when (the words) *whoever among you hereafter disbelieves, verily I will chastise him with a chastisement wherewith I chastise no other being* were spoken to the people, they prayed for forgiveness but the table did not come down. . . .

(Aṭ-Ṭabarī concludes:) According to our view it is correct to say the following: God (actually) sent down the table to those who asked Jesus to request it from his Lord. We maintain this in view of the information concerning this which we have related from the Messenger of God, his Companions, and after them the exegetes, since these do not occupy any special position in the interpretation mentioned above. Furthermore, God breaks no promise, and there will not be any contradiction in what he announces. God proclaims in his Book that he will fulfil the request of his prophet Jesus, when he says: *Verily I do send it down on you.* It is impossible that God would say 'verily I do send it down on you', and then not send it down. This verse deals with a proclamation of God; thus nothing that contradicts it can ensure from him. Were it possible for God to say 'verily I do send it down on you', and then not send it down, then he could also say: 'Whoever among you hereafter disbelieves, verily I will chastise him with a chastisement wherewith I chastise no other being', and someone thereafter could disbelieve without being punished by God. In this case neither the promise nor the threat of God would become true and valid; however, such things cannot be ascribed to God.

Concerning what was on the table, some say correctly that there was food on it. It could have been fish and bread, or it could have been fruit from paradise. It is to no advantage if one knows what it was; neither is it any harm if one does not know, so long as the conclusions drawn from the verse correspond with the external wording of the revelation.

God said: (Aṭ-Ṭabarī says that) here God gives to the people an answer to their demand which is addressed to his prophet Jesus, that he ask their Lord to send down to them a table. God says: *Verily I do send it down on you*, you disciples, and you are to eat from it.

Whoever among you hereafter disbelieves: that is, whoever among you, after I have sent down the table to you and you have eaten from it, denies that I have sent Jesus as a messenger, and whoever does not acknowledge the prophethood of my prophet Jesus, and whoever refuses obedience to me in my commands and prohibitions.

Verily I will chastise him with a chastisement wherewith I chastise no other being: that is, in the world at the time of Jesus. The people, however, did (disbelieve, in spite of this warning). After the table had been sent down to them, they denied (the miracle) and remained unbelieving, so that it was restored back to us, and, as it returned to us, they were punished so that they were transformed into monkeys and swine.

11. Jesus is not God's son

Zamakhsharī on Sūra 4:171/169

People of the Book, do not go too far in your religion, and say nothing about God but the truth. The Messiah, Jesus son of Mary, was only the messenger of God, and His word which He committed to Mary, and a spirit from Him. So believe in God and His messengers, and say not: 'Three.' Refrain! Better is it for you. God is only One God. Glory be to Him—that He should have a son! To Him belongs all that is in the heavens and in the earth; God suffices for a guardian.

Do not go too far in your religion: The Jews went too far in that they degraded Christ in his position, since they regarded him as an illegitimate child (of Mary). And the Christians went too far in that they elevated him unduly, since they regarded him as a god.

And say nothing about God but the truth: Here is declared that God is exalted high above having a (divine) associate and a child. . . . Jesus is designated as 'the word of God' and as 'a word from Him' (see Sūra 3:39/34), because he alone originated through the word and the command of God, rather than through a father and a sperm. For this reason he is (also) designated as 'the spirit of God' (see Sūra 66:12, etc.) and as 'a spirit from Him', since Jesus was a spirit-endowed man (*dhū rūḥ*) who originated without any element from a spirit-endowed man, such as the sperm that is discharged from an earthly father. He was created through a new act of creation by God whose power (*qudra*) is unlimited.

Which He committed to Mary: which he delivered to her and permitted to enter into her.

(The word) *three* is the predicate to an understood subject. If one accepts the Christian view that God exists in one nature (*jauhar*) with three divine persons, namely the Father, the Son, and the Holy Spirit, and (if one accepts) the opinion that the person of the Father represents (God's) being (*dhāt*), the person of the Son represents (his) knowledge (*'ilm*), and the person of the Holy Spirit represents (his) life (*ḥayāt*), then one must supply the subject as follows: 'God is three(fold).' Otherwise, one must supply (the subject) thus: 'The gods are three.' According to the evidence of the Qur'ān, the Christians maintain that God, Christ, and Mary are three gods, and that Christ is the child of God by Mary, as

God says (in the Qur'ān): 'O Jesus son of Mary, didst thou say unto men: "Take me and my mother as gods, apart from God"?' (Sūra 5:116), or: 'The Christians say: "The Messiah is the Son of God"' (Sūra 9:30). Moreover, it is well known that the Christians maintain that in Jesus are (combined) a divine nature derived from the Father and a human nature derived from his mother. God's words: *The Messiah, Jesus son of Mary, was only the messenger of God* are (also) explained on the basis of such an interpretation (of the Christians). These words confirm (the Christian view) that Jesus was a child of Mary, that he had with her the usual relationship between children and (their) mothers, and that his relationship to God was that he was his messenger and that he became a living being through God's command and new act of creation without a father. At the same time, these words exclude (the Christian view) that Jesus had with God the usual relationship between sons and (their) fathers. Also God's words: *Glory be to Him—that He should have a son* (are explained on the basis of such an interpretation of the Christians). However, what is reported by God must be regarded as having more validity than what is reported by others. . . .

To Him belongs all that is in the heavens and in the earth: Here is set forth why God is free from what was ascribed to him (by the Christians). If everything that is in the heavens and the earth is God's creation and possession, how then can one of his possessions be a part of him when one can properly speak of a part only regarding bodies, while God is exalted above the properties (*ṣifāt*) of corporeality and inconstant attributes (*a'rāḍ*)[53]? . . .

12. The death of Jesus

Baiḍāwī on Sūra 4:157f./156

And because they said: 'We slew the Messiah, Jesus son of Mary,
the messenger of God.' But they did not slay him, nor did they
crucify him; for only a likeness of him was shown to them.
Those who disagree concerning it surely are in doubt regarding
him. They have no knowledge of him, but only follow surmise.
And it is certain that they did not slay him!
No indeed, God raised him up to Himself. God is All-mighty,
All-wise.

And because they said: We slew the Messiah, Jesus son of Mary, the messenger of God: (that is) because the Jews asserted this. It is (however also) possible that the Jews said this (only) scornfully as is the case in a similar situation with (the words of Pharaoh concerning Moses): 'Surely your messenger who was sent to you is possessed!' (Sūra 26:27/26), and that God took up this assertion (of the Jews) again in order to praise Jesus or to replace their evil account with a good one.

But they did not slay him, nor did they crucify him; for only a likeness of him was shown to them. It is related that a group of Jews insulted Jesus and his mother, whereupon he appealed to God against them. When God turned (those who insulted Jesus and his mother) into monkeys and swine, the Jews came to an agreement to kill Jesus. Then God informed Jesus that he would raise him up to heaven; so Jesus said to his disciples: 'Who among you will agree to take a form similar to mine and die (in my place) and be crucified and then go (straight) to paradise?' A man among them offered himself, so God changed him into a form to look like Jesus, and he was killed and crucified.

Others say that a man pretended (to be a believer) before Jesus and then went away denouncing him, whereupon God changed this man into a form similar to that of Jesus, and then he was seized and crucified. (Still) others say that the Jew Titanus entered a house where Jesus was (with a treacherous intention) but could not find him. Then God changed him into a form similar to that of Jesus, and when he came outside people thought he was Jesus and so they seized and crucified him.

Similar unusual things which one may not find improbable for the time of the prophets (have been reported on this subject). When God blames the Jews (here), (it is) only because their words showed that they acted impudently towards God, wishing to kill his prophet in spite of the confirmation (of the prophethood of Jesus) through overwhelming miracles (*mu'jizāt*), and (furthermore they) rejoiced in doing so. (God blames them) not because their assertion (to have Jesus killed) was (merely) an opinion.

Those who disagree concerning it: (that is) concerning the state in which Jesus was. For as soon as this event (the crucifixion of another person in Jesus' place) occurred, the people disagreed (concerning it). Some Jews said: 'Jesus was a liar (when he said God would raise him up to heaven), for we certainly killed him!'

Others hesitated, and some of these said: 'If this (crucified person) is Jesus, then where is our companion (who wanted to betray him)?' Others said: 'That is the face of Jesus, but the body is that of our companion.' Those, however, who had heard Jesus when he said: 'God will raise me up into heaven', said: 'He was raised up into heaven.' Certain people believed (also) that his human nature was crucified, while his divine nature rose up to heaven. ...

13. Jesus as the herald of the Day of Judgment

Baiḍāwī on Sūra 43:61

And he (hu) *is the sign of the Hour. Doubt not concerning it, and follow me! This is a straight path.*

And he, that is Jesus, *is the sign of the Hour* (of judgment), since his appearance or his coming down (from heaven) is among the signs which will announce that the Hour (of judgment) is near. Or: (Jesus is a sign of the Hour) because he showed through his resurrection from the dead that God has the power to raise the dead (on the Day of Judgment). ...

In the Tradition (*ḥadīth*) it is reported that Jesus will come down over a mountain pass in the Holy Land called Afīq, and in his hand he will carry a spear with which he will kill the Antichrist (*dajjāl*[54]). He will then go to Jerusalem (*bait al-muqaddas*) just when the inhabitants are performing the morning prayer. The prayer leader (*imām*) will want to step back (in view of Jesus' appearance), but Jesus will give precedence to him and perform the prayer behind him according to the rite (*sharī'a*) of Muḥammad. Then he will kill the swine, dash to pieces the crucifix, demolish the churches and synagogues, and kill the Christians who do not have (correct) belief in him.

Others say that the pronoun *hu* ('he' or 'it') refers to the Qur'ān, since signs of the Hour are given in it and it points the way to it. ...

IV

ISLAM, THE 'BOOK RELIGIONS', AND PAGANISM

1. The religions

Zamakhsharī on Sūra 22:17[1]

Surely they that believe, and those who are Jewish, the Sabaeans, the Christians, the Zoroastrians, and those who associate (other gods with God)—God will distinguish (yafṣilu) *between them on the day of resurrection. Surely God witnesses everything.*

The distinction (which God will make between them) is unlimited and will involve the condition as well as the (future) abode of those in question. God will neither reward them (*ghazā*) uniformly without differentiation, nor bring them together to the same place. It is said that there are five religions, four of which belong to Satan and one to the Compassionate One. According to this view the Sabaeans[2] are considered to be Christians, constituting one branch of them.

It is also said that (the word) *yafṣilu* means that God will 'distinguish' between the believers and the unbelievers. . . .

2. The Muslims

Baiḍāwī on Sūra 2:142/136–143/138

The fools among the people will say: 'What has turned them
from the direction they were facing in their prayers before?'
Say: 'To God belong the East and the West; He guides whomever
He wills on a straight path.'
Thus We have made you (Muslims) into a community in the
middle that you may be witnesses to the people, and that the
Messenger may be a witness to you; and We established the

direction of prayer thou wast facing only in order to discover who would follow the Messenger and who would turn on his heels—though it were a grave thing except for those whom God has guided; but God would never leave your faith to waste—truly, God is All-gentle with the people, All-compassionate.

The fools among the people will say: those (people) who exhibit (only) little capacity for insight (*aḥlām*) and who depreciate even this through their blind acceptance (*taqlīd*) (of other views) and their neglect of (any) examination (*naẓar*) (of such views on their own). Referred to are those among the hypocrites (*munāfiqūn*), Jews, and pagans, who want to know nothing of the change of the direction of prayer. That this (i.e., what the fools will say later) is reported of them here in anticipation (of the future) is advantageous because one can be ready for it spiritually and can prepare an answer, and because this (report concerning a future event) exhibits the miracle (*mu'jiza*) (of divine revelation).

What has turned them from the direction they were facing in their prayers before: ... meaning the direction of prayer towards Jerusalem (*bait al-muqaddas*[3]). (The word) *qibla* originally designated the position (*ḥāla*) of a man when he looked towards (*istaqbala*) (a thing). It then became a useful designation for the place towards which one turns while praying.

Say: To God belong the East and the West: No place is so constituted by its nature that it belongs especially to God more than another place and would not be interchangeable with another such (place). The concern here is not to designate a special place but to portray God's dominion (*amr*) (over all places of the world).

He guides whomever He wills on a straight path: The straight path consists in the fact that wisdom approves, and benefit demands, that in prayer one turns towards Jerusalem at one time and towards the Ka'ba at another time.

Thus: referring to the content of the preceding verse. It means: thus as we have made you (Muslims) to be people who will be led on a straight path. Or: thus as we have made your direction of prayer to be the most excellent, so have we made you (Muslims) to be a community situated in the middle (*umma wasaṭ*), that is, good and just (*'udūl*) people who are blameless in knowledge and actions. (The word) *wasaṭ* (middle, in the middle) was originally a designation for a place with equal surfaces on the sides. Then it came to refer to (certain) praiseworthy attributes of character because these lie (in the middle) between the extremes of excess and exaggeration on both sides. Thus, generosity lies between wastefulness and stinginess, and boldness lies between foolhardy recklessness and cowardice. This word is now (also) applied to the person who possesses such characteristics. . . . From the present words of God one can draw the conclusion that consensus (*ijmā'*) is a valid authority (*ḥujja*) (in questions of faith), since if that on which the Muslims are agreed were delusion (*bāṭil*), then a gap would be created in their integrity (*'adāla*) (and they would not stand in the middle).

That you may be witnesses to the people, and that the Messenger may be a witness to you: Here is stated God's motive (for making the Muslims a community in the middle). What is meant is: in order that you (Muslims) may come to know, through a weighing of the evidence which God has prepared for you and through the Book (*al-kitāb*) which he has sent down to you, that God has done no injustice to anyone, nor has he been miserly towards anyone, but that (on the contrary) his ways have been set forth clearly and he has sent the messengers who have fulfilled their mission and have warned (the people); but still the unbelievers have let themselves be led astray through their evil ways, to follow their own desires, and to disregard the signs (of God). Herein you will be witnesses to your contemporaries, ancestors, and descendants.

It is related that on the day of resurrection the communities (of unbelievers) will dispute (the claim) that the prophets fulfilled their mission. Then God will demand of the prophets an appropriate proof—whereby he knows very well how one proceeds in the use of proofs against the disavowing (unbelievers)—and the community of Muḥammad will be produced as witnesses. When the (other) communities say: 'How did you come to know (what you bear witness to)?', the community of Muḥammad will answer: 'We know this from the information given by God in his Book which was spoken by the tongue of his faithful Prophet.' Then Muḥammad will be brought forward and asked about the conduct of his community and he will bear witness to their justness. . . .

And We established the direction of prayer (qibla) thou wast facing: that is, (we have now instituted as the final, obligatory direction of prayer) the direction which you faced originally, that is, towards the Ka'ba. The direction of prayer which Muḥammad observed in Mecca was towards the Ka'ba; then when he emigrated (to Medina) he was ordered to face in prayer towards the (Dome of the) Rock (*aṣ-ṣakhra*) (in Jerusalem), in order to establish a bond with the Jews. Or, (in this verse) the (temporary) direction towards the (Dome of the) Rock is meant, since, according to Ibn 'Abbās, Muḥammad observed the direction towards Jerusalem (also) in Mecca. To be sure, he positioned himself so that the Ka'ba came to stand between him and the (Dome of the) Rock. Thus, in the first case, the institution finally abolishing would be meant, and in the second, the one abolished would be meant. The meaning is (in the last case): Actually you are to adopt the direction of prayer towards the Ka'ba, for we made (Jerusalem) your direction of prayer (for a time), *only in order to discover who would follow the Messenger and who would turn on his heels*: (that is) in order to put the people to a test and in order to ascertain who follows you in facing towards Jerusalem in prayer and who is faithless regarding your religion out of devotion to the direction of prayer of his (unbelieving) forefathers. Or (what is meant is): in order to ascertain now (after the abrogation of the temporary direction towards Jerusalem) who follows the Messenger of God and who does not, and which followers are to be attributed to a temporary condition and (thus) disappear when the condition does. In the first case the meaning is: We have instructed you to turn back again (towards the Ka'ba) in the direction of prayer which you adopted (originally), in order to ascertain who would persevere in Islam and would not execute an about face as a result of inner uncertainty and weakness of faith. . . .

But God would never leave your faith to waste: that is, your firm perseverance in belief. Others say: your belief in the direction of prayer which was abrogated and the prayers which you performed facing in that direction. It is related that when the Messenger of God (changed the direction of prayer and) finally turned towards the Ka'ba, someone asked him: 'Messenger of God, what is the condition of those of our brothers who died before this change?' Then came down (from God the following words): *Truly, God is All-gentle with the people, All-compassionate*, and will not let their reward come to nothing nor overlook their uprightness. . . .

3. *Jews and Christians*

Zamakhsharī on Sūra 5:82f./85f.

Thou wilt surely find that the most hostile of men to the believers

are the Jews and the idolaters; and thou wilt surely find the nearest of them in love to the believers are those who say: 'We are Christians.' This is because some of them are priests and monks, and they wax not proud,
and when they hear what has been sent down to the Messenger, thou seest their eyes overflow with tears because of the truth they recognize. They say: 'Our Lord, we believe; so do Thou write us down among the witnesses.'

Here God portrays the Jews as being unyielding and as acknowledging the truth only grudgingly, while the Christians are (portrayed as) of gentle disposition, easily guided, and having an inclination towards Islam.[4] On account of their vehement enmity against the believers, God places the Jews together with the idolaters; indeed, going even further, he shows them to be at the head, since they are mentioned before the idolaters. God does the same in his words: 'And thou shalt find them (the Jews) the eagerest of men for life—even more so than the idolaters. Each of them wishes he could be given a life of a thousand years; but, the grant of such life would not save him from chastisement—for God sees well all that they do!' (Sūra 2:96/90). The Jews are surely like this, and even worse! From the Prophet (the following is related): 'If a Muslim is alone with two Jews, they will try to kill him.'

That the Christians are to be treated kindly and are held in high esteem by the Muslims, God bases on the fact that there are priests and monks among them, that is, men of learning (*'ulamā'*) and servants, and that they are modest and humble people who know no arrogance, while the Jews are just the opposite. Here is a clear example showing that the struggle for knowledge (*ta'allum*) is exceedingly useful, leading first to good and then to success, even among the (non-Muslim) priests. The same is true also of concern for the hereafter and speaking about the end, possibly another characteristic of the monk, just like freedom from haughtiness—even though a Christian is involved here.

God's characterization of the Christians as being tender-hearted and as weeping when they hear the Qur'ān is in accordance with what is reported concerning an-Najāshī (the Negus of Ethiopia). When the immigrants to Ethiopia (in 615) appeared before him with the idolaters (curses be upon them), the latter tried to stir him up against the immigrants, demanding that he use measures of force against them. He said to Ja'far ibn Abī Ṭālib: 'Is Mary mentioned in your scripture?' To this Ja'far answered: 'In our scripture one sūra is devoted to Mary', and he began to recite this sūra (Sūra 19) up to the words: 'That is Jesus, son of Mary, in word of truth' (verse 34/35). Then he recited Sūra Ṭā Hā (Sūra 20) up to the words: 'Hast thou received the story of Moses?' (verse 9/8), and an-Najāshī wept. His seventy men who came as emissaries to the Messenger of God also did the same, (for) when the Messenger recited to them Sūra Yā Sīn (Sūra 36), they then wept. . . .

Zamakhsharī on Sūra 5:44/48

Surely We sent down the Torah, wherein is guidance and light; thereby the prophets, who had surrendered themselves, gave judgment against those who were Jewish, as did the masters (of the law) and the rabbis, following the portion of God's Book that was entrusted to them and to which they were witnesses. So fear not men, but fear you Me; and sell not My signs for a little price. Whoever judges not according to what God has sent down—they are the unbelievers.

. . . *The prophets, who had surrendered themselves* (*aslama*, 'to become Muslim')[5]: an attribute which is used in praise of the prophets and not as a distinguishing characteristic (that is, distinguishing some prophets from others, since according to Muslim dogma all true prophets in all ages have been Muslims), just as is the case with attributes one uses in reference to the Eternal One.[6] The use of this attribute (of true prophets) shows that the Jews are far from acknowledging Islam, which is the (true) religion of the prophets in both ancient and modern times, and that Judaism is separated from this acknowledgment. God's words: *The prophets, who had surrendered themselves, gave judgment against those who were Jewish* emphasizes this forcibly (through the contrast of the two groups).

As did the masters (of the law) and the rabbis: as did the ascetics (*zuhhād*) and the learned men (*'ulamā'*) among the descendants of Aaron, who remained faithful to the way of the prophets and have remained aloof from the religion of the Jews.

Following the portion of God's Book that was entrusted to them: (the portion of God's Book) that the prophets had instructed the rabbis and masters (of the law) to preserve as the Torah. That is, their prophets had ordered them to preserve the Torah from change and distortion.

And to which they were witnesses: people who watched over it so it would not be distorted. The meaning is that the prophets between Moses and Jesus, of which there were a thousand, as well as Jesus, were to judge the Jews on the basis of the statements of the Torah, forcing them to observe its regulations and allowing no deviation from it. The Messenger of God did precisely the same when he held the Muslims to the observance of death by stoning (for adultery), defying them and refusing to them (the punishment of) flogging which they wanted to have (instituted as a milder punishment).[7] In the same way the judgment of the rabbis, masters (of the law), and Muslims should result, because the Book of God and the fulfilment of its regulations were entrusted to the prophets, and because they were made witnesses to it.

The pronoun in (the phrase) *that was entrusted to them* may possibly refer to the prophets, rabbis, and masters (of the law) all together, while the entrusting comes from God. (Thus) this means: God ordered them to preserve the Book and to be witnesses to it.

So fear not men, but fear you Me: Here those who make judgments are forbidden from every fear except the fear of God. In their judgments they should be incorruptible and should not deviate from the fairness which is commanded to them, out of fear before a tyrannical master or because they are afraid one of their relatives or friends might become angry.

And sell not My signs: and do not exchange the signs of God and his regulations, nor pawn them!

For a little price: such as corruptibility or striving after esteem and pleasure which is exhibited by men. Thus the masters (of the law) among the Jews falsified the Book of God in their desire for this world and in their striving for mastery, and they distorted its regulations and then perished.

Whoever judges not according to what God has sent down (in his Book), because they attach little value to it, *they are the unbelievers* (*kāfirūn*) and the transgressors (*ẓālimūn*) and the wicked ones (*fāsiqūn*).[8] They are here characterized as disobedient in their unbelief because they transgressed and were rebellious through their disdain for the signs of God, since they did not judge according to these signs. According to Ibn 'Abbās, the unbelievers, transgressors, and wicked ones are the People of the Book. (The following is related) from him: '(Muslims,) you are good people. What is agreeable belongs to you; what is disagreeable belongs to the People of the Book. Whoever denies the regulations of God is an unbeliever. Whoever recognizes it but does not judge according to it is a wicked transgressor.' According to ash-Sha'bī, the unbelievers are found among the people of Islam, the transgressors among the Jews, and the wicked ones among the Christians. According to Ibn Mas'ūd, the statement refers to the Jews and others altogether. (The following saying is related) from Ḥudhaifa: '(Muslims,) among the (religious) communities (*umam*) you are the closest to the Children of Israel in your behaviour. You follow their way as close as a hair, but I do not know whether or not you (also) worship the calf.'

Zamakhsharī on Sūra 4:51/54

> *Hast thou not regarded those who were given a share of the Book believing in demons* (al-jibt) *and idols* (aṭ-ṭāghūt), *and saying to the unbelievers: 'These are more rightly guided on the way than the believers'?*

Al-jibt are the idols as well as all who are worshipped besides God; and *aṭ-ṭāghūt* is Satan.[9] This passage refers to the following: the two (Medinan) Jews, Ḥuyayy ibn Aḥṭab and Ka'b ibn al-Ashrāf, went to Mecca with a group of (their) fellow believers in order to conclude a covenant with the (unbelieving members of the tribe of) Quraish to fight the Messenger of God. Then (the members of the tribe of) Quraish said: 'You are people who possess a book and thus stand closer to Muḥammad than to us. We feel uncertain as to whether you will betray us. Throw yourselves down before our gods, so we can feel assured before you.' So the Jews did this, and in so doing they placed their faith in *al-jibt* and *aṭ-ṭāghūt*. That is, they threw themselves down before the idols and obeyed Iblīs in their deeds. Abū Sufyān (the leader of the pagan Meccans) then said: 'Are we or is Muḥammad on the right path?' Then when Ka'b asked: 'What then does Muḥammad teach?', the (members of the tribe of) Quraish answered: 'He commands that God alone be worshipped and forbids associating (other gods with him).' In reply to this Ka'b asked (further): 'And of what does your religion consist?' They replied: 'We administer the House (of the Ka'ba), provide drinking water for travellers, show hospitality to guests, and provide ransom for those who are captured.' When they thus enumerated their deeds, Ka'b suggested: 'You (rather than Muḥammad and his followers) are on the right path.'

Baiḍāwī on Sūra 9:29

Fight those who believe not in God and the Last Day and do not forbid[10] *what God and His Messenger have forbidden—such men as practise not the religion of truth, being of those who have been given the Book—until they pay the tribute out of hand and have been humbled.*

... *Who believe not in God and the Last Day*: that is, who do not believe in it as is required according to our statement at the beginning of Sūrat al-Baqara (Sūra 2, 'The Cow'); for the belief of such people is no belief at all.

And (who) do not forbid what God and His Messenger have forbidden: (that is) what is firmly (and finally) forbidden according to the Book and the *sunna*. Others say that God's 'messenger' (here is the messenger whom they assert to follow. This would mean that they had deviated in their belief (*i'tiqād*) and their practice of the true form (*aṣl*) of their (own) religion, which has now been annulled (through Islam).

Such men as practise not the religion of truth: the firm (and final religion of Islam), which annuls and destroys the other religions. ...

Until they pay the tribute: (until they pay) what is imposed upon them (by the religious law)[11]. ...

Out of hand (yad): indicating the condition of those who pay the tribute. (The meaning is) then (either): out of a hand which offers willingly, thus indicating that they submit obediently; or, out of their hand in the sense that they pay the tribute with their (own) hands, rather than sending it by the hands of others. Thus one is here forbidden to claim a proxy in this regard. Or: out of abundance (*'an ghinā*).[12] Thus some say that the tribute should not be taken from the poor. Or: by a hand which has power over them, thus indicating that they are humbled and powerless. On the other hand, (the expression 'out of hand') can also refer to the condition of the tribute. This would mean (either): (until they pay the tribute) as ready cash which is handed over from hand to hand; or, as a charity, which is permitted to the one who is obliged to pay tribute. It is thus a great charity that they are spared from the tribute.

And have been humbled: brought low. According to Ibn 'Abbās the *dhimmī* (one of the People of the Book living under Muslim rule and paying tribute in return for protection) is struck on the neck (with the hand) when the tribute is collected from him.

According to the meaning of the verse, the tribute is restricted to the People of the Book. This is confirmed through the fact that 'Umar accepted no tribute from the Zoroastrians until 'Abd ar-Raḥmān ibn 'Auf testified that the Prophet had collected tribute from the Zoroastrians of Hajar (in southern Bahrain) and had said: 'Establish for them the same custom as for the People of the Book, for they have a similar book.' Thus they are regarded as possessing the Book. However, according to our view, tribute may not be collected from other unbelievers. According to Abū Ḥanīfa (on the other hand), it should be collected from them, except not from the pagan Arabs, for az-Zuhrī relates that the Prophet concluded peace treaties with the idolaters who were not Arabs. According to Mālik (ibn Anas), the tribute is to be collected from all unbelievers except the apostates. The minimum tribute amounts to one dinar per year, with the rich and poor being treated equally. Abū Ḥanīfa (however) says that it amounts to forty-eight dirhams for the rich, one half of that amount for those who are moderately well-to-do, one quarter of that amount for the poor who are capable of earning a living, and nothing for the poor who are not capable of earning a living.

4. The pagans and their idols

Baiḍāwī on Sūra 2:170f./165f.

And when it is said to them: 'Follow what God has sent down', they say: 'No, but we will follow such things as we found our fathers doing.' What? Even if their fathers had no understanding of anything? And even if they were not guided?
Those who disbelieve are like those who shout to something that hears nothing—except a call and a cry. Deaf, dumb, blind—they do not understand!

. . . *They say: No, but we will follow such things as we found our fathers doing*: ... This verse was sent down concerning the pagans, who were ordered to follow the Qur'ān and the other evidences and signs which had been sent down by God, but who had held instead to the blind acceptance (*taqlīd*) (of traditional beliefs and practices). Others say (that the verse was sent down) concerning a group of Jews whom the Messenger of God urged to accept Islam, but who answered: 'No, we will follow such things as we found our fathers doing, since they were better and had more knowledge than we.' However, what God sent down (as revelation) includes also the Torah, since it also summons people to the acceptance of Islam (in the sense of a state of surrender to God).

What? Even if their fathers had no understanding of anything? And even if they were not guided: ... The final clause to this conditional clause is omitted. What is meant is: If their fathers had been ignorant, had not reflected on religion, and had not been rightly guided to the truth, then they (still) would have followed them. This (passage) shows that blind acceptance[13] of what is capable of (individual) insight (*naẓar*) and independent research (*ijtihād*) is to be rejected. If one follows freely in the religion of another and thus has assurance through some kind of proof that he is correct, as is the case with the prophets and those who investigate the statements (of revelation) independently, then it is not in fact a matter of blind acceptance, but on the contrary one then follows what God has sent down. ...

Zamakhsharī on Sūra 46:4f./3f.

Say: 'Have you considered what you call upon apart from God?
Show me what they have created of the earth; or have they a
partnership in the heavens? Bring me a book which precedes this,
or some remnant of knowledge, if you speak truly.'
And who is further astray than one who calls upon, apart from
God, such as will not answer him till the day of resurrection, and
are heedless of the calling (of their worshippers)![14]

... *Bring me a book which precedes this*: that is, which precedes this Book, namely the Qur'ān. What is meant is: This Book speaks of the unity of God and the futility of polytheism. Among the books of God which had been sent down earlier there is not one which speaks contrary to this. Thus (the meaning is): Bring (only) one single book which was sent down earlier and which is a witness for the legitimacy of your worshipping beings other than God.

Or some remnant of knowledge: or some vestige (*baqiyya*) of knowledge which remains with you from the knowledge of the ancients. . . .

And who is further astray: The question posed here has its significance in the disavowal (of the assumption) that among all errors there may be one greater than idolatry. For idolaters do not call upon (him who is) All-hearing and All-granting, who (alone) has the power to fulfil every wish and every request. Instead of calling upon him, they call upon lifeless beings who do not hear them and who have no power to grant the requests of even one of their servants so long as the world remains and until the resurrection occurs. And when the resurrection occurs and the people crowd together, then the false gods will step forth as enemies and opponents of those who served them. Thus, the latter will have only burden and harm in both worlds (this world and the hereafter), since the false gods do not grant their requests in this world, and speak against them as enemies in the hereafter, and will disavow the worship which was paid to them . . . as in God's words: 'If you call upon them, they will not hear your prayer, and if they heard, they would not answer you; and on the day of resurrection they will disown your partnership' (Sūra 35:14/15). . . .

Zamakhsharī on Sūra 53:19–23

Have you considered al-Lāt and al-'Uzzā
and Manāt the third, the other?
What, have you males, and He females?
That were indeed an unjust division.
They are naught but names you yourselves and your fathers have named; God has sent down no authority concerning them. They[15] *follow only surmise and what the souls desire; and yet guidance has come to them from their Lord.*

Have you considered al-Lāt and al-'Uzzā and Manāt: the female idols of the pagan Arabs.[16] Al-Lāt was worshipped by (the tribe of) Thaqīf in aṭ-Ṭā'if. Others say that she was to be found in (the valley of) Nakhla (near Mecca), where (the tribe of) Quraish worshipped her. (The name) al-Lāt is the *fa'la* form from (the root) *l-w-y* (to turn, curve, bend, rotate), since one turned to her in order to worship her, or one circled around her, that is, made the circumambulation around her. (This name also) is read al-Lāttu (the mixer) and it is held that this idol bore the name of a man who at this location used to mix butter with olive oil and give it to pilgrims for food. According to Mujāhid (however), there used to be a man in aṭ-Ṭā'if who made a mixture (out of wheat or barley), and (later) people began to worship at his grave and then they made an idol out of him.

Al-'Uzzā was worshipped by (the tribe of) Ghaṭafān and was an acacia tree. This name was originally the feminine of *al-a'azzu* (the most powerful one). The Messenger of God sent Khālid ibn al-Walīd to her to destroy her.[17] (When he arrived) a female demon came forth out of her and tore her hair, bewailing the calamity (which was about to occur) and placing her hands on her head. Then Khālid struck her with his sword until he killed her and said (in *rajaz* verse):

> 'Uzzā, not praise but curses upon you!
> I see that God surely hath humbled you.

When Khālid returned and made his report to the Messenger of God, the latter said: 'That was al-'Uzzā. She will never again be worshipped!'

Manāt was a stone which was worshipped by (the tribes of) Hudhail and Khuzā'a and according to Ibn 'Abbās (also) by (the tribe of) Thaqīf.[18] Some read (the name Manāt in the written form) *m-n-'-t* (instead of *m-n-w-t*). It appears that this goddess Manāt was so named because the blood of the sacrifice was spilled (*amnā*) before her. . . . (Others read) in addition *manā'a* (which is the) *maf'ala* form of *nau'* (stormy weather, rain, storm), suggesting that the people sought rain from her while imploring her blessing.

The third, the other (al-ukhrā): a deprecatory designation in the sense of one who is put back (*al-muta'akhkhira*) on a lower rank.[19] Similar is (the linguistic usage in) God's words: 'The first of them shall say to the last of them (*ukhrāhum*)' (Sūra 7:38/36), that is, last regarding importance and rank. It is possible that al-Lāt and al-'Uzzā held priority and pre-eminence among the pagan Arabs. The Arabs used to say that the angels and these (three) idols were daughters of God (*banāt Allāh*). They worshipped them and maintained that they were their intercessors before God, even though they buried alive their (unwanted) newborn daughters.[20]

Thus, they were asked: *What, have you males, and He females?* What may be meant here is: Al-Lāt, al-'Uzzā, and Manāt are female beings whom you have placed alongside God as female associates. At the same time, you have the custom of despising and burying (alive) female beings who are born to you and are thus your relatives. How can you now regard these female beings as equal partners of God and designate them as goddesses? . . .

Zamakhsharī on Sūra 71:21/20–23

Noah said: 'My Lord, they have rebelled against me, and followed
him whose wealth and children increase him only in loss,
and have devised a mighty device
and have said: 'Do not leave your gods, and do not leave Wadd,
nor Suwā', Yaghūth, Ya'ūq, nor Nasr.'

. . . *And do not leave Wadd, nor Suwā', Yaghūth, Ya'ūq, nor Nasr*: It appears that these who are named were the most important and significant idols and are thus enumerated after the words *Do not leave your gods.* These idols of the (pagan) fellow tribesmen (*qaum*) of Noah reached the Arabs, so that (the tribe of) Kalb accepted Wadd, (the tribe of) Hamdān accepted Suwā', (the tribe of) Madhḥij accepted Yaghūth, (the tribe of) Murād accepted Ya'ūq, and (the tribe of) Ḥimyar accepted Nasr.[21] Thus an Arab may be named 'Abd Wadd (the servant of Wadd) or 'Abd Yaghūth (the servant of Yaghūth). Some say that these are the names of certain righteous men. Others say that these were among the descendants of Adam, and after they died, Iblīs[22] said to their descendants: 'If you make for yourselves images (*ṣuwar*) of them, you can look at them.' This they did and after they died, Iblīs said to their descendants: 'Your parents worshipped these images.' Thereupon they began to worship them. (Still) others say that Wadd had the form (*ṣūra*) of a man, Suwā' that of a woman, Yaghūth that of a lion, Ya'ūq that of a horse, and Nasr that of an eagle (*nasr*). . . .

5. *Superstition*

Zamakhsharī on Sūra 113:1–5

Say: 'I take refuge with the Lord of the Daybreak
from the evil of what He has created,

from the evil of darkness when it gathers,
from the evil of the women who blow on knots,
from the evil of an envier when he envies.'

... *From the evil of the women who blow on knots (an-naffāthāti fī l-'uqad)*: By those who blow is meant the women who practise sorcery, (either) individuals (*nufūs*) or groups (*jamā'āt*) who make knots in ropes and then blow on them as a means of practising sorcery.[23] (The word) *nafatha* signifies blowing with spittle. This (practice) has an effect in the working of magic only if one eats, drinks, smells, or takes in in some other way something noxious. God still may effect something with the blowing as a test through which those who persevere in the truth can be distinguished from those who just talk and the fools among the common people. The talkers and the (ignorant) populace ascribe this result to the sorcerers and their blowing, while those who persevere in the firmly established words of God give no attention or consideration to such sorcery.

If one now asks about the meaning (of the statement) about seeking refuge from the evil which results from (such sorcery), then I answer that there are three possible interpretations (*aujuh*): The first is that one seeks refuge from their action as a (forbidden) practice of sorcery and (thus) from the sin that lies therein. The second is that one seeks refuge from the delusion of men through sorcery and from the deception by which the sorcerers delude people. And the third is that one seeks refuge from the evil that God allows to occur out of their blowing. The reference to the sorcerers may possibly (also) include the cunning women, as are mentioned in God's words: 'When (Joseph) saw his shirt was torn from behind, he said: "This is of your women's guile; surely your guile is great"' (Sūra 12:28). In this case her guile represents something comparable to sorcery and blowing on knots. Or, it may refer to the women who deceive men by offering themselves to them, exhibiting their beauty and thus bewitching them so to speak. ...

Baiḍāwī on the same passage

... *From the evil of the women who blow on knots*: from the evil that proceeds from the women or other sorcerers who make knots in rope and blow on them. (The word) *nafatha* signifies blowing with spittle. The specific occasion of this (verse) is found in the following

Tradition: A Jew practised an act of sorcery against the Prophet by making eleven knots in a string and placing this in a well. Then, when the Prophet became ill, the two sūras of refuge (sūras 113 and 114) came down. Gabriel (who transmitted this revelation) reported the act of sorcery to the Prophet, who then sent 'Alī who immediately brought back the string. When the Prophet then recited the (eleven verses of) the two sūras, each verse of the recitation loosened one knot, and the Prophet noticed (as each verse was recited) a steady alleviation (of his illness). From this it does not at all necessarily follow that the unbelievers were speaking the truth when they accused the Prophet of being bewitched (in regard to the source of his revelation), meaning that as a result of an act of sorcery he was jinn-possessed (*majnūn*) (so that his revelations were inspired by one of the jinn).

Others say that the statement about blowing on knots refers to the women who frustrate the resolve of men through cunning. Thus the reference would be a metaphor suggesting the softening of the knots by blowing on them for the purpose of loosening them more easily. . . .

V

GOD

1. God's greatness and power

Zamakhsharī on Sūra 2:255/256

There is no god but God, the Living, the Everlasting. Neither slumber nor sleep seizes Him. To Him belongs all that is in the heavens and the earth. Who is there who shall intercede with Him except by His leave? He knows what lies before them and what is after them, and they comprehend nothing of His knowledge[1] *except such as He wills. His Chair* (kursī) *extends over the heavens and earth. The preserving of them*[2] *oppresses Him not. He is the All-high, the All-glorious.*

. . . In God's words *His Chair (kursī) extends over the heavens and earth* lie four possible interpretations (*aujuh*):

(1) His Chair[3] is not confined enough (to be included within) the heavens and earth, because it extends too far and is too wide. Moreover, this is nothing but a vivid description (*taṣwīr*) and fanciful image (*takhyīl*) of his greatness. In fact, there is no such Chair, no sitting (*qu'ūd*) (on such a Chair), and no-one seated (*qā'id*). Thus, God says: '(The unbelievers) measure not God with His true measure. The earth altogether shall be His handful on the day of resurrection, and the heavens shall be rolled up in His right hand' (Sūra 39:67), without proposing the idea (*taṣawwur*) of an (actual) holding-in-one's-hand, an (actual) rolling up (of the heavens), or an (actual) right hand. Rather this is a fanciful image and a physical simile (*tamthīl ḥissī*) of the greatness of his affairs, as God says: 'They measure not God with His true measure.'

(2) His knowledge is extensive. According to this interpretation, knowledge is characterized as a place, namely the Chair of the Wise One.

(3) His sovereignty (*mulk*) extends far. According to this interpretation, sovereignty is characterized as a place, namely the Chair of the Sovereign One.

(4) (It is to be taken into consideration) that it is related that God created the Chair (*kursī*) which stands before the Throne (*'arsh*) (of God) and under which lie the heavens and the earth. This Chair is something very much smaller in proportion to the Throne. According to al-Ḥasan (al-Baṣrī), however, the Chair is identical with the Throne. . . .

Zamakhsharī on Sūra 11:44/46

And it is said: 'Earth, swallow thy waters! Heaven, hold (the rain)!' And the waters subsided, and the affair was accomplished. And the Ark (of Noah)[4] *settled on (the mountain) al-Jūdī. And it was said: 'Away with the people of the evildoers!'*

Since the earth and heaven are addressed here in the vocative with expressions of more precision (*takhṣīṣ*) than (are addressed to) sensible living beings, and since special attention is devoted to them among all the subjects of creation through the (specific) address with the words *earth* and *heaven*, and since they are commanded to do something in the same manner as beings with reason and intellect, in that they are commanded: *swallow thy waters!* and *hold (the rain)!*, then this is an indication of the vast power (*iqtidār*) (of God) and (an indication) that heaven, the earth, and (other) such powerful bodies allow themselves to be led by God in such a manner that he can cause to originate from them whatever he wills, and that they do not refuse (to do what he commands). (It is as if) they are rational and intelligent beings who have knowledge of his greatness and pre-eminence, and his reward and punishment, as well as his power (*qudra*) over everything, which succumbs (*maqdūr*) to it. And (it is) as if they recognized the duty to obey him and allow themselves to be led by him, and as if they feared him and shrank back before him, with submission and the immediate yielding to his will. Thus, as soon as God issues a command to them, those who are commanded obey without hesitation and without delay in its execution. The swallowing (*bal'*) (of the water) is an expression for absorption, while the restraining (*iqlā'*) signifies the holding back (of rain). . . .

And the affair was accomplished (*quḍiya-l-amru*): and what God had promised Noah concerning the downfall of his people was accomplished.

And the Ark (of Noah) settled on (the mountain) al-Jūdī: that is, on a mountain near Mosul.

And it was said: Away (buʿdan): . . . God's statement (in this verse) with verbs in the passive form (with the names of the divine subject omitted) is an indication of the pre-eminence and greatness (of God) and (an indication) that such powerful things (as are portrayed here) appear only through the action of a powerful actor and only through the creation of an irresistible creator. (It should be shown) further, that the one who accomplishes these things is a unique actor in whose deeds no-one can have a share. One cannot go so far as to presume that someone other than God would say: 'Earth, swallow thy waters! Heaven, hold (the rain)!' Also (one cannot imagine) that anyone other than God would carry through this frightful affair as he did, or that the Ark would land and remain on the ridge (of Mount) al-Jūdī, unless he caused it to land and remain (there).

Regarding the meaning (*maʿānī*) (of this verse) and other points (*nukat*) which we could enumerate, the rhetoricians consider this verse to be linguistically perfect (*istafṣaḥa*) and they applaud it, (but surely) not on account of the assonance of the two words *iblaʿī* (swallow) and *aqliʿī* (retain). Although this assonance does not destroy the overall beauty of the words, it stands over against the beauty that constitutes the kernel of the rest (of the verse) and thus appears superficial, that is, not noteworthy. . . .

2. *God the creator*

Baiḍāwī on Sūra 7:54/52

*Surely your Lord is God, who created the heavens and the earth in six days, then sat Himself upon the Throne (*ʿarsh*). He draweth the night as a veil over the day, each seeking the other in rapid succession. (He created) the sun, and the moon, and the stars, (all) governed by laws under His command. Verily, His are the creation and the command. Blessed be God, the Lord of all the world.*[5]

Surely your Lord is God, who created the heavens and the earth in six days: in six periods of time . . . or in one time period corresponding to six days.[6] What one usually understands by a day consists of the time between the rising and setting of the sun; but at that time this did not yet exist. That God created things in stages, even though he had the power to call everything into being at once, is (on the one hand) a sign of the possession of free will (*ikhtiyār*) (by God), and (on the other hand) it is advice and a stimulus for the wise to maintain thoughtfulness in (all) things.

Then sat Himself upon the Throne ('arsh): Then his power (*amr*) was placed (on the Throne), or he took possession (of the Throne). According to our followers, the sitting upon the Throne is an attribute of God (which one accepts) 'without (asking) how' (*bi-lā kaifa*).[7] This means that when one says that God sits upon the Throne, then, in the same manner as he himself has said this (in the Qur'ān), in so doing one must keep free from (the idea) of residing or of being settled in a place. The Throne is the substance which surrounds all other substances. It is so designated because it is high, or as a simile for the seat of the ruler, since all things and regulations come down from it. Others say that the Throne signifies the lordship (*mulk*) (of God). . . .

Blessed be God (tabāraka Allāh) the Lord of all the world (rabbu-l-'ālamīn): He is considered as exalted on account of his uniqueness as God and is to be praised because he alone is Lord (of the world). The specific meaning of the verse is—to be sure God knows it better—as follows: The unbelievers had provided for themselves (more divine) lords. Then God showed them that only one is worthy of being Lord, namely he, since it is he to whom the act of creation and the command (*amr*) are suited, and he created the world according to a proper order and a wise plan. He brought forth the heavenly domain and then embellished it with stars, as he shows in his words: 'So He determined them as seven heavens in two days, and revealed its commandments in every heaven; and We adorned the lower heaven with lamps' (Sūra 41:12/11). After he made these, he called into being the lower substances. Thus he created (first) a substance which was susceptible to the changing forms and the various shapes. This he then subdivided into the various species, each with its specific form and functions. God refers to this in his words: 'Who created the earth—(that is, what is below) in two days' (Sūra 41:9/8). Then he brought forth the three kingdoms of nature (mineral, plant, and animal), first by combining their matter together in the first act (of creation), and then by giving them (specific) form in a second act (of creation). Appropriately God continues after the words 'who created the earth in two days' with: 'And he set therein firm mountains over it, and He blessed it, and He ordained therein its diverse sustenance in four days' (Sūra 41:10/9). The meaning is: (He created the earth and the kingdoms of nature in four days altogether) in addition to the first two days (during which he created the seven heavens), for God says in the sūra (called) 'The Prostration': 'God is He who created the heavens and the earth, and what between them is, in six days, then seated Himself upon the Throne' (Sūra 32:4/3). As soon as the world was created completely, he established his lordship over it, ruling it like a ruler who sits on his throne in order to rule his kingdom. And he directed his command from heaven to the earth, setting the spheres in motion, sending the stars on their journeys, and veiling the days with the nights as one seeks the other (in rapid succession). Then he told, as the confirmation (of the week of creation), and acknowledged, as the consequence that follows from it, who he is, saying: *Verily, His (alone) are the creation (of the world) and the command (over it). Blessed be God, the Lord of all the world!* Then he commanded all the people in the world to worship him in humility and sincerity, saying: 'Call on your Lord, humbly and in private; He loves not transgressors' (Sūra 7:55/53).

Zamakhsharī on Sūra 41:11/10

(God created the earth in two days.[8]) Then He lifted Himself to heaven when it was smoke, and said to it and to the earth: 'Come willingly, or unwillingly!' They said: 'We come willingly.'

Then He lifted Himself to heaven when it was smoke . . . : The meaning is: Then, after he had created the earth and what is on it, his wisdom led him to the creation of heaven without there being anything that could have dissuaded him from it. Some say that God's Throne (*'arshuhu*) was on the water before the creation of heaven and earth, and that God then caused a (pillar of) smoke to rise up out of the water, which arose over the water and remained (suspended) over it. Then God caused the water to dry up and made from it (the various) regions of the earth (*araḍūn*); and finally God created heaven out of the smoke which had risen up.

God's commanding of heaven and earth to come into being and the fact that both submitted (and obeyed his command) have the following meaning: God wished to call both into being and they did not refuse him. They were called into being as God wished them to be, and they responded (to his command) like someone who obeys a command from one in authority over him just as soon as the effect (*fi'l*) of the command makes its impression on him. What is involved here is a metaphor (*majāz*) which one characterizes as simile (*tamthīl*). It can (however also) pertain to a fanciful image (*takhyīl*),[9] in which case the meaning would be as follows: God speaks to heaven and the earth, saying: 'Come willingly, or unwillingly!', and they reply: 'We come willingly and not unwillingly.' The meaning is to be seen exclusively in the fact that God's power (*qudra*) upon the things which had been established is described clearly, without thereby implying that an actual statement and answer are meant. This is like when one says that the wall (of a tent) says to the (tent-)peg: 'Why do you split me?', and the peg replies: 'Ask that which pounds me! The stone which is behind me does not follow my will.'

One may now ask: Why does God mention the earth together with heaven and place them together in the command to come into being? Was the earth not already created in two days before heaven (was created)? To this I answer: God had created the material (*ghirm*) of the earth at first without spreading it out. He spread out the earth only after the creation of heaven, for God says: 'And after that (that is, after the creation of heaven) He spread out the earth' (Sūra 79:30). Thus the meaning is: 'Come forth in the form and condition in which you are to be made. Earth, come forth spread out as the resting-place and dwelling-place for your inhabitants! Heaven, come forth arched as a roof for her!' By coming forth is meant that something originates and appears, as when one says: 'His work had come forth in a satisfactory and welcome manner.' . . .

Zamakhsharī on Sūra 32:7/6–9/8

(He) who has created all things well and who originated the creation of man out of clay,

then fashioned his progeny of an extraction of mean water (min sulālatin min mā'in mahīnin[10]),
then shaped him, and breathed His spirit in him, and appointed for you hearing, and sight, and hearts.[11] *Little thanks you show!*

Who has created all things well (alladhī aḥsana kulla shai'in khalqahū[12]*)*: ... that is, there is nothing in his creation that would not be so arranged as required by wisdom and demanded for well-being. All creatures are (created) well, even though they show variation with regard to the good and the better. Thus God says: 'We indeed created man in the best form' (Sūra 95:4). ...

That (in this verse) God presents the spirit (which he breathes into man) as his own shows that what is involved is a wondrous creation whose nature no-one knows but (God). Thus God says: 'They will question thee (Muḥammad) concerning the spirit. Say: "The spirit is of the bidding (*amr*) of my Lord. You have been given only a little knowledge"' (Sūra 17:85/87). Thus, it is as if God had said: and (who) breathed something into him which he himself and his knowledge withheld.

3. *The creation as evidence for God*

Baiḍāwī on Sūra 2:164/159

Surely in the creation of the heavens and the earth and the alternation of night and day and the ship that runs in the sea with profit to men, and the water God sends down from heaven therewith reviving the earth after it is dead and His scattering abroad in it all manner of crawling things, and the turning about of the winds and the clouds compelled between heaven and earth—[13] *surely (in all this) are signs for a people having understanding.*

... *Surely (in all this) are signs for a people having understanding*: (for people) who ponder over these things and consider them with eyes of understanding. From the Prophet (the following) is related: Woe to him who recites this verse but pays no attention to it—that is, who does not ponder over it. One notes that these signs show the existence and unity of God in so many ways that a detailed description would be too extensive here. The general theological meaning (*al-kalām al-mujmal*) is as follows: The manifestations which are mentioned are types of possible existence, each within (the realm) of the conceivable manner and of the various ways in which a specific thing has come into being. By way of example, it would also be possible that heaven or its parts could move as little as the earth, that they could move in the opposite direction, that the revolving part (of the earth) could cross the two poles, or that heaven could possess neither an apogee nor a perigee. Since (this however is not the case, but) they are uncomplicated and similar in their parts, they must have a powerful and wise creator, who calls them into being according to the demands of his wisdom and the requisites of his will, and who is too exalted for anything to be able to oppose him. If there were in addition to this creator (yet) a (another) God who had the ability to do the same things (then there would exist various possibilities). First, their wills could agree, (in which case) if both were acting, then the two actors must have called forth a single action (which is absurd). Furthermore, were (only) one of the two acting, then the acting one would be predominant, and there would have to be something that calls forth this predominance, and there would be (at the same time) a weakness in the other which would not be consistent with his divine character. Or, the wills (of the two divine beings) could not agree, which would necessarily lead to mutual encumbrance and persecution, as God indicates with the following words: 'Had there been in them gods other than God, the heavens and earth surely would have gone to ruin' (Sūra 21:22). In the verse (under discussion) lies instruction concerning the high rank of the science of theology (*'ilm al-kalām*) and its representatives, as well as a stimulus for the pursuit of research and study.

4. God's support and benevolence

Zamakhsharī on Sūra 2:269/272

He gives wisdom to whomever He will, and whoever is given wisdom has been given much good. Yet none remembers except those who have understanding.

He gives wisdom: He grants his support (*waffaqa*)[14] in (the form of) knowledge and action according to (this knowledge). He is wise before God who is knowing and acting (according to this knowledge). . . .

Zamakhsharī on Sūra 2:272/274

Thou (Muḥammad) art not responsible for guiding the unbelievers[15] *(to belief); but God guides whomever He wills. . . .*

. . . *But God guides whomever He wills*: He grants his benevolence (*luṭf*) to him of whom he knows (1) that the benevolence will bring gain and (2) that he keeps far away from what is forbidden.

Zamakhsharī on Sūra 5:41/45

. . . Whomever God desires to try, thou (Muḥammad) canst not avail him anything with God. Those are they whose hearts God desires not to purify; for them is degradation in this world; and in the world to come awaits them a mighty chastisement.

Whomever God desires to try: when God leaves someone in the condition of temptation and wishes to leave him in the lurch.

Thou (Muḥammad) canst not avail him anything with God: you can do nothing for him to obtain God's support and benevolence.

Those are they whom God desires not to grant his benevolence through which he would *purify their hearts*. They do not belong among the people who are worthy of his benevolence, since God knows that his benevolence would remain without gain or effect. . . .

Ibn al-Munayyir on this verse

How often people fall into stuttering even though the truth is certain! This verse is to be understood in accordance with the doctrines of the people of the *sunna*, who say that God (himself) wills it when people succumb to temptation, and that he (is the one who) does not wish to purify their hearts from the impurity of temptation and the filth of unbelief. (On the contrary the verse is) not (to be understood) in the sense of the assertion of the Mu'tazilites, which is as follows: God wills that no-one should succumb to temptation, but he wills that everyone should believe and have a pure heart. If someone succumbs to temptation, then this happens against the will of God. And it would also be in accordance with his will if the hearts of the unbelievers remain pure. However this does not happen!

This verse and similar verses should suffice for the Mu'tazilites (as insight into the falsity of their assertion). If only God had willed to purify their hearts from the filth of (heretical) innovations (*bida'*)! Do they not ponder upon the consequences from the Qur'ān, or do they do it with hearts that are closed through (heretical) innovation? How loathsome it is when az-Zamakhsharī treats the present verse contrary to the external meaning of the words, saying: God does not wish to grant his benevolence to them because he knows that his benevolence would remain without gain or effect for them! God is exalted high above what the blasphemers say. If God's benevolence remains without gain and effect, whose benevolence shall then be profitable, and whose will grants success, when there is nothing beyond God that man could pursue?

Zamakhsharī on Sūra 6:125f.

Whomever God desires to guide, He expands his breast to Islam.
Whomever He desires to lead astray, He makes his breast narrow, tight, as if he were climbing to heaven. So God lays abomination upon those who believe not.
This is the path of thy Lord, straight. We have distinguished the signs to a people who remember.

Whomever God desires to guide: him to whom God bestows his benevolence. God wishes to bestow his benevolence only on him who is worthy.

He expands his breast to Islam: he bestows his benevolence upon him so that he feels a longing for Islam, his soul feels at home therein, and he desires to be a Muslim.

Whomever He desires to lead astray: him whom he leaves in the lurch and wishes to abandon to his own deeds. What is meant is one who is not worthy of his benevolence.

He makes his breast narrow, tight: he withholds his benevolence from him so that his heart hardens and he refuses and resists the reception of truth. Then faith finds no access in him. ...

As if he were climbing to heaven: as if he were pursuing something impossible. That is, climbing up to heaven is simply a simile for anything impossible, which exceeds one's capability and surpasses one's power.

So God lays abomination (rijs): that is, the abandoning and withdrawing of support. God distinguishes this from its opposite, that is, from what characterizes support. Or, God means the act of vacillating (*irtijās*) ..., which leads to punishment *(rijs)*. ...

This is the path of thy Lord: This is the path that is required by his wisdom and custom regarding his support. ...

5. *The attributes of God*

Ṭabarī on Sūra 6:102f.

This then is God your Lord. There is no god but He, the Creator of everything. So serve Him, for He is Guardian over everything. The vision (of men) reaches Him not, but He reaches the vision (of men).

... The exegetes disagree concerning the meaning of God's words *The vision (al-abṣār) (of men) reaches (tudrikuhū*[16]*) Him not, but He reaches the vision (of men)*. Some exegetes maintain that the meaning is as follows: The vision (of men) does not fully grasp (*aḥāṭa*[17]) him, but will be grasped by him. To be cited (as authorities) for this view are (the following):[18]

... Yūnus ibn 'Abd Allāh ibn 'Abd al-Ḥakam has related to us on the basis of (a chain of authorities going back to) Khālid ibn 'Abd ar-Raḥmān and Abū 'Arfaja the following quotation from 'Aṭiyya al-'Aufī concerning God's words: 'Upon that day (of resurrection) there will be radiant faces, gazing (*nāẓiratun*) upon their Lord' (Sūra 75:22f.):[19] 'They shall gaze upon God, yet their vision shall not reach him because of his greatness, while his vision shall reach them. This is mentioned in God's words: "The vision (of men) reaches Him not, but He reaches the vision"'. ...

The proponents of this view give reasons for their interpretation by saying that God has said: 'And We brought the Children of Israel over the sea; and Pharaoh and his hosts followed them insolently and impetuously until when the drowning reached him (*adrakahū*), he said: "I believe that there is no god but He in whom the Children of Israel believe. I am of those that surrender"' (Sūra 10:90). Here, so they say, God ascribes to the drowning the characteristic that it reached the Pharaoh. There is no doubt, however, that the drowning is not ascribed the characteristic that it saw the Pharaoh, and (there is no doubt) that it belongs among those things of which one cannot ascribe the characteristic that it sees anything. They continue by saying that it is far from one's thoughts that God's words 'the vision (of men) reaches Him not' have the meaning 'does not see him', since one thing may reach something else without seeing it. Thus, God says in his proclamation concerning the story of Moses and his companions when the people of Pharaoh approached: 'And when the two hosts sighted each other, the companions of Moses said: "We are reached (*la-mudra-kūna*)!"' (Sūra 26:61). God had told his prophet Moses that they would not be reached, as it is said: 'Also, We revealed to Moses: "Go with My servants (out of the land of the Pharaoh)! And strike (with your staff) for them a dry path in the sea, fearing not being reached (*darak*), neither being afraid"' (Sūra 20:77/79–80).

The proponents of this view say (further) that since one thing can see something else without reaching it and can reach it without seeing it, then interpreting God's words 'the vision (of men) reaches Him not' to mean 'the vision does not see him' gives an entirely isolated meaning, and that the (actual) meaning of these words is: 'the vision apprehends him not', since it is impossible for it to apprehend him. Since the believers and the inhabitants of paradise, so they say, see their Lord with their vision, although their vision does not reach him, this means that it will not apprehend him since it is impossible to ascribe to God the characteristic that anything can apprehend him.

They maintain that since it is permissible to ascribe to God the characteristic that he appears although he cannot be reached, then this is in accordance with the possibility of ascribing to him the characteristic that one knows of him without apprehending his knowledge. Thus, God says: 'And they apprehend nothing of His knowledge[20] except what He wills' (Sūra 2:255/256). God, so they say, therefore excludes (the possibility) that his creatures apprehend anything of his knowledge except what he wills. Thus is meant, according to their view of this passage, the knowledge of the contents of (his) knowledge (*ma'lūm*). Although God, so they continue, excludes (the possibility) that his creatures apprehend anything of his knowledge except what he wills, it is not excluded that they know him. (Further) they maintain that since the exclusion of (the possibility of) apprehending anything with regard to his knowledge does not exclude (the possibility) that one may know him, then the exclusion of (the possibility of) reaching God with the vision just as little excludes (the possibility) that the vision sees him. They say that just as it is possible for (God's) creatures to know things without apprehending their knowledge, it is (also) possible for them to see their Lord with their vision without its reaching him, since the (word) 'seeing' (*ru'ya*) has another meaning than the (word) 'reaching' (*idrāk*), and the (word) 'reaching' has another meaning than the (word) 'seeing'. Therefore (it is possible) that by 'reaching' what is meant is 'apprehending'. . . .

They continue: One may ask us: Do you not deny that God's words 'the vision reaches Him not' have the meaning 'the vision sees Him not'? To this we answer: We deny this, since God proclaims in his Book that there will be faces (*wujūh*) in the resurrection which look upon him, and his Messenger has proclaimed to his community that on the day of resurrection they shall see their Lord, as one sees the moon on a full-moon night and as one sees the sun when it is not obscured by a cloud. Since, so they say, God proclaims this in his Book and since the statements of his Messenger . . . confirm that God's words 'upon that day there will be radiant faces (*wujūh*), gazing upon their Lord' are to be interpreted so that the vision of the eyes will look upon God, and since in the Book of God one (statement) rests upon another within his truth and it is impossible that one of the two statements (of God) discussed here abrogates the other—which is simply impossible with the(se two) proclamations[21] . . ., then one knows that his words 'the vision (of men) reaches Him not' have another meaning than his words 'upon that day there will be radiant faces, gazing upon their Lord'. Consequently, on the day of resurrection the inhabitants of paradise will look on God with their vision, but will not reach him with it. (One must accept this) in order to agree with God in these two passages, and in order to be able to consider the revelation in the form in which it was delivered in these two sūras.

Other exegetes maintain that the verse under discussion has the meaning: 'The vision (of men) sees Him not, although He sees the vision (of men).' To be cited (as authorities) for this view are (the following):

. . . Hannād has related to us on the authority of (a chain of witnesses going back to) Wakīʿ, Ismāʿīl ibn Abī Khālid, ʿĀmir (ash-Shaʿbī), and Masrūq, the following words of ʿĀʾisha: 'If someone reports to you that the Messenger of God has seen his Lord, then he lies.' (God's words however read:) *The vision (of men) reaches Him not, but He reaches the vision (of men)* as well as: 'It belongs not to any mortal that God should speak to him, except by inspiration, or from behind a veil' (Sūra 42:51/50).[22] On the other hand, Gabriel appeared to Muḥammad twice in his (true) form[23]. . . .

The proponents of this view say that the meaning of (the word) 'reaching' (*idrāk*) in this passage is 'seeing' (*ru'ya*), and they deny that God can be seen by the vision (of men) in this world or in the hereafter. They interpret God's words: 'Upon that day there will be radiant faces, gazing (*nāẓiratun*) upon their Lord' in the sense that they hope for (*intaẓara*)[24] God's goodness and reward.

(Aṭ-Ṭabarī concludes that) some exegetes place a false interpretation on the statements which are related here from the Messenger of God, by reinterpreting the statement that the inhabitants of paradise will see their Lord on the day of resurrection. Other exegetes (simply) reject such statements of the Messenger of God, disputing them on (the basis of) their reason (*'aql*). They maintain that (reason) eliminates the possibility that one could see God with the vision, and they put forward all sorts of falsifications, using various derivations of many words. The most important argument by which they, so they say, know about the correctness of this assertion of theirs is the following: They find that their vision can see only something that is removed from them spatially and not something that has direct contact with it, for the vision cannot see anything that has direct contact with it. Thus, so they say, whatever is removed spatially from one's vision belongs to the category of things that can be seen with one's own eyes, since empty spaces and a gap lie between the object and the eyes. Now, so they continue, if the vision should see their Lord on the day of resurrection in the same manner as it sees shapes today, then the Creator would have to be (spatially) limited (*mahdūd*). But, so they say, whoever ascribes this characteristic to (God), (thereby) ascribes to him the characteristic of corporeality, which also includes increase and decrease (which is absurd).

They say that the ability to 'reach' (*adraka*) colours is given to the vision just as (the ability to reach) tones is given to hearing and (the ability to reach) smells is given to the respiratory organ. Then they continue that in the same manner as it is invalid for the hearing to give an opinion without reaching the tones and for the respiratory organ (to give an opinion) without reaching smells, so also is it invalid for the vision to give an opinion without reaching colours. They maintain that in the same way as it is impossible to characterize

God as possessing colour, it is (also) correct to say that it is impossible to characterize him as something visible.

(Still) other exegetes maintain that the verse under discussion has the meaning: The vision of (God's) creatures cannot reach him in this world but can in the hereafter. The proponents of this view say that the (word) 'reaching' (*idrāk*) in this place means 'seeing' (*ru'ya*). As a basis for their view they cite the following: Although the (word) 'reaching' has in some contexts another meaning than the (word) 'seeing', 'to see' is still one of its meanings. Thus it is impossible for the vision of men to see and contact something without this (object) being reached when it is observed and viewed, even when it is not apprehended as something seen in all its parts. Therefore, so they continue, if someone sees something he has looked at, then this means that he has reached it, that is, except for what he did not see. They say that God has proclaimed that on the day of resurrection there will be faces which will look upon him. Now according to their view, it is absurd (to conclude) that the faces should look upon him without reaching him as something that is visible. They say that because of this and because it is impossible that one could find any contradiction or disagreement in what God proclaims, then it is necessary and correct that God's words 'the vision (of men) reaches Him not' be interpreted in a special and not general sense, and mean: The vision (of men) does not reach him in this world, but he reaches the vision (of men) in this world and in the hereafter. That is, with his words: 'Upon that day there will be radiant faces, gazing upon their Lord' (Sūra 75:22f.), God has made an exception, so that (seeing God in this world) is excluded.

Other proponents of this point of view maintain that the verse under discussion is meant in a special sense, but that it may be possible that it has the following meaning: The vision of the evildoer does not reach him in this world or in the hereafter, while the vision of the believers and those who trust in God does reach him. They say (further) that the verse may possibly have the meaning: The vision does not reach him until the end and until (there is complete) comprehension (*iḥāṭa*), and indeed until (there is actual) vision. (Further) according to their view, the verse could mean that the vision (of men) does not reach him in this world, but indeed in the hereafter. (Also) the verse could have the meaning: The vision of the one who sees him does not reach him in the (same) way that the

Eternal one reaches the vision of his creatures. The one (i.e., God) who has excluded (the possibility) that the vision of his creatures may reach him is the one who has acknowledged this himself, since their vision is weak and can penetrate only that to which their God has given the power. On the other hand, they stand there completely open before his vision, and to his vision nothing of them remains hidden. There is no doubt, so they maintain, that God's words: 'the vision (of men) reaches Him not' are meant in a special sense, and that those who trust in God will reach him with their vision on the day of resurrection. Only we do not know which of the four special meanings (which have been mentioned) is intended in the verse (under discussion). As an argument for the truth of the assertion that God will be seen in the hereafter they cite reasons corresponding to those mentioned above.

(Still) other exegetes maintain that the verse is meant in the general sense and that no-one's vision will reach God in this world or in the hereafter. Rather God will create a sixth sense for his companions on the day of resurrection, which will be different from their five senses. With this they will see God. As a basis for this view, they cite the following: God has excluded (the possibility) that the vision of men should reach him except that in this or one other verse an indication is given that this is meant in a special sense. The same God has, so they say, proclaimed in another verse that on the day of resurrection there will be faces which will look upon him. Now, so they continue, since the proclamations of God do not annul each other reciprocally and cannot contradict each other, then the meanings of both proclamations are correct just as revelation brought them down. (Also) they present an argument based on reason (*'aql*) in that they say: If it is possible for us to see him in the hereafter with our vision, then, under the assumption that (at that time) this (same vision) will be increased, we must also be able to see him in this world, although the power of sight is weak. For all of the senses were created for the (purpose of) 'reaching' (*idrāk*) specific sense-objects (*ma'ān*, sing. *ma'nā*). Even if it is weak, in spite of its weakness it reaches what it is intended to reach according to its specific purpose—that is, as long as it does not cease to exist. They say (further): Were it ascribed to the vision that it reaches its creator and sees him in a certain situation and time, it must (also) reach and see him in this world, although it would reach him only weakly. They continue: Accordingly, if there were nothing of that kind for our vision in this world, there could be nothing of that kind in the hereafter, because (our vision) is created as it is in this world so that it can reach only what is to be reached in this world. Thus, this is now the case, they say, and God has proclaimed that in the hereafter there will be faces which look upon him, (although) one knows that they will see him with another sense than the sense of sight, since what God proclaims can be nothing other than true.

(Aṭ-Ṭabarī concludes:) What is correct concerning this, in our opinion, is what the accounts of the Prophet often bear witness to, namely that he said: 'You will see your Lord on the day of resurrection, as one sees the moon on a full-moon night and the sun when it is not obscured by a cloud.' Thus, the believers will see him, while the unbelievers will be veiled from him on that day, for God says: 'No, indeed! Upon that day they shall be veiled from their Lord, then they shall roast in hell!' (Sūra 83:15–16)[25]. . . .

Zamakhsharī on Sūra 75:22–25

Upon that day there will be radiant faces,
gazing upon their Lord.
And upon that day faces shall be scowling;
thou mightest think that upon them is about to
be inflicted some back-breaking calamity.

The reference here to the face is a (metaphorical) expression for the entire man. With the (expression) radiant (faces) one thinks of rays of happiness.

Gazing upon their Lord (ilā rabbihā nāẓiratun):[26] They finally look upon their Lord and upon nothing else. This is the sense of the object (being placed) in front (of the subject in Arabic). . . . It is (however) certain that the people will look upon boundless and numberless things in the gathering (on judgment day) during which all creatures will meet. The believers will gaze especially fully on that day, since they will feel confident and will not be living in fear and sorrow. It would be absurd (to think) that God would confine the gazing of the believers to himself alone, since this would mean that he would be something on which one could gaze (in the literal sense). Thus, one must comprehend this gazing in the sense in which the limitation (of the one looking) is properly taken into consideration. This proper perspective is achieved when one sees the gazing in connection with the following saying of men: 'I gaze (in my thoughts) on this and that, which he will perhaps do to me.' Here one means (not literal sight, but) expecting and hoping. Such a meaning is in the words (of the poet):

> And since I look on you as a king
> whom the sea (of generosity) never fills up,
> grant to me further favours.

One has heard how a woman of the Sarw in Mecca asked for a gift at noon, when the people closed their doors and proceeded to their places of rest, saying: 'My eyes gaze a little on God and on you.' Such is the meaning (of the verse under discussion): They will (on that day) await the generosity and favour exclusively from their Lord, just as they have placed their fear and hope only on him in this world. . . .

Thou mightest think: you might expect *that upon them is about to be inflicted* something violent and dreadful like *a back-breaking calamity (fāqira)*,[27] that is, like a sickness which shatters the spine, just as the radiant faces expect that to them will occur every kind of good.

VI

ANGELS, SPIRITS, AND MANKIND

1. The angels

Zamakhsharī on Sūra 40:7

Those who bear the Throne and those who surround it proclaim the praise of their Lord, and believe in Him, and they ask forgiveness for those who believe: 'Our Lord, Thou embracest everything in mercy and knowledge; therefore, forgive those who have repented and follow Thy way, and guard them against the chastisement of hell.'

It is related that the feet of those (angels) who bear the Throne[1] are in the underworld, while their heads tower above the Throne; yet, they are humble and do not look up. From the Prophet (is related the following): Think not of the greatness of our Lord, but of the angels whom he created! One of the angels named Isrāfīl[2] has one of the corners of the Throne on his shoulders while his feet are in the underworld and his head extends through the seven heavens; yet, in relation to the greatness of God, he is as small as a little bird (*waṣ'*).

In the Tradition (*ḥadīth*) it is reported (furthermore) that God has commanded all the angels to offer salutations to the bearers of the Throne in the morning and evening in order to distinguish them from the rest of the angels. Others say that God created the Throne out of a green gem and that (it is so large that) in order to fly back and forth between its two posts requires eighty thousand years for fast birds. (Still) others say that around the Throne are seventy thousand rows of angels who circle around it while praising and glorifying (God). Behind them are seventy thousand rows (of angels) who have placed their hands on their shoulders and lift their voices with praise and glory (to God). Behind them are (another) seventy thousand rows (of angels) who have their right hands placed on their left (hands) and glorify (God) in a different manner at any given time. . . .

One may now ask: What is the use of the words *and (they) believe in Him*, since no-one is prevented from knowing that the bearers of the Throne and the angels who surround the Throne while singing praises to their Lord are believing ones? To this I answer: These words should clearly inspire the high position and superiority of faith. Thus in other passages of his Book, God presents the prophets as upright on account of (their) faith; and thus he adds to the good deeds (which are enumerated in Sūra 90 in the portrayal of the 'steep path') the following words: 'Then that he (also) became of those who believe and counsel each other to be steadfast' (Sūra 90:17). In this God shows clearly the superiority of faith.

The words *and (they) believe in Him* also provide the following information: If what the anthropomorphists (*al-mujassima*) assert were correct, then *those who bear the Throne and those (angels) who surround it* would see and perceive God with their own eyes. In that case, however, they could not have been characterized as believing, since only one who is not present (directly with the object of faith) can be characterized as believing. Now, since the angels are characterized in a commendable manner as believing, one may know that their faith and the faith of those who are on the earth, as well as the faith of every being who is not present at that place, are similar in this respect. For the faith of all arises exclusively through reflection (*naẓar*) and deduction (*istidlāl*),[3] and there is no other path to knowledge of God. Further (one may know) that one must not ascribe to God any characteristics of the body.

Also, in the words *and (they) believe in Him* and the words *and they ask forgiveness for those who believe*, a mutual relationship (*tanāsub*) is established (between the angels and the other believers). It is the same as if it were said: 'And they believe and ask forgiveness for those who are like them regarding circumstance and condition.' Herein lies instruction concerning the fact that it is the partnership in faith which on most occasions must lead to friendly advice and, sooner than anything else, to sincere sympathy, even though there may be a distinction between the kinds (*ajnās*) (of believers) based on origin, and also their places of residence may be far removed from one another. Between angels and men, the celestial and terrestrial, there never existed any relationship of nature (*tajānus*).[4] Yet, after the uniting bond of faith came into being, there has existed with it a general relationship of kind and a real mutual relationship, so that those (angels) who surround the Throne ask forgiveness for those (believers) on earth. . . .

Zamakhsharī on Sūra 53:4–10

This[5] is naught but a revelation revealed,
taught him[6] by one terrible in power,
one very strong; he stood poised,
on the highest (point of the) horizon.
Then he drew near and hung suspended,
two bows'-length away or nearer;
then he revealed to his servant what he revealed.

By one terrible in power: . . . that is, Gabriel.[7] It conforms to his power that he snatched up the villages of Lot's people[8] out of the black water and, carrying them on his wings, raised them up to heaven and then hurled them down again (to the earth). He burst forth with a loud cry against the people (of the tribe of) Thamūd, so that they fell to the ground. Whenever he came down to the prophets and ascended again, this lasted for (only) an instant at the most. (Once) he saw Iblīs[9] on a steep path in the Holy Land speaking with Jesus and knocked against Iblīs with his wings and flung him onto the most distant mountain of India.

One very strong (dhū mirratin): who is endowed with right judgment in his understanding and opinion and is steadfast in his religion.

He stood poised (fa-stawā): He stood there erect in his true form rather than in the form that he used to assume (at other times) when he came down with the revelation, when he appeared in the form of Diḥya (ibn Khalīfa al-Kalbī). The Messenger of God wanted to see him in the form in which he was created; so he stood there upright before him *on the highest (point of the) horizon*, that is, the horizon of the sun, and filled out the horizon. Some say that the only one of the prophets who saw Gabriel in his true form was Muḥammad, who saw him thus twice,[10] once on earth and the other time in heaven.

Then he drew near to the Messenger of God *and hung suspended (fa-tadallā)*: and hung over him in the air. . . .

2. *The disobedience of Iblīs*[11]

Zamakhsharī on Sūra 38:71–76/77

When the Lord said to the angels: 'See, I am creating a mortal out of clay.
When I have shaped him and breathed My spirit into him, fall down, bowing before him.'
Then the angels bowed themselves all together,
except Iblīs; he waxed proud and was one of the unbelievers.
God[12] *said: 'Iblīs, what prevented thee from bowing thyself*
before what I created with My own hands? Hast thou waxed proud, or art thou of the lofty ones?'
He answered: 'I am better than he; thou createdst me of fire, and him Thou createdst of clay.'

... If one asks what the meaning is of God's words: *what I created with My own hands*, then I answer: We have already demonstrated earlier that one endowed with hands performs most of his acts with his hands. Therefore, action with the hands predominates over against other actions that one performs with something else. Thus one can say of the deed of the heart (which God has just as little as hands): 'It belongs to what your hands perform'; and one can say to one who has no hands (but is responsible for his misfortune): 'Your hands have tied up (the tube) and your mouth has blown.' Thus, there is no distinction between the two expressions 'that is something that you have done' and 'that is something that your hands have done'. The same is true of the two statements of God: 'what We created for them of what Our hands made' (Sūra 36:71) and 'what I created with My own hands'.

One may ask (further): What is the meaning of God's words: *What prevented thee from bowing thyself before what I created with My own hands?* To this I answer: The reason why Iblīs detested and scorned bowing down before Adam is that this would be prostration before something created; thus, he held back arrogantly and was too proud to bow down before another being besides the Creator. Add to this that Adam was created out of clay whereas Iblīs was created out of fire[13] and that Iblīs believed that fire was superior to clay. Thus, it was on the basis of his higher rank that he was too proud to bow himself before this creature. In this Iblīs did not take into consideration the following: God gave the command to bow down (before Adam) to those among his servants who are dearest to him and closest to him in favour, namely the angels.[14] These, rather than all others, would have been entitled to be too proud to humble themselves before the small man and to scorn bowing down before him. But they did not do so; on the contrary, they followed God's command and kept it in mind, while disregarding the distance between those who bowed down and the one before whom they bowed. For they wished to esteem the words of their Lord and honour his command. Thus, it would be proper for Iblīs, whose position is lower than that of the angels, to emulate and follow them. He should have known that, by bowing down before a lower being at the command of God, the angels devoted themselves more strongly to the service of God than if they had bowed down before God himself. This meant laying aside their pride and humiliation. For this reason Iblīs was asked: 'What prevented thee from bowing thyself before what I created with My own hands?' That is, what prevented you from bowing yourself before him who you say is a creature whom I have created with my own hands—and he is indeed a creature (of God)—if you wanted to submit yourself to my command and wished to honour my words as the angels did?

Iblīs is told that he refused to bow himself, and, at the same time, the reason through which he was led astray is mentioned. Thus he is asked: Why have you failed to bow yourself while putting forward this reason, when God has commanded you to do this? What is meant is: You had the command of God and should not take this reason into consideration. An example (*mithāl*) for this is the following: A king commanded his vizier to go in search of one of the lowest servants; but the vizier refused, citing the low rank of this (servant). Then the king said to the vizier: 'What prevents you from humbling yourself before someone whose low rank is not hidden from me?' What is meant is: Will you respect my command and my words and disregard consideration for his low rank! Accordingly, the words of God (under discussion) mean the following: I have created this creature with my own hands and thus have complete knowledge concerning his state. In spite of this, I have commanded the angels, on the basis of a wise reason which prompted me to do this, to bow themselves before him. Through this (action) Adam was supposed to receive the gift of a high token of esteem, while the angels were to be subjected to a test. But who are you that something which has not dissuaded me from (giving) such a command dissuades you from bowing yourself before him?

(Still) others say that (the words) 'what I have created with My own hands' mean: what I have created without anything interceding. . . .

3. *The jinn*[15]

Baiḍāwī on Sūra 72:1f.

Say: 'It has been revealed to me that (as a portion of the Qur'ān was being revealed to me) a company of the jinn gave ear;
then they said: "We have indeed heard a qur'ān *wonderful,*
guiding to rectitude. We believe in it, and we will not associate
with our Lord anyone!"'

. . . *That a company (nafar) of jinn gave ear*: (The word) *nafar* indicates (a number) between three and ten. The jinn are reason-endowed, invisible bodies in which the nature of fire or air predominates. Others say that they are a kind of pure spirit (*arwāḥ mujarrada*). (Still) others say that they are human souls who have left their bodies. This shows why the Prophet did not see them and (thus also) could not expound (the Qur'ān) especially for them. Rather (what occurred was that) they happened to be present once when (Muḥammad was) reciting and they heard him. (Here) God informs his Messenger of this. . . .

4. *Man and jinn*

Baiḍāwī on Sūra 15:26f.

We created man out of clay (formed) from mud moulded (into shape);
and the jinn We created before out of fire flaming.

We created man out of clay (ṣalṣāl): out of dried clay that rings (*yuṣalṣilu*, perfect form: *ṣalṣala*), that is, rings (*yaṣawwitu*) when one strikes it. . . .

(Formed) from mud: from clay that was transformed and became black because it lay near water for a long time. . . .

Moulded (masnūn): formed (out of mud) . . . or out of something that is moulded in order to dry and take shape, like the loosened materials that one pours into moulding castings. . . . It is thus as if God poured mud (into a mould) and from this shaped the statue (*timthāl*) of a hollow man, which then was dried until it rang when struck. Then God continued to transform it until finally he had made it completely proportionate and could breathe into it some of his spirit (*rūḥ*). . . .

And the jinn (jānn): the father of the jinn.[16] Some say (that the term *jānn* here refers to) Iblīs. However, the (entire) race of jinn may be meant as is evidently the case with (the term) man (*insān*) (in the preceding verse). Since the expansion of the race proceeded from a single individual who was created out of a single substance, then the entire race is also created out of it. . . .

We created before: before the creation of man.

Out of fire flaming (nār as-samūm): out of the fire of intense heat which penetrates the pores of the skin (*masāmm*). The creation of life in simple bodies (*ajrām basīṭa*)[17] is just as much possible as his creation into pure substances (*jawāhir mujarrada*), to say nothing of (the creation of life in) those compound bodies (*ajsād mu'allafa*) in which the fiery element (*juz' nārī*) predominates. These bodies (because of their warmth) are more suited for the reception of life than those in which the earthen element (*juz' arḍī*) predominates. God's expression 'out of fire' indicates that (element) which predominates in the body. This is also the significance of his words: 'He created you out of earth' (Sūra 35:11/12). Just as this verse provides evidence of the completeness of God's omnipotence and the explanation of the origin of the creation of man and the jinn, so also it provides evidence concerning the second assumption on which the possibility of the gathering (of the dead on the day of resurrection) rests, namely, that the material could be joined together and caused to revive.

5. *The temptation of Adam and Eve*

Baiḍāwī on Sūra 7:19f./18f.

(God said:) 'O Adam, inherit, thou and thy wife, the garden, and eat thereof where you will, but come not near this tree, lest you be of the evildoers.'

*Then Satan whispered (*waswasa*) to them in order to reveal to* *them what was hidden from them of their shameful parts. He said: 'Your Lord has only prohibited you from this tree lest you become angels, or lest you become immortals.'*

... *In order (li-) to reveal to them*: in order to disclose to them. (The conjunction) *li-* has a consecutive meaning; or, it has a final meaning, because in his insinuation (*waswasa*) (Satan) also had the intention to do something wicked to them by disclosing their nakedness. It is for this reason that he speaks of their shameful parts. There is here an indication that it is unnatural to appear naked and that this is something detestable and objectionable even when one is alone or before one's marriage partner, unless there is a need for it.

What was hidden from them of their shameful parts (sau'āt)[18]: what remained concealed to them concerning their nakedness. Neither of them yet perceived it in himself or in his partner. ...

He said: Your Lord has only prohibited you from this tree lest you become: only because he did not permit you to become *angels, or lest you become immortals*: beings who do not die or who live forever in paradise. Some have concluded from this that the angels have a higher rank than the prophets.[19] However, against this is the following: It is certain that the realities cannot be reversed. Adam and Eve simply had the wish to obtain the same natural perfection as the angels so that (like them) they would be able to do without food and drink. There is no evidence here for the absolute superiority of the angels.

VII

ESCHATOLOGY

1. The moment of the Last Judgment

Baiḍāwī on Sūra 7:187/186f.

> *They will question thee concerning the Hour, when it shall berth. Say: 'The knowledge of it is only with my Lord; none shall reveal it at its proper time, but He. Heavy is it in the heavens and the earth; it will not come on you but—suddenly!' They will question thee, as though thou art well-informed of it. Say: 'The knowledge of it is only with God; but most men know not.'*

They will question thee concerning the Hour: concerning the resurrection. (The word) 'the Hour' (*as-sā'a*) occurs frequently as a designation (of the resurrection), and it is employed for this because the resurrection takes place suddenly, or because the settling of accounts, which follows it, proceeds quickly, or because the resurrection is like an hour to God regardless of its actual duration. . . .

Say: *The knowledge of it is only with my Lord*: He has reserved the knowledge of it for himself alone and discloses it neither to an angel who stands near,[1] nor to a prophet whom he has sent.

None shall reveal it at its proper time: No-one shall disclose it and its time *but He*. By this is meant that it remains hidden to everyone except him until it takes place. . . .

Heavy is it in the heavens and the earth: It distresses intensely through the fear which people have concerning it—all of whom are perplexed, including both the angels and the jinn and men (*thaqalān*). This is, as it were, an indication of the wisdom (of God) in concealing it.

It will not come on you but—suddenly!: (It will come) unexpectedly and surprisingly, as the Prophet has said: 'Surely the Hour will startle mankind—one man will be digging his well, another will be watering his animals, another will be spreading out his goods at the market, and another will be adjusting his scales up and down.'

They will question thee, as though thou art well-informed of it (ḥafiyyun 'anhā): as though you knew it. (The word *ḥafī*) is the *fa'īl* form from (*ḥafiya*, as in the expression) *ḥafiya 'ani sh-shai'i* ('he gets sore feet from something'), (which one says) when someone inquires earnestly about something. That is, when someone investigates and inquires into something intensely, then he obtains a thorough knowledge of it. ... It is said that *'anhā* (regarding it) is linked with *yas'alūnaka* (they will question you); (also) it is said that *ḥafī* means *ḥafāwa* (good). The Quraish are reported to have said to the Prophet: 'We are, after all, related to each other; therefore, tell us when the Hour will come!' In this case, the meaning (of the sentence) would be as follows: 'They question you regarding it, as though you were a good person who had shown himself to be affectionate (*taḥaffā*) to them, and who would disclose the knowledge of the moment of the Hour to them alone as relatives.' Others say the meaning may be: 'as though you would be pleased by the question', that is, 'as though you would like it'. (The word *ḥafī*) would then be derived from (*ḥafiya* as in the expression) *ḥafiya bi-sh-shai'i* ('he welcomes something'), (which one says) when someone is pleased. (In this case) it would mean that you (actually) detest the question, since the moment of the Hour is among those things which God has reserved to himself alone in his hidden knowledge. ...

But most men know not: that knowledge regarding the Hour lies with God (alone), and that he has conveyed it to none of his creatures.

2. *The situation in the grave*

Zamakhsharī on Sūra 40:11

They[2] shall say: 'Our Lord, Thou hast caused us to die two deaths and twice Thou hast caused us to live; now we confess our sins. Is there any way to go forth?'

... In saying that he causes men to die two deaths, God means that he created them as if dead at the beginning (before birth) and that he causes them to die when their appointed times have come.

In saying that he causes men to live twice, he means the first act of bringing to life (at birth) and the bringing back to life at the resurrection. Support for this interpretation is found above all in God's saying: 'How do you disbelieve in God, seeing you were dead and He gave you life, then He shall make you dead, then He shall give you life, then unto Him you shall be returned?' (Sūra 2:28/26). . . .

Anyone who holds that the two deaths refer (here) to the death that follows the life of this world and the death that follows the life in the grave,[3] must accept (all together) three acts of bringing to life, and this contradicts what is stated in the Qur'ān. He can then at best seek support (for his view that there is life in the grave) by considering one of the (three) acts of bringing to life as not being included in the reckoning, or, on the other hand, by asserting that God brings the dead to life in the grave and that thereafter they will not die again. In this case he would consider them to be among those whom God calls forth with the blast of the trumpet, as he has said: 'For the trumpet shall be blown, and whoever is in the heavens and whoever is in the earth shall swoon, except those whom God wills. Then it shall be blown again, and lo, they shall stand, beholding' (Sūra 39:68).

One may now ask how this (that is, the statement: 'Thou hast caused us to die two deaths and twice Thou hast caused us to live') leads to the further statement in God's saying: 'Now we confess our sins.' To this I answer that they had disavowed the resurrection and were unbelievers; then, countless sins followed upon this, because one who does not fear the results (of his actions) transgresses excessively. Then, when they perceived that the act of causing death and the act of bringing to life are brought about again and again, then they knew that through his power (*qudra*) God is able to cause (man) to be brought back to life as a (new) creation. Thus, they (now) become well aware of the sin they had committed when they disavowed the resurrection, and also their subsequent transgression. . . .

3. The resurrection and judgment

Zamakhsharī on Sūra 36:81

Is not He, who created the heavens and earth, able to create the like of them? Yes indeed; He is the All-creator, the All-knowing.

... God's saying *able to create the like of them* can have two meanings: He creates something which in its insignificance and contemptuousness resembles men, when they did not exist in the heavens and the earth; or, he causes men to be brought back to life, since this reappearance is indeed similar to the original creation, although not identical with it[4]. ...

Zamakhsharī on Sūra 41:19/18–21/20

Upon the day when God's enemies are mustered to the fire,
held in order,
till when they are come to it, their hearing, their eyes and their
skins bear witness against them concerning what they have been
doing,
and they will say to their skins[5]*: 'Why have you borne witness*
against us?' They shall say: 'God gave us speech, as He gave
everything speech. He created you the first time, and unto Him
you shall be returned.'

... *God's enemies*: the unbelievers among those who come first and those who come last.

Held in order: that is, those who come first will be held back until the last arrive. Those who are at the head will be stopped until those who follow later have closed ranks with them. What is involved in this expression is a large number of inhabitants of hell-fire. We implore God to protect us from it through his far-reaching compassion. ...

Then, if one asks how their organs can bear witness against them and how they are able to speak, I answer: God will grant to them the ability to speak as he did to the bush (which spoke to Moses on Mount Sinai)[6] in that he created in it the ability to speak. Some say that the expression 'skins' may refer to the limbs. Others assert that it is an allusion to the female genitals.

By *everything* God means everything among living creatures, just as his saying: 'Truly, God is powerful over everything' (Sūra 2:20/19 and often) means everything which can be subjugated to his power. The meaning is this: In view of his power, there is no cause for surprise that we (the skins) have the ability to speak, for he certainly has the power to grant this ability to every living creature, just as, in the first place, he caused you to be created and to grow up, and he caused you to come back to life and to be brought to his judgment.

The men say to their skins: *Why have you borne witness against us* because their witness distresses them, and because the degradation through the speech of their own limbs appears intolerable to them.

Zamakhsharī on Sūra 101:1–11/8

*The pounder (*al-qāri'a*)!*[7]
What is the pounder?
And what shall teach thee what the pounder is?
The day that men shall be like scattered moths,
and the mountains shall be like plucked wool ('ihn*).*
*Then he whose deeds weigh heavy in the balance (*mawāzīn*)*
shall inherit a pleasing life (in paradise).
But he whose deeds weight light in the balance,
*his mother shall be (the) abyss (*hāwiya*).*
And what shall teach thee what the abyss is?
(It is) a blazing fire!

... *The day that men shall be like scattered moths*: God likens men to moths on the basis of their number, diffusion, weakness, and lowliness, and (also) in that they fly in every direction from which they will be called, just as the moths fly to the fire. (The poet) Jarīr said (concerning his poetic adversary al-Farazdaq):

> Al-Farazdaq and his people are, as far as I know, like moths,
> who conceal the fire of the glowing firebrand.

Among the similes (of the Arabs) are the following: (He is) weaker than a moth, lower than a moth, more ignorant than a moth. ...

God likens the mountains to *'ihn*, that is, dyed wool (*ṣūf*), because they will be colourful, and to dishevelled wool (*manfūsh*) because they will be split into pieces. ...

(The word) *mawāzīn* is either the plural of *mauzūn*, which denotes an action endowed with weight and importance before God, or the plural of *mīzān* (scales, a balance). The heaviness of the scales means that they sink down. To this refers the Tradition that Abū Bakr told to 'Umar in his will: The balance of those who on the day of resurrection will have a heavy scale will be so because these men have followed the truth (*ḥaqq*) and had heavy scales in this world. It is true (*ḥaqq*) that a scale in which only good words are placed is heavy. On the other hand, the balances which have light scales (on the day of resurrection) are light because these men followed futility and had light scales in this world. It is (likewise) true that a scale in which only evil deeds are placed remains light.

His mother shall be (the) abyss (*fa-ummuhū hāwiyatun*): (This expression) is related to what one says of someone whose destruction one wishes: 'May his mother perish!' If a man perishes, that is, suffers a downfall and is destroyed, then his mother also will perish as a result of grief at his loss. (The poet Ka'b ibn Sa'd al-Ghanawī) said:

> May his mother perish!
> What will the morning conjure up at its daybreak?
> And what will the night bring back when it returns?

Thus it is said likewise (here in the Qur'ān): 'But he whose deeds weigh light in the balance, he has already perished.' Others say that *hāwiya* is one of the designations for hell-fire[8] and that it is thus the deep fire, since the inhabitants of hell-fire fall down deep (*hawā*) into it. Thus (the saying) has been handed down that one will fall down seventy autumns deep. It means then: His dwelling-place (*ma'wā*) is the fire. Some speak of the dwelling-place as 'mother' metaphorically because she is a lodging and resting place for the child. According to Qatāda, (the phrase) *fa-ummuhū hāwiyatun* means: With him the 'mother of the head' (that is, the skull) is hurled down to the bottom of hell. That is, he will be thrown into it head first.

From the Messenger of God (the following is related): Whoever recites the sūra (called) 'The Pounder', to him God will make the scales heavy on the day of resurrection.

Baidāwī on Sūra 99:6–8

On that day men shall issue forth separately to be shown their works,
and whoever has done an atom's weight of good shall see it,
and whoever has done an atom's weight of evil shall see it.

On that day men shall issue forth out of the exits of their graves to the place (of judgment).

Separately: divided up (into various groups) according to their standing.

To be shown (li-yurau) their works: (to be shown) the rewards for their works. Others read: 'in order to see' (*li-yarau*).

And whoever has done an atom's weight of good shall see it (yarahū), and whoever had done an atom's weight of evil shall see it (yarahū): (Here the statement is) divided in order to clarify (its contents). Thus others read: 'he will be shown it' (*yurahū*). Perhaps the good deed of the unbeliever and the evil deed of him who keeps away from major sins[9] will bring about some lessening of punishment and reward. However, others say that the verse is to be interpreted with the understanding that there will be no cancellation (of good deeds) and no forgiveness (for evil deeds). Or, the first 'and whoever' may refer exclusively to the blessed, and the second to the damned, because previously it is said that they will come forth separately (in various groups). . . .

From the Prophet (the following is related): Whoever recites four times (the sūra beginning with the words) 'When the earth is shaken with a mighty shaking' will be rewarded just as much as one who recites the entire Qur'ān.

Zamakhsharī on the same passage

. . . One may now say: The good deeds of the unbeliever are devalued through his unbelief, while the evil deeds of the believer are forgiven if he has kept away from the major sins. What then is the meaning of the recompense according to the atom's weight of good and evil? To this I answer: (The passage) *whoever has done an atom's weight of good* refers to the group of the blessed, and (the passage) *whoever has done an atom's weight of evil* refers to the group of the damned. . . .

Zamakhsharī on Sūra 56:4–14

When the earth is shaken
and the mountains are crumbled
and become dust scattered,
and you are three groups:
Those on the right side, who are they?
Those on the left side, who are they?
Those who go before are (indeed) those who go before.
They are the ones who stand near (God),

in the gardens of delight—
a throng (thulla) *from former generations,*
but (only) a few from the later ones.

. . . *Those on the right side*: those who show their right sides. *Those on the left side*: those who show their left sides. Or, it may concern those of high rank and those of low rank, as one says: 'So and so is to the right and so and so is to the left of me', when one wishes to designate those who are higher and those who are lower in rank. The right side constitutes a good sign and the left side constitutes a bad sign. . . . Others say that those on the right and those on the left are those who experience happiness and unhappiness, since the blessed ones are happy with themselves because of their obedience, while the damned are unhappy with themselves because of their disobedience. (Still) others say that the inhabitants of paradise come to stand on the right and those of hell-fire come to stand on the left.

Those who go before (*as-sābiqun*): those with pious hearts, who arrived there first (*sabaqū*), for God summoned them, and who were not to be surpassed in striving according to God's pleasure. Some say that there are three classes of men: (1) the one who entered into good very early at a youthful age and remained in it until he left this world. This is the one who goes on before and stands near (God). (2) The one who came into sin early in his life and was remiss for a long time, but then turned in repentance (to God). This is the one on the right side. (3) The one who entered into evil very early at a youthful age and who thereafter was unable to keep away from it until he left this world. This is the one on the left side.

(The questions) *Who are those on the right side?* and *Who are those on the left side?* should awaken curious wonder concerning the condition of the two groups in happiness and unhappiness. The meaning is: What kind of people are they?

(The statement) *Those who go before are (indeed) those who go before* means: Those who go before are the ones whose condition you know and concerning whose peculiarity you have informed. The Prophet said: "Abd Allāh is (indeed) 'Abd Allāh', and Abū n-Najm said: 'My poetry is (indeed) my poetry.' Thereby he would, as it were, say: My poetry is that of which you already have knowledge and of whose purity of language (*faṣāḥa*) and aptness you have already heard. . . .

The ones who stand near (God) (al-muqarrabūn) in the gardens of delight: whose stairs in paradise[10] stand near the Throne (of God) and whose positions are high. Others read: in the garden of delight.

(The word) *thulla* designates a numerous community (*umma*). . . . What is meant is: Those who go before among the former generations are numerous. These are the communities from Adam to Muḥammad.

But (only) a few from the later (generations): thus referring to the community of Muḥammad. Others say that the former generations and the later ones refer to the older and younger members of this community. From the Prophet (the following is related): 'Both groups belong to my community.'

One may now ask: How can God say: 'But (only) a few from the later (generations)' and then say: 'And a throng of the later (generations)' (verse 40/39 of the same sūra)? To this I answer: The first refers to 'those who go before' (*as-sābiqūn*) and the last refers to 'those on the right side'. The latter increase not only through the former generations but also through the later ones.

One can say (further): It is related that the Muslims were severely persecuted when this verse came down, and that, for this reason, the Messenger of God conferred again and again with his Lord until (the following came down): 'A throng from former generations, and (also) a throng from the later ones' (verses 39f./38f. of the same sūra). To this I answer: This is not feasible for two reasons: first, because the passage under discussion (in v. 10) refers clearly to 'those who go before', while the second verse (40/39) refers to 'those on the right side' . . . ; and second, because abrogation is possible (to be sure, in the case of commands, but) not with information (which is reported).[11] According to al-Ḥasan (al-Baṣrī) 'those who go before' are as numerous in the (former) communities as in ours; and, at the same time, those who remain behind are (also) as numerous as in our community. . . .

4. Paradise and hell

Zamakhsharī on Sūra 47:15/16f.

This is what 'the garden' (of paradise) (al-janna), *which the godfearing have been promised, is like: therein are rivers of water not going stale, rivers of milk not changing in flavour, and rivers of wine, a delight to the drinkers; rivers, too, of honey purified. And therein are for them*[12] *every fruit and forgiveness from their*

Lord. Are they, as he who dwells forever in the fire, such as are given to drink boiling water that tears their bowels asunder?

... *Rivers of milk not changing in flavour*: as is the case with milk in this world. It is neither bitter nor sour nor in any way disagreeable as food.

A delight: ... What is meant is that the wine is a pure pleasure which is accompanied by neither loss of consciousness nor crapulence nor headache nor any other ill effect of wine.

Honey purified: which does not come from the bodies of bees and is thus without wax and other things.

Boiling water: Some say that when it comes near them it will scorch their faces and peel off their scalps. When they drink it, it will tear their bowls asunder.

Zamakhsharī on Sūra 11:106f./108f.

As for the wretched, they shall be in the fire, wherein there shall be for them moaning and sighing,
therein dwelling forever, so long as the heavens and earth abide,
except as thy Lord wills. Surely thy Lord accomplishes what He desires.

...*So long as the heavens and earth abide*: For this there are two possible meanings (*wajhān*):

(1) The heavens and the earth of the hereafter (*al-ākhira*) are meant, since these abide forever and are created for eternity. That the hereafter possesses heavens and earth is shown by the (following) words of God: 'Upon the day the earth shall be changed to other than the earth, and (also) the heavens ... and thou shalt see the sinner that day coupled in fetters' (Sūra 14:48f./49f.), and: 'Praise belongs to God, who has been true in His promise to us and has bequeathed upon us the earth (of paradise), for us to make our dwelling wherever we will in the garden (of paradise)' (Sūra 39:74). Since it is essential for the inhabitants of the hereafter that something must exist that will bear and shelter them, then either there must be existing a heaven that God has created, or the Throne (of God) must shelter them. Everything that shelters one is (however) a (kind of) heaven.

(2) This is an expression for the affirmation and for the negation of the end. Thus the Arabs say: 'So long as there is a bleat (of an

animal)', 'So long as (Mount) Thabīr[13] exists', 'So long as a star shines', and other similar formulas of affirmation.

One may now ask: Wherein lies the meaning of the exception (which is referred to) in God's words: *except as thy Lord wills*? For it is certain that the 'inhabitants of paradise' (*ahl al-janna*) and those of the hell-fire will remain there forever without exception. To this I answer: The exception refers to the eternal stay in the punishment by the fire and the eternal stay in the blessing of 'the garden' (of paradise) (*al-janna*). The inhabitants of the hell-fire will not always remain only in the punishment of the fire; rather, they will also be punished through severe frost and in other ways, (especially) through a punishment which is stronger than all these kinds, namely, in that God will be angry with them, will reject them, and will regard them as contemptible. At the same time, the 'inhabitants of paradise' (*ahl al-janna*) will have, in addition to 'the garden', something that is more important than this and will affect them more strongly, namely, the satisfaction that God will have (for them). Thus God says: 'God has promised the believers, both men and women, gardens in which rivers flow, forever therein to dwell, and goodly dwelling-places in the gardens of Eden—but even greater, God's good pleasure; that is the mighty triumph' (Sūra 9:72/73). Thus, in addition to the reward of the garden, they also receive yet another benevolent gift of God, the nature of which (certainly) no-one knows but him. This is what is meant by the exception. Evidence for this is (seen in) God's words: 'And as for the blessed, they shall be in the garden (of paradise), therein dwelling forever, so long as the heavens and earth abide, except as thy Lord wills—for a gift unbroken!' (verse 108/110, which follows the passage under discussion).

The meaning of God's words: *Surely thy Lord accomplishes what He desires*, which are a counterpart to the words (just discussed above), is as follows: He allots whatever he wills as punishment to the inhabitants of the hell-fire, just as he grants his gifts unceasingly to the 'inhabitants of paradise' (*ahl al-janna*). One should reflect upon this, since in the Qur'ān one part explains another. One is not to be deceived here by the assertion of the Mujbira[14] (who maintain) that the exception means that the people of grave sins (*ahl al-kabā'ir*) will be brought out of the hell-fire through intercession (*bi-sh-shafā'a*). For the second exception (seen in the statement:

'Surely thy Lord accomplishes what He desires') clearly accuses them of falsehood and proves that they lie.

But what must one think of people who repudiate the Book of God on the basis of a Tradition which has come down to them from a non-expert like 'Abd Allāh ibn 'Amr ibn al-'Āṣ? According to this Tradition, a day will come when the gates of hell[15] will be closed and no longer will anyone be inside; and this is to happen after the inhabitants have been there for a very long time. It has come to my attention that those who let themselves be misled by this Tradition and believe that the unbelievers will not remain forever in hell-fire have fallen prey to this error. This and similar (views) are clear deceptions, from which may God preserve us! May God increase to us guidance to the truth, knowledge of his Book, and the admonition to be gained from understanding it! If this Tradition according to ('Abd Allāh) ibn ('Amr) ibn al-'Āṣ is sound, then its meaning can only be that the unbelievers will come out of the heat of the fire (and) into the cold of severe frost. Thus hell would be empty and its gates would be closed. . . .

Ṭabarī on Sūra 23:105/107–108/110

(God shall say:) 'What, were My signs not recited to you, and did you not say they were lies?'
They shall say: 'Our Lord, our adversity prevailed over us; we were an erring people.
Our Lord, bring us forth out of it! Then, if we revert, we shall be evildoers indeed.'
'Away with you into hell,'[16] *He shall say, 'and do not speak to Me.'*

. . . *They shall say: Our Lord, our adversity (shiqwatunā)*[17] *prevailed over us*: The Qur'ānic readers disagree concerning the reading of this passage. The majority of the Medinan and Baṣran readers as well as some Kūfans read: *ghalabat 'alainā shiqwatunā*. . . . On the other hand, the majority of the Kūfan readers read: *ghalabat 'alainā shaqāwatunā*. . . . Some say correctly that here there are two canonical readings, both of which are read with the same meaning by well-informed readers. Whichever of the two one may read is correct.

The interpretation of the passage is as follows: They shall say: 'Our Lord, whatever precedes us in your knowledge and whatever is prescribed for us in the *umm al-kitāb*[18] prevailed over us.' The (early) exegetes (also) expressed opinions corresponding to this interpretation. To be cited (as authorities) for this view are (the following):[19]

... 'Abd al-Marwazī has related to us ... the following words of Muḥammad ibn Ka'b: To my attention has come, or it has been mentioned to me, that the inhabitants of hell-fire call to the wardens for help (saying): 'Call on your Lord, to lighten for us one day of the chastisement' (Sūra 40:49/52). Then, the wardens refer them to what God has said.[20] When they have reached despair, they cry: 'Mālik!' This one (as the angel of hell) is over them and has a seat in the midst of the hell-fire and the embankments down which the punishment angels move along (the damned). From there he oversees the farthest part of the hell-fire just as (well as) the nearest (part). (Thus) they say: 'O Mālik, let thy Lord have done with us' (Sūra 43:77). They beg for death (in order to find release), but after eighty thousand years of the hereafter Mālik gives them ... no answer. Then, he lowers himself to them and says: '(No) surely you will tarry (here)' (Sūra 43:77). When they hear this, they will say: 'Have patience as the people of this world have, in obedience to God; perhaps patience is profitable to us.' ... So they then have patience, and when they have persevered in patience for a long time, they cry: 'For us it is the same whether we cannot endure or whether we are patient; we have no asylum'—that is, no escape (Sūra 14:21/25). Now Iblīs rises up and delivers the following words to them: 'God surely promised you a true promise; and I promised you, then I failed you, for I had no authority over you' (Sūra 14:22/26). When they have understood his words, they will loathe themselves. It is to them that the following will be said: 'Surely God's hatred is greater than your hatred for one another, when you were called to belief but you disbelieved' (Sūra 40:10).

They will say: 'Our Lord, Thou hast caused us to die two deaths, and twice Thou hast caused us to live;[21] now we confess our sins. Is there any way to go forth (from here and escape the punishment of hell)?' (Sūra 40–11). ... Then God will say to them: 'That is because you disbelieved when God was called upon alone; but if others are associated with Him, then you believe. Judgment belongs to God, the All-high, the All-great' (Sūra 40:12). ... Then they say: 'We have not yet (completely) given up hope.' ... They call to God another time and say: 'Our Lord, we have (now) seen and heard; return us (again to life) that we may do righteousness, for we have sure faith' (Sūra 32:12). ... To this God answers: 'If We had so willed, We could have given every soul its guidance' (Sūra 32:13), whereby the Lord wishes to say: If I had so willed, I would have rightly guided all men so that none of you would have gone astray. 'But, (God continues) My word is now realized (when I said): "Surely I shall fill Jahannam with jinn and men all together." So now taste (the chastisement of hell, for) you forgot the encounter of this your day!' (Sūra 32:13f.). Thereby God wishes to say: (Now taste the chastisement) for what you have failed to do in anticipation of this day of yours. (God continues:) 'We indeed have forgotten you'—that is, we have forsaken you—'Taste the chastisement of eternity for what you were doing!' (Sūra 32:14). ...

Then they say (again): 'We have not yet (completely) given up hope.' ... And they call (to God) another time (with the words): 'Our Lord, defer us to a shorter term, and we will answer Thy call and follow the messengers' (Sūra 14:44/45). ... To this God will say to them: 'Ah, but did you not swear aforetime that there should be no removing for you? And you dwelt in the dwelling-places of those who wronged themselves. And it became clear to you what We did with them and how We struck examples for you' (Sūra 14:44f./45f.) ... Now they say (yet again): 'We (still) have not yet (completely) given up hope.' And they say again: 'Our Lord, bring us forth (out of hell), and we will do righteousness, other than what we have done' (Sūra 35:37/34). ... To this God says: 'What, did We not give you long life, enough to remember in for him who would remember? To you the warner came; so taste you now! The evildoers shall have no helper' (Sūra 35:37/34f.). Then God remains silent before them as long as he wills until (finally) he calls to them: *What, were My signs (āyāt) not recited to you (again and again), and (every-time) did you not say they were lies?*

After they have heard this, they will say: 'Now He will have mercy upon us', and they will continue: *Our Lord, our adversity*, that is, the Book in which things concerning us are written down, *prevailed over us; we were an erring people*. (They say further:) *Our Lord, bring us forth out of it! Then, if we revert, we shall be evildoers indeed.* To this God says: *Away with you into hell, and do not speak to Me!* . . . Henceforth they will speak no more in hell, since for them entreaty and hope have ended. Some of them will begin to yelp in the faces of others; then their mouths will be closed. . . .

VIII

DUTIES AND PROHIBITIONS

1. The grave and the light sins

Baiḍāwī on Sūra 4:31/35

If you avoid the grave sins (kabā'ir) *which are forbidden to you, We will acquit you of your evil deeds (which are not so grave) and admit you by the gate of honour (into paradise).*

... There is disagreement concerning the grave sins. Most natural is (the interpretation) that a grave sin is every sin for which the Lawgiver prescribed a specific punishment (*ḥadd*) or pronounced a threat of punishment.[1] Others say that what is meant is that whose inviolability is clearly acknowledged. According to the Prophet there are seven (grave sins): associating (other gods) with God, killing a person (*nafs*) whom God declared inviolable, slandering a blameless woman, consuming the wealth of an orphan, (charging) interest (*ribā*), deserting a cause, and being obstinate towards one's parents. According to Ibn 'Abbās, the number of grave sins lies closer to seven hundred than to seven. (Still) others say that God means here the (various) kinds of association, for his words say: 'God forgives not that anything should be associated with Him; less than that He forgives to whomever He wills' (Sūra 4:48/51 and 4:116).

Some say (further): The insignificance and gravity of sins is in relation to the sins that are above them and the sins that are below them. The gravest sin is associating (other gods with God), and the lightest is that the soul shelters sinful thoughts (*ḥadīth an-nafs*). Between these two (gravest and lightest sins) lie the middle ones of which there are two (kinds, those that are graver and those that are lighter). If two (such kinds) present themselves to someone and his soul draws towards them because he does not have control over it, and he restrains his soul from the graver of the two, then what he committed will be blotted out (of his record) as a reward for avoiding the graver sin. This is among those matters which vary in different people and situations, for God reproved his Prophet for many of his thoughts which would not count as sin in another and surely would not lead to their punishment. . . .

2. The motivation behind actions

Zamakhsharī on Sūra 11:15f./18f.

> *Whoever desires the present life and its adornment, We will pay them in full for their works therein,*[2] *and they shall not be defrauded there.*
> *These are they for whom in the hereafter there is nothing but the fire; there what they have done will have failed, and futile will be what they are doing.*

We will pay them in full: We will deliver the reward for their deeds in this world, whole, complete, and without diminution, in that health and sustenance will be bestowed upon them here. Some say that the hypocrites are meant here. When someone praises those who recite the Qur'ān,[3] doing so (only) in order that people will say of him: 'So and so recites the Qur'ān', then this is already said (and they have their reward). And when one speaks well of those who do good deeds and give gifts (*taṣaddaqa*) (only) in order that people will speak of it, then people have already spoken of it. And when it is said to one who fights and dies that he should fight so that people will say: 'So and so is brave', then people have already spoken of it.

According to Anas ibn Mālik, the Jews and Christians are meant (here). When they grant a request or do a good deed, they receive the reward for it immediately in the form of ample sustenance and physical health. Others say that those among the 'hypocrites' (*munāfiqūn*) who fought on the side of the Messenger of God are meant (here), for he gave to them their share of the booty. . . .

There what they have done will have failed: What they have done will fail in the hereafter . . ., by which is meant that they will receive (no further) reward, since they aimed their deeds not towards the hereafter but towards this world, and since they have already received the reward for that for which they aimed.

And futile will be what they are doing: that is, their deeds are futile in themselves, since they are not done in the right manner. For a futile action, however, there is no reward. . . .

Zamakhsharī on Sūra 2:262f./264f.

> *Those who contribute their wealth in the way of God, and then* (thumma) *do not follow up their gifts with reminders of their generosity or with injury, their reward is with their Lord; and no fear shall be on them, neither shall they sorrow.*
> *Honourable words and forgiveness are better than a freewill offering followed by injury. And God is All-sufficient, All-clement.*

(The phrase) *reminders of their generosity* signifies that one points out his good deed to the one for whom it was done; that is, that one points it out in order thereby to gain a binding claim on the other. (The Arabs) used to say: 'If you point out a good deed (after you have done it), then forget it!' And from one (of their poets) comes (the verse):

> A man who points out a good deed (of his) to me and calls my attention to it (even) once is truly a scoundrel.

Among the excellent sayings (of the Arabs) count the following: 'Twins are he who grants a gift to one who asks, and then brags about it, and he who gives nothing and is miserly.' . . .

Follow up . . . with injury signifies that one becomes arrogant towards the one receiving the gift, because one gave something to him. (The expression) *and then (thumma)* is to make it clear that when one contributes something, there is a distinction between renouncing claim to it and reminding of one's generosity and adding injury (to the one who receives the gift). Further (it is to make clear) that this renouncing of claim is better than the contribution itself, just as God has presented those who go straight in faith, in his words: 'Those who have said: "Our Lord is God" and then have gone straight' (Sūra 41:30; 46:12), as better than those who (merely) accept faith. . . .

Honourable words: a polite refusal.

And forgiveness: and that one forgives the one who requests a gift if his request proves to be annoying for the one approached, or that one receives forgiveness from God because one refuses politely, or that the one who requests a gift forgives (the one solicited) because he regarded the polite refusal as sufficient. . . .

3. Spending and hoarding

Zamakhsharī on Sūra 9:34f.

O believers, many of the rabbis (aḥbār) *and monks indeed consume the goods of the people in vanity and bar from God's way. Those who hoard gold and silver, and do not spend it in the way of God—give them the good tidings of a painful chastisement,*
on the day they[4] *shall be heated in the fire of Jahannam and therewith their foreheads and their sides and their backs shall be branded: 'This is the thing you have treasured up for yourselves; therefore taste you now what you were treasuring!'*

When one speaks of the consumption of goods, this can have a double meaning: Either one speaks of the consumption as a metaphor for taking something (which rightfully belongs to others) . . ., or one concludes from it that one receives something for consumption through the goods, so that the goods constitute the basis for the fact that one consumes (something). . . . If it means that they consume in a deceitful manner, then it is thus meant that they take gifts of bribery in the administration of justice and grant mitigation and alleviation in the sphere of religious laws (*sharā'i'*).

Those who hoard: It is possible that here is an allusion to many of the rabbis (of the Jews) and monks (of the Christians) in order to show that in them are combined two blameworthy characteristics: They accept gifts of bribery, and they hoard wealth which they hold back covetously and do not spend for the sake of good. It is (however also) possible that the Muslims who hoard and do not spend wealth are meant. They would then be classed together with the Jews and Christians who accept gifts of bribery, namely in the sense of being more uncouth (*taghlīẓ*) and as an indication of the fact that those among the Jews and Christians who accept forbidden goods, and those among you who do not hand over the appropriate part of your wealth, have earned in like manner the announcement of a painful punishment.

Some say that the (institution of the) legal alms (*zakāt*)[5] abrogated the verse about hoarding. (However) it is (also) said that this verse remains in effect and that (the statement referring to) failure to spend for the sake of God means the refusal to pay the legal alms. From the Prophet (the following is related): If a man paid the legal alms for something (which he now possesses), then this is not hoarding, even if it is kept secret. If, however, something reaches the stage that one must pay the legal alms for it but it is not paid, then this is hoarding, even if it lies there openly. From 'Umar (is related) that a man asked him about a piece of land that he had sold. To this 'Umar said: 'Keep the money that you received! Bury it under your wife's bed!' When the man asked whether this then would not be hoarding, 'Umar answered: 'If one has paid the legal alms for something, this is not hoarding.' From 'Umar (is also related): 'Everything for which one has paid the legal alms is not hoarded, even if it lies under seven earths. If, however, one has not paid the legal alms, then this is what God has mentioned (as hoarding), even if it lies on top of the ground.'

One may now ask what is to be done with the following Tradition of Sālim ibn Abī l-Ja'd (who reports): As the present verse was coming down, the Messenger of God said: 'Perish, the gold! Perish, the silver!' This he said three times. Then someone asked him: 'Then what kind of wealth should we cherish?', to which he answered: 'A tongue that mentions (God), a submissive heart, and a wife who supports (her husband) in his religion.'

Again (one may ask what one should do) with the following words of the Prophet: 'Whoever leaves behind (at death) a piece of yellow or white gold is to be branded on that account.' A man then died and a dinar was found in his loin-cloth. At this the Messenger of God said: '(That causes) a branding mark (*kayya*)!' Then, another died and two dinars were found in his loin-cloth. To this the Messenger of God said: '(That causes) two branding marks.'

(To these questions) I answer: That was before the legal alms were introduced as a duty. Regarding the situation afterwards, God is too just and too exalted to punish a servant (*'abd*) of his who accumulates wealth that is lawful and pays the legal alms that are imposed upon it. Many of the Companions of the Prophet, like 'Abd ar-Raḥmān ibn 'Auf, Ṭalḥa ibn 'Ubaid Allāh, and 'Ubaid Allāh (ibn Jaḥsh), acquired wealth and spent it, without being criticized for it by those who renounced claim to the acquisition of wealth. The renouncing (of wealth) is a free choice (*ikhtiyār*) for the most excellent (*al-afḍal*), who enter more into piety and asceticism in this world. The acquisition (of wealth) is completely permissible, and those who do this should not be criticized. (Certainly) everything has its limit. When from 'Alī (the following) is related: 'Four thousand (dirhams) and less than that are acceptable expenses (for the cost of living); whatever goes over that is hoarding', then this is a statement concerning the most excellent. . . .

(Further) one may say: Why are gold and silver mentioned specifically among the various objects of wealth? To this I answer: because they constitute the standard of wealth and the price for (all) things. Only (the possession of) that which constitutes more than the necessities of life is (considered) hoarding. If then someone possesses enough so that he can hoard it, then he also does not lack the remaining kinds of wealth. Accordingly, the mentioning of hoarding (gold and silver specifically) refers to the other kinds (also). . . .

4. The prohibition against interest

Zamakhsharī on Sūra 30:39/38

> *And what you give in interest* (ribā), *that it may increase the people's wealth, increases not with God. But what you give in alms, seeking (only) the pleasure of God*[6] *— those (who do this will) receive recompense manifold.*[7]

This verse is exactly in accordance with the meaning of God's words: 'God blots out interest (*ribā*), but freewill offerings (*ṣadaqāt*) He augments with interest (in paradise)' (Sūra 2:276/277). What is meant is: what you give (away) in interest charges.

In interest (ribā), that it may increase the people's wealth: so that it will increase and augment their wealth. (What you give for this purpose) does not increase with God and he does not bless it.

But what you give in alms (zakāt): that is, what you contribute freely (*ṣadaqa*) while seeking only God's pleasure, rather than seeking reward, or favour in the eyes of men, or fame. . . .

Some say that this verse came down on account of (the people of the tribe of) Thaqīf, and that they had practised business transactions with interest. Others say that what is meant is that a man gives (*yahabu*) or presents (*yuhdī*) (something) to another so that the latter will return more than he was given or presented. Such an increase is not forbidden; yet the one who makes the repayment for this increase will not be rewarded. (Also) others say that there are two kinds of interest: Forbidden interest is every loan (*qarḍ*) for which one receives more (in return) or from which one makes a profit. The interest which is not forbidden consists of giving or presenting something (to another) and requiring more (in return) for it.[8] In the Tradition (*ḥadīth*) it is reported: Whoever seeks to obtain more through a small gift receives a reward for it. . . .

Zamakhsharī on Sūra 2:275/276

> *Those who consume interest* (ar-ribā) *shall not rise again (on the day of resurrection), except as one arises whom Satan has prostrated by the touch (that is, one who is demon-possessed); that is because they have said: 'Bargaining is just the same as interest', even though God has permitted bargaining but has forbidden interest. Now whoever receives an admonition from his Lord and then desists (from the practice), he shall retain his past gains,*[9] *and his affair is committed to God. But whoever repeats (the offence)*[10]*—those are the inhabitants of the fire, therein dwelling forever.*

Shall not rise again: when they are awakened out of their graves.

Except as one arises whom Satan has prostrated: that is, (as one) who is cast down to the ground. . . .

That is the punishment *because they have said: Bargaining is just the same as interest.* One may now ask: Why is it not said that interest and bargaining are just the same (reversing the order of bargaining and interest), since (in the present context) the discussion is about interest and not about bargaining? It should have been said that those who charge interest liken it to bargaining and thus regard interest as permissible. Their (misleading) argument apparently consists in saying that: If someone were to purchase for two dirhams something that is worth only one dirham, then that would be permissible. It is the same if one sells one dirham for two. To this I reply: This is a kind of exaggeration (*mubālagha*), namely, in the direction that, in their firm belief that interest is justifiable, they have reached such a stage that they charge interest as the basis (*aṣl*) and standard of what is allowable, in order to liken it to bargaining.

Even though God has permitted bargaining but has forbidden interest: Through these words of God it is denied that they may both be treated as the same, and it is shown that a conclusion from analogy (*qiyās*) (as is represented by the apparent argument of those who charge interest) is nullified through an explicit statement (*naṣṣ*). For these words of God show that their conclusion from analogy concerning what is permitted and what is prohibited by God is invalid. . . .

5. *Capital punishment and blood revenge*

Baiḍāwī on Sūra 17:33/35

> *Do not kill the person God has forbidden (to kill), except with justification. Whoever is killed unjustly, We have appointed to his next-of-kin authority (for revenge) but let him not be extravagant in killing—surely he is helped.*

Do not kill the person God has forbidden (to kill), except with justification: except in one of the following three cases:[11] unbelief after (previous) belief, adultery after having led a virtuous life, and the intentional homicide of a believer who is protected (through blood revenge).

Whoever is killed unjustly: without the death being deserved (according to the law).

We have appointed to his next-of-kin (walī): to him who administers (*waliya*) his affairs after his death, that is, the heir.

Authority (for revenge): authority to carry out the punishment prescribed for homicide on him who is to be punished, or to undertake retaliation (*qiṣāṣ*) upon the one who committed homicide. Since God says (in this verse): (whoever is killed) *unjustly*, this shows that the killing must be an intentionally hostile act, since a (mere) error is not characterized as unjust.

But let him not be extravagant: that is, the one who kills (in one of the three cases mentioned above is justified).

In killing: in that he may (perhaps) kill someone whom it is not justified to kill. The prudent person thus will do nothing that brings destruction to him. Or, the *walī* (who is not to be extravagant) is meant, when he inflicts mutilation while killing, or when he kills another than the one who committed the homicide. The first meaning (namely, that one of the three cases of justified killing is meant) is supported by the reading of Ubayy: 'You (pl.) shall (however) not be extravagant.' Ḥamza and al-Kisā'ī read: 'You (sing.) shall not be extravagant', whereby one of the two would be addressed.

Surely he is helped (innahu kāna manṣūr): Here the motive for the prohibition (of extravagance) is stated in a new sentence. The pronoun 'he' refers either to the one who is killed (unjustly), since he is helped in this world through the retaliation for the death which is established (by God for the sake of justice), and he will be helped in the hereafter through the reward (of paradise). Or, the pronoun refers to his *walī*, since God has helped the latter in that he granted him the retaliation and commanded (other) *walīs* to assist him. Or, the pronoun refers to those whom the *walī* kills in extravagance, because (they are helped in that) retaliation in extravagance or punishment and responsibility for the extravagance are accepted.

Zamakhsharī on Sūra 2:178f./173–175

O believers, retaliation (qiṣāṣ) *is prescribed for you regarding the slain: freeman for freeman, slave for slave, female for female. But if anyone is granted any remission*[12] *by his brother,*[13] *the matter is to be pursued with equity, and the payment (of blood money) is to be made with kindness. This is a concession and a mercy granted to you by your Lord: and for him who commits aggression after that—for him there awaits a painful chastisement.*

In retaliation there is life for you who have insight; perhaps you will be godfearing.

According to 'Umar ibn 'Abd al-'Azīz, al-Ḥasan al-Baṣrī, 'Aṭā', and 'Ikrima, as well as the legal schools of Mālik (ibn Anas) and ash-Shāfi'ī, a freeman may not be killed (in retaliation) for a slave and a man may not be killed for a woman, specifically on the basis of this verse. They say that this verse is a clear commentary on what is unclear in God's words: 'Therein (that is, in the Torah), We have prescribed for them: a life for a life, an eye for an eye, a nose for a nose, an ear for an ear, a tooth for a tooth, and for wounds, retaliation' (Sūra 5:45/49). This verse (just quoted) may have been revealed in order to inform through it what is prescribed in the Torah for its people. Here, on the other hand, the Muslims would be addressed and would receive what appears as regulation in this verse.

On the other hand, according to Sa'īd ibn al-Musayyab, ash-Sha'bī, an-Nakh'ī, Qatāda, and ath-Thaurī, as well as the legal school of Abū Ḥanīfa and his followers, the present verse should be (regarded as having been) abrogated by God's words 'a life for a life ...' (Sūra 5:45/49). Accordingly, retaliation between slaves and freemen and between men and women would remain. Thus, from the words of the Prophet: 'The murder of Muslims is all the same', and from the fact that no relative position of superiority is taken into consideration concerning the soul, (these authorities) conclude that if a (whole) crowd (of people) murdered an individual, they could (all) be killed on his account.

It is related that a blood feud existed between two Arab tribes in pre-Islamic times and one gained power over the other and swore: 'We will kill your freemen for our slaves, your men for our women, and two (of yours) for one (of ours)!' Then, someone confronted the Messenger of God with this legal matter, (that is, for a decision) concerning the time since God brought Islam. It was on this occasion that the present verse came down; and the Prophet commanded them to place everyone on an equal footing.

But if anyone is granted any remission by his brother: ... The brother is the *walī* of the one who was killed. He is called his brother because he stands near him in so far as he is his blood revenger (*walī ad-dam*) and carries out his claim in this regard. ... Or, God mentions the *walī* with the designation of brotherhood so that the one may do what is to be done for the other with the thought that between the two exists a community relationship (*jinsiyya*) and Islam. ...

The matter is to be pursued with equity, and the payment is to be made with kindness: ... This is an instruction to the one who is granted the remission and concerns also those who grant the remission. That is, the *walī* is to pursue (the matter) in the right manner (with) the one who has taken a life, in that he is not to deal (too) severely with him, and (he is to) demand from him only what can be demanded in a good manner. And the one who has killed is to make good the equivalent for the (shed) blood in a respectable manner, in that he is not to postpone or reduce it.

This: the decision that is mentioned concerning the remission and the blood money.

Is a concession and a mercy granted to you by your Lord: since he specifically prescribed retaliation to the people of the Torah and forbade remission as well as the taking of blood money, while he prescribed remission to the people of the Gospel and forbade retaliation and the (taking of) blood money. The community (of Muslims), however, have the choice among (all) three: retaliation, blood money, and remission, which represents for them a magnanimity and a concession.

And for him who commits aggression after that: after the mitigation is put into effect and a man goes beyond what he is ordered to do, by killing someone who had not killed or by killing after receiving blood money. In pre-Islamic times the *walī* would sometimes accept blood money and lead the one who had killed to think that he was safe, (only) in order then to subdue and kill him.

For him there awaits a painful punishment: some kind of very painful punishment in the hereafter. According to Qatāda the 'painful punishment' is that he will certainly be killed, but no blood money will be accepted for him, since the Prophet said: 'I will grant remission to no-one who has killed after receiving blood money.'

In retaliation (qiṣāṣ) there is life for you: ... The meaning is: In this kind of regulation, as (for instance) represented by retaliation, you have strong life. That is, previously for a single (person killed), one killed a (whole) group (in retaliation). How many, after all, did (the poet) Muhalhil kill for his brother Kulaib, so that (the relatives of) Bakr ibn Wā'il nearly disappeared! For the one person murdered he killed (also) people who had not participated in the murder. This led to civil war and mutual slaughter among them.[14] Then when Islam brought the law of retaliation, therein lay a life for each life, or a (specific) kind of life, namely the life that results from the fact that a man is restrained from taking a life because he knows that retaliation will be inflicted against the one who takes a life. That is, if he plots a homicide, knowing that he will suffer retaliation, and is thus deterred from taking a life, then his companion is saved from murder and he himself is saved from retaliation. Thus, the (fear of) retaliation is the occasion for (saving) the life of two people.

Abū l-Jauzā' read: 'In the account (*qaṣāṣ*) there is life for you.' That is: in that which is reported to you about the regulation concerning homicide. . . .

6. *The prohibition against infanticide*

Baiḍāwī on Sūra 17:31/33

And slay not your children for fear of poverty; We will provide for you and them. Surely the slaying of them is a grievous sin.

And slay not your children for fear of poverty: for fear of scarcity. When (this verse states that) they (that is, the unbelieving Arabs) killed their children, this means that they buried their (newborn) daughters alive out of fear of poverty. God now prohibits this and promises to them the necessities of life, by saying:

We will provide for you and them. Surely the slaying of them is a grievous sin: a grievous transgression, since through it is brought about the cessation of reproduction and the extinction of the species. . . .

7. *The prohibition against the flesh of swine*

Rāzī on Sūra 2:172f./167f.

O believers, eat of the good things wherewith We have provided you, and give thanks to God, if it be Him that you serve.
These things only has He forbidden you: carrion, blood, the flesh of swine, and that over which any other name than that of God has been invoked. But if anyone is forced by necessity, without his own desire or deliberate transgression, then no sin shall be on him. God is All-forgiving, All-compassionate.

. . . Section concerning swine (*khinzīr*). There are here (various) complex questions:

(1) The community (*umma*) (of Muslims) agree that all parts of the swine are forbidden. God speaks of the flesh (and not of the other parts) of the swine because the main use (of the swine) derives from its flesh. This way of speaking is similar to the words of God: 'O believers, when proclamation is made for prayer on the day of assembly (that is, Friday), hasten to God's remembrance and leave

bargaining aside' (Sūra 62:9), where in this case God has specifically forbidden bargaining because it represents the main occupation of the people. Although the bristles of swine are not involved according to the (precise) wording, they (too) are unanimously regarded as forbidden and impure. There is a difference of opinion concerning whether one may use them for sewing (*kharz*) (of leather). Abū Ḥanīfa and Muḥammad (ibn al-Ḥasan ash-Shaibānī) regard this as permissible while ash-Shāfi'ī does not. Abū Yūsuf said: 'I regard sewing with swine bristles to be objectionable'; however, it is (also) related that he regarded it as permissible. The arguments of Abū Ḥanīfa and Muḥammad are as follows: We see that the use of swine bristles is conceded to the shoemakers among the Muslims and is not explicitly condemned. There (even) exists an urgent necessity for it. When ash-Shāfi'ī says that the blood of fleas does not contaminate the clothing because it is difficult to protect oneself from it, why then in the same manner are swine bristles not to be permissible, since one sews with them?

(2) There is disagreement concerning the 'water swine' (*khinzīr al-mā'*, that is, the hippopotamus). Ibn Abī Lailā, Mālik (ibn Anas), ash-Shāfi'ī, and al-Auzā'ī maintain that there is no objection about it, since one eats something that is derived from the water. Abū Ḥanīfa and his followers say that one may not eat it. Ash-Shāfi'ī bases his argument on God's words: 'Permitted to you is the game of the sea and the food of it as a provision for you and for the journeyers (who are going on the pilgrimage)' (Sūra 5:96/97). Abū Ḥanīfa (on the other hand) regards the 'water swine' as a swine and, for this reason, forbids (its use for food), according to God's words: 'Forbidden to you are carrion, blood, the flesh of swine, and that over which any other name than that of God has been invoked' (Sūra 5:3/4). Ash-Shāfi'ī says: When one speaks of swine alone, one knows immediately that the land swine and not the 'water swine' is meant, just as one knows immediately when meat alone is mentioned that it is a usage appropriate to other than fish meat, but not to this. (In the same way) one never refers to 'water swine' simply as swine, but (precisely) as 'water swine'.

(3) To the question whether one must purify seven times a container which has been licked by a swine, there are two statements by ash-Shāfi'ī. The first says: Yes, because one can liken it to the dog.[15] The second says: No, since that strictness (with which they consider contact with dogs) is for the purpose of deterring the people

from having contact with dogs. Regarding swine, however, one has no contact, and the distinction (between swine and dogs) is thus evident. . . .

8. The prohibition against wine

Rāzī on Sūra 2:219/216

They question thee concerning wine (khamr)[16] *and games of chance* (maisir).[17] *Say*: '*In both are great sin and some uses for men. But the sin in them is greater than their usefulness.*' . . .

Some note that in God's words *They question thee concerning wine and games of chance* (precisely) what the people have asked about is not made clear. It is possible that they have asked about the true character and nature of wine. (Also) they could have asked whether it is permissible to make use of wine. And (finally) they could have asked whether it is permissible or sinful to drink it. However, since God answers (the question) by indicating the sinfulness (of these two), the special emphasis of the answer provides proof that the questions concerned permission and sinfulness. In this verse there are (various) complex questions.

I. Some maintain: Concerning wine four verses have been sent down. In Mecca the following verse came down: 'And (We give you) the fruits of the palms and the vines, from which you obtain an intoxicant as well as wholesome food. Surely in this is a sign for people who understand' (Sūra 16:67/69). (On the basis of this) the Muslims drank such drinks, since they were permitted (or at least not explicitly prohibited). Then, however, 'Umar, Mu'ādh, and a group of the (other) Companions of the Prophet said: 'Messenger of God, render to us an opinion concerning wine, since it seizes the mind and steals the wealth!' Then came down the following words of God concerning wine: *In both are great sin and some uses for men*. Henceforth, some people continued to drink it, while others abstained from it. Then, 'Abd ar-Raḥmān ibn 'Auf invited some people (to drink wine), and they drank it and became intoxicated. One of them arose in order to perform the prayer and recited (falsely): 'Say: O unbelievers, I worship (instead of: I do not worship) what you worship' (Sūra 109:1f.). At this point, the (following) verse came down: 'O believers, draw not near to prayer when you are intoxicated until you know what you are saying' (Sūra 4:43/46), and the number (of Muslims) who continued to drink (wine) decreased. Then some Helpers (*anṣār*) came together, and among them was Sa'd ibn Abī Waqqāṣ. When they had become drunk, they boasted and recited poetry to each other, until finally Sa'd recited a poem that included a slander against the Helpers. Then when one of the Helpers struck Sa'd with the jaw-bone of a camel and inflicted a deep head wound, the latter complained to the Messenger of God, and 'Umar said: 'God, give us a conclusive statement concerning wine!' Then came down (the verse): 'O believers, wine (*khamr*), games of chance (*maisir*), idols (*anṣāb*), and divining-arrows (*azlām*) are (a clear) abomination (*rijs*) and some of Satan's work. So avoid it! Perhaps you will (then) prosper. Satan desires only to precipitate enmity and hatred among you, with wine and games of chance, and to bar you from the remembrance of God and from prayer. Will you then not desist?' (Sūra 5:90f./92f.). 'Umar added: 'Will we desist, Lord?'

Al-Qaffāl said that the wisdom of issuing the prohibition (against drinking wine) in these stages lies in the following: God knew that the people had been accustomed to drinking wine and drawing from it its many uses. Thus he (also) knew that it would be unbearable for them if he had prohibited them all at once (from the use of wine), and thus unquestionably (for this reason) he made use of these stages and kindness in the prohibition (against drinking wine). There are (however also) people who maintain that God forbids wine and games of chance in the present verse (Sūra 2:219/216), and that his words: 'Draw not near to prayer when you are intoxicated' came down after it. That is, the demand that the drinking of wine is forbidden during the time of prayer is connected with these words, since one who drinks wine would be performing his prayer while intoxicated. If therefore intoxication is forbidden, then the prohibition against drinking (wine) is also included. The verse (regarding the prohibition of wine) in (the sūra called) 'The Table' (5:90f./92f.) came down after the verse under discussion. It represents the strongest possible form of the prohibition. According to ar-Rabī' ibn Anas, the present verse (Sūra 2:219/216) came down after the prohibition against wine.

II. One should take note, according to our view, that the present verse shows the (existence of the) prohibition against wine. It lacks (however) the (more precise) explanation of what wine (*khamr*) is, and then (also) the (more precise) explanation of the fact that this verse shows the (existence of the) prohibition against wine.

(1) On the first point, namely the (more precise) explanation of what wine is (the following is offered): Ash-Shāfi'ī said that every intoxicating drink (*muskir*) is wine. Abū Ḥanīfa said that wine is equivalent to a strong grape juice which develops foam (as a result of fermentation).

(1A) The evidence on which ash-Shāfi'ī supports his opinion consists of various aspects (*wujūh*, sing. *wajh*):

(1AA) The first aspect is presented in what Abū Dāwūd relates in his (work on Tradition called) *Sunan*, from ash-Sha'bī, from Ibn 'Umar, who said (that 'Umar said the following): On one particular day, the prohibition against wine came down (from God, stating that wine is prohibited) whenever made out of five kinds of things: grapes, dates, wheat, barley, and millet (*dhura*). (At that time) one understood as wine that which clouds (*khamara*) the mind. From this one can draw three kinds of conclusions:

(a) The first is as follows: 'Umar reported that on a specific day wine was prohibited, whenever made out of wheat, barley (and millet) as well as grapes and dates. This shows that all of these were designated as wine.

(b) The second is as follows: 'Umar said that on a specific day wine was prohibited, whenever it was made out of these five things. This is as good as an explicit declaration that the prohibition of wine includes the prohibition of these five kinds.

(c) The third is as follows: 'Umar spoke also of every type of drink that 'clouds' the mind. Doubtlessly 'Umar knew the correct linguistic usage. Consequently, his Tradition indicates that 'wine' is a designation for all (drinks) that 'cloud' the mind. And so forth.

(1AB) The second (portion of) evidence (on which ash-Shāfi'ī bases his opinion) is this: Abū Dāwūd relates from an-Nu'mān ibn Bashīr the following statement: The Messenger of God said: 'Wine is made out of grapes, dates, honey, wheat, and barley.' From this one can draw two kinds of conclusions:

(a) The first is as follows: This is an explicit explanation that these things fall under the designation 'wine' and thus are also included in the verse that establishes the prohibition against wine.

(b) The second is as follows: It is not the intention of the Lawgiver (*shāriʿ*) to give instruction concerning the (various) expressions (for wine and similar drinks). Thus, in the present case he cannot have wished other than to explain that the decision which applies to wine (made from grape juice) also applies to these (other kinds of wine). If the known decision, which is meant specifically for wine (made from grape juice), pertains to the wickedness of drinking, it must therefore be applied in like manner for these (other) types of drinks.

Al-Khaṭṭābī said that (the reason) the Messenger of God used (the word) 'wine' specifically for these five things (was) not because wine is produced only from these five (raw materials). Rather, these are specially mentioned because they were well known at that time. Therefore, the decision concerning these five (raw materials) applies to all that are like them, such as millet, sult (-barley), and tree sap. . . .

(1AC) The third (portion of) evidence (on which ash-Shāfiʿī bases his opinion) is as follows: Abū Dāwūd relates also from Nāfiʿ who relates from Ibn ʿUmar: The Messenger of God said that every intoxicating drink (*muskir*) is wine and that every type of intoxicating drink is forbidden. Al-Khaṭṭābī said the following: If the Messenger of God states that every type of intoxicating drink is to be considered wine, then this leads to two possible interpretations (*wajhān*):

(a) First: (The word) 'wine' designates all drinks that cause intoxication. This is based on the following: After the verse had proclaimed the prohibition against wine, the people did not know the (exact) meaning which God meant to express with the (word) 'wine', that is, whether the Lawgiver (*shāriʿ*) was using this expression according to the usual meaning in the Arabic language, or was producing a legal designation through a creation (of a new definition of the word 'wine'), as is also the case with (the terms) 'prayer' (*ṣalāt*), 'fast' (*ṣaum*), and others.

(b) Second: The meaning of the statement (of the Messenger of God) consists in the following: that every intoxicating drink is to be treated like wine regarding the sinfulness (of its use). That is, when the Messenger of God says that this (that is, every intoxicating drink) is wine, then the literal meaning of this expression would signify that these are actually (different kinds of) wine. It is now evident that this (narrow interpretation) is not meant, so one must take it as a figurative expression (*majāz*) for whatever is equivalent, and this remains as the authoritative decision.

(1AD) The fourth (portion of) evidence (on which ash-Shāfi'ī bases his opinion) is this: Abū Dāwūd related the following from 'Ā'isha: The Messenger of God was asked about (the drink) *bita'*, and he answered: 'Every drink that intoxicates is prohibited.' Al-Khaṭṭābī said: *Bita'* is a drink that one makes out of honey. This statement (of the Messenger of God) refutes every interpretation that is put forward by those who declare the (wine) *nabīdh* (a type which includes *bita'*) to be permitted. This (statement also) refutes the assertion of those who say that a small amount of an intoxicating drink is allowed. The Messenger of God was asked only about a single kind, the (wine) *nabīdh*, but answered with a prohibition against the (entire) class (of intoxicating drinks). This includes not only a large amount of it but also a small amount. If separate classifications according to kind and amount were intended here, then the Messenger of God would have mentioned this and not neglected it.

(1AE) The fifth (portion of) evidence (on which ash-Shāfi'ī bases his opinion) is this: Abū Dāwūd related the following from Jābir ibn 'Abd Allāh: The Messenger of God said that whatever intoxicates in large amounts is also prohibited in small amounts.

(1AF) The sixth (portion of) evidence (on which ash-Shāfi'ī bases his opinion) is this: Abū Dāwūd related further from al-Qāsim who related from 'Ā'isha (who said): I heard how the Messenger of God said: 'Every intoxicant is forbidden. Whatever intoxicates in the amount of a *farq* is also forbidden in the (smaller) amount of a handful.' Al-Khaṭṭābī said that a *farq*[18] is a measure that comprises sixteen *raṭl*. Here then it is most clearly evident that sinfulness extends to all parts of (intoxicating) drinks.

(1AG) The seventh (portion of) evidence (on which ash-Shāfi'ī bases his opinion) is this: Abū Dāwūd related also from Shahr ibn Ḥaushab who related from Umm Salama that the Messenger of God prohibited every intoxicating and weakening (drink). Al-Khaṭṭābī said that by 'weakening' is to be understood every drink that brings about weakness and stiffness in the joints. It doubtlessly includes all kinds of drinks. All these reports indicate that every intoxicating drink (*muskir*) is wine, and is thus prohibited.

(1B) The second kind of argument which indicates (in addition to the material cited above) that every intoxicating drink (*muskir*) is wine (*khamr*) is seen when one considers the etymology. The lexicographers maintain that the basic meaning of the consonantal group *kh-m-r* is 'to cover'. The head veil (of women) is called *khimār* because it covers the head of the woman, while *khamar* may be a shrub, or a ground depression or hill, which conceals somebody. ... The etymology shows that by 'wine' is to be understood that which 'veils' (*satara*) the mind, just as one designates wine as an intoxicating drink (*muskir*) because it 'closes' (*sakara*) the mind. ...

(1C) The third kind of argument which indicates that by 'wine' is to be understood (simply) whatever (drink) intoxicates is based on the fact that the (Islamic) community agree in the following: There are three verses which refer to wine, in two of which it is mentioned explicitly (as *khamr*). The first is the verse presently under discussion (Sūra 2:219/216), and the second is the verse in (the sūra called) 'The Table' (5:90f./92f.). The third verse refers to intoxication and contains God's words: 'Draw not near to prayer when you are intoxicated' (Sūra 4:43/46). This shows that by 'wine' is meant (simply) whatever (drink) intoxicates.

(1D) The fourth kind of argument is as follows: The occasion for the prohibition of wine was when 'Umar and Mu'ādh said: 'Messenger of God, wine seizes the mind and steals the wealth. Give us an explanation concerning it!' Thus, they asked for a judgment from God and his Messenger because wine seizes the mind. Hence it follows necessarily that all that is like wine in this sense is either wine or is equivalent to it in view of the present decision.

(1E) The fifth kind of argument is as follows: God has confirmed his prohibition of wine through his words: 'Satan desires only to precipitate enmity and hatred among you, with wine and games of chance, and to bar you from the remembrance of God and from prayer' (Sūra 5:91/93). Doubtless, such kinds of acts are motivated by intoxication. This cause is certain. Accordingly, the present verse (Sūra 2:219/216) presents more precise evidence of the fact that the sinfulness of (the use of) wine lies in the fact that it intoxicates. Whether it is now unconditionally necessary that every intoxicating (drink) is wine, or whether this is not so, in all cases the present decision has validity for every intoxicating drink. Whoever thinks correctly and is free from stubbornness knows that these aspects (*wujūh*) (of evidence) are given clearly and distinctly along with the (clear) statement of this problem.

(1F) The evidence of Abū Ḥanīfa is (likewise) of various aspects:

(1FA) The first aspect is as follows: When God said: 'And (We give you) the fruits of the palms and the vines, from which you obtain an intoxicant as well as wholesome food' (Sūra 16:67/69), then he granted a favour to us in that we (may) make an intoxicating drink and wholesome food. (Therefore) that through which we have an intoxicating drink and wholesome food must be permitted, since a benefaction (which God grants) cannot be other than permitted.

(1FB) The second (portion of) evidence (on which Abū Ḥanīfa bases his opinion) is that Ibn ʿAbbās related the following: In the year of the farewell pilgrimage, the Messenger of God came to the drinking place (of the pilgrims in Mecca, that is, the well Zamzam), leaned against it, and said: 'Give me a drink!' Then al-ʿAbbās asked: 'Should I not give you a drink from what we pressed (from the grapes) (*nabadha*) in our houses?' Then when the Messenger of God replied: '(Give me a drink of) what you usually give the people to drink!', al-ʿAbbās brought a cup of (the wine) *nabīdh*. The Messenger of God smelled it, made a gloomy face, and handed back the cup, whereupon al-ʿAbbās said: 'Messenger of God, do you want to destroy the drink of the inhabitants of Mecca?' Then the Messenger of God said: 'Give me the cup!', and it was handed to him. He ordered water out of (the well) Zamzam, poured it into it, drank it, and said: 'If these drinks climb to your head, break their benefit with water!' From this one draws the following conclusion: The Messenger of God made a gloomy face solely because the (wine) *nabīdh* was strong. Mixing it with water was done clearly for the purpose of diluting it. That a drink climbs to the head means that it is strong.

(1FC) The third (portion of) evidence (on which Abū Ḥanīfa bases his opinion) is that one accepts the Traditions of the Companions of the Prophet (which are not specifically mentioned here).

(Concerning 1FA) To the first aspect (of the evidence of Abū Ḥanīfa) is to be answered: When God says: 'And (We give you the fruits of the palms and the vines, from which you obtain an intoxicant as well as wholesome food', there is uncertainty in the acknowledgment (of the kind of drink and food). Why do you now say that this intoxicating drink and wholesome food are identical with (the wine) *nabīdh*? After all, the Qur'ānic exegetes agree that this verse (Sūra 16:67/69) came down before the (other) three verses mentioned which indicate the prohibition of wine. Thus, these three verses must either abrogate or elucidate the (first) verse.

(Concerning lFB) The (wine) *nabīdh* with which the Tradition (from Ibn 'Abbās) is concerned could be water into which one had tossed (*nabadha*) dates in order to remove its brackishness. Then the taste of the water could have changed by becoming a little tart. Now the Messenger of God was extremely gifted with his sensitive taste, and so his noble nature could not stand that taste; so he made a gloomy face. Furthermore, he wanted to decrease the tartness and smell by pouring in that amount of water. To sum up, every reasonable person knows that it is impossible to refute the arguments which we have mentioned with such a (small) amount of weak evidence.

(Concerning 1FC) Thus (in conclusion), the Traditions of the Companions of the Prophet contradict and refute one another. One must therefore disregard them and hold to that which is evident through the Book of God and the *sunna* of his Messenger. Thus concludes the discussion concerning the true nature of wine.

(2) Concerning the second point, namely the (more precise) explanation of what the present verse (Sūra 2:219/216) indicates concerning the prohibition against wine (the following may be cited). The explanation concerning this has various aspects:

(2AA) The first aspect is as follows: The verse shows that wine in itself contains sin (*ithm*). And sin is forbidden according to God's words: 'Say: My Lord has forbidden all indecencies, open and hidden, and sin (*ithm*), and unjust insolence (*baghy*)' (Sūra 7:33/31). Taking both verses together, they prove the prohibition of wine.

(2AB) The second aspect is this: With (the word) *ithm* one sometimes means punishment and sometimes transgression (*dhanb*) that deserves punishment. Whichever of the two (meanings) may be intended here, one can correctly interpret it only as referring to something that is forbidden.

(2AC) The third aspect is as follows: God said: 'But the sin in them is greater than their usefulness.' (With this) he expressed clearly the predominance of the sin and the punishment, and this makes the prohibition (under discussion) necessary.

One can now say (to us): This verse does not indicate that the drinking of wine (in itself) is a sin, but (only) that therein lies a sin. Let us suppose that that sin is forbidden. Why then do you maintain that the drinking of wine is necessarily forbidden because that sin occurs in it? To this I answer: (This is so) because the question (at the beginning of the verse) is directed towards wine in general (and not to its nature, sanction, or sinfulness). When God now reveals that therein lies a sin, what is meant is that that sin is inseparably linked with it, in all its implications (which one could develop here). The drinking of wine thus leads necessarily to this complex of prohibitions; and whatever necessarily leads to something prohibited is (itself) prohibited. Consequently, the drinking of wine must be prohibited.

There are also people who maintain that this verse does not indicate the sinfulness of wine and who argue for this in various ways:

(2BA) The first way is as follows: God established (in the present verse) that wine and games of chance can be useful for man; however, no usefulness lies in something which is forbidden.

(2BB) The second way is as follows: If this verse indicated the prohibition of wine, why then were the Muslims (at the time of Muḥammad) not satisfied with it, before the verse in (the sūra called) 'The Table' (5:90f./92f.) and the verse concerning the prohibition (of drunkenness) at prayer (Sūra 4:43/46) came down?

(2BC) The third way is as follows: God has indicated that a great sin lies in wine and games of chance. This requires that the great sin (which lies therein) occurs as long as these two exist. Now if this great sin were the basis for the (general) sinfulness of (the use of) wine, then God would have to have spoken of the existence of such sinfulness (also earlier) in the other revelations (which were issued before the Qur'ān).

(Concerning 2BA) To the first (of these arguments) is to be answered: That a temporary usefulness appears in the present world with something that is prohibited does not alter the fact that it is prohibited. Since this is so, then the fact that usefulness (sometimes) occurs with wine and games of chance also does not alter the fact that both are sinful. From the legality (of something that is prohibited) in particular (namely, without the usefulness connected with it) follows necessarily the legality in general.

(Concerning 2BB) To the second (of these arguments) is to be answered: We have a Tradition of Ibn 'Abbās according to which the present verse came down for the purpose of prohibiting wine, while the objection cited by me (above) is not related by Ibn 'Abbās and his followers (and therefore does not have such good support through ancient authorities). Naturally it is possible that (after the revelation of this verse) the more important Companions of the Prophet desired that a statement would come down which would contain a more emphatic prohibition (against wine) than this verse (contains), just as Abraham asked to be able to see the quickening of the dead in order to gain greater peace and resignation.[19]

(Concerning 2BC) To the third (of these arguments) is to be answered: When God says: 'In them lies a great sin', he thereby proclaims something concerning the present condition and not concerning the past. According to our view, God knew that drinking wine would bring ruin to the people in that time; and he also knew that it was not injurious for the people before this (religious) community (of Muslims). Herewith this chapter may be concluded.

9. *The emancipation of slaves*

Zamakhsharī on Sūra 24:33

And let those who find not the means to marry be abstinent until God enriches them through His bounty. Those your right hands own (as slaves) who seek emancipation, contract with them accordingly, if you know some good in them; and give to them some of the wealth of God that He has given you. And constrain not your slavegirls (fatayāt) *to prostitution, if they desire to live in chastity, that you may seek the chance goods* ('arad) *of the present life. Whoever constrains them, surely God, after their being constrained, is All-forgiving, All-compassionate.*

... *Contract with them accordingly*: ... This means that the man is to say to his slave (*mamlūk*): 'I issue to you a letter of emancipation for the price of a thousand dirhams', and that the slave will then be free when he pays the amount.[20] The meaning is: I write down in your behalf that you will be free from me when you pay the money; and I write down in my behalf that you will pay it. Or, I write down for you the payment of the money and for me the emancipation. According to Abū Ḥanīfa, this is to be effected either immediately or later, as well as by instalments or not by instalments. Since God has not in any way mentioned division into instalments, this (interpretation) is reached through 'conclusion from analogy' (*qiyās*) based on other agreements. According to ash-Shāfi'ī (on the other hand) this (agreement) is effected only at a later time and only by instalments. According to his view, the payment is not to be made in a single instalment, since the slave possesses nothing[21] and consequently an agreement to be completed at once would prevent the realization of the desired goal, since the slave could not make a full payment all at once.

The agreement may be concluded with him for a small or large (amount of) money, and for a specific period of service or for a specific, temporary, designated task, as for example the digging of a well at a designated place, whereby also the length and width (of the well) must be specified. ... If the master contracts a letter of emancipation with the slave in the amount of his value (without this being specified more precisely), this is not permissible. If (however) the slave pays this price, he is free. If the master contracts with him a letter of emancipation for the value of a young slave (*waṣīf*) (who has just become capable of work), this is permissible, because the amount which is left undetermined is small and the average value is low. It is not proper for the master to disregard the emancipation agreement. If the slave (in such a case) pays, he is free. The patronage (*wilā'*) concerning the (freed) slave falls to (the lot of) the master (*maulā*),[22] who grants to him the profit that he originally had (been able to keep) for himself.

According to the view of the majority of scholars, the command under discussion here is to be understood as a recommendation (and not an obligation). According to al-Ḥasan (al-Baṣrī), it is not a final decision. If the master wishes, he may contract the letter of emancipation, and if he wishes, he may not do so. According to 'Umar (on the other hand) this belongs among the strict commands of God. Ibn Sīrīn is of the same view, and it is also interpreted likewise by the legal school of Dāwūd.

(If you know some) good (in them): an ability to pay that for which they are set free. Some say (also that it means): credit and earnings. It is related by Salmān that he had a slave who asked for a letter of emancipation from him. Then Salmān said: 'Do you have the means?' When the slave answered in the negative, Salmān said: 'Then do you want to command me to consume the dirty hand-washing water of the people?'

And give to them: According to the view of Abū Ḥanīfa and his followers, God has commanded the Muslims, in the sense of a strict obligation, to help those who possess letters of emancipation and to hand over to them their share of what God has allotted to the Muslims out of the public treasury (*bait al-māl*[23]). Thus God says: 'The freewill offerings (*ṣadaqāt*) are for the poor and needy, for those who work to collect them, for those whose hearts are brought together, for the ransoming of slaves, (for paying the debts of) debtors, in God's way, and for the traveller. Thus God ordains!' (Sūra 9:60; cf. 2:177/172). If I am asked whether it is permissible for a rich master to accept contributions[24] that are given to him on behalf of his slave, then I answer in the affirmative. A charitable contribution that does not amount to the full price (of a slave), and does not prove to be sufficient for the payment of the remainder, proves to be a blessing for the master, since he accepts the money not because it is a charitable contribution, but in regard to the emancipation agreement, just like someone who has received a charitable contribution which was given to a poor person, whether acquired by purchase, received by inheritance, or as a present (but not as charity). To this refer the words of the Prophet in the Tradition concerning the (emancipation of the slave girl) Barīra: 'It is a charity for her and a present for us.'

According to ash-Shāfi'ī, the present words of God signify an obligation for the masters to decrease the amount for the emancipation of slaves. If they do not do this, they should be forced (to do so). According to 'Alī, one should remit one-fourth to the slave. According to Ibn 'Abbās, one should give a small present to the slave with his letter of emancipation. From 'Umar (is related) that he contracted a letter of emancipation with his slave named Abū Umayya, who was the first slave in Islam to receive a letter of emancipation. When the letter came to 'Umar with the first instalment, 'Umar gave it back to him and said: 'Take it as help for your emancipation agreement!' To this the slave replied: 'Why did you not defer that until the final instalment?' 'Umar answered: 'I fear that I may not come to that (point).'

According to the view of Abū Ḥanīfa, this is to be understood as a recommendation. He said: (In the letter of emancipation) what is involved is a mutual agreement for the exchange of the value of property, and one is just as likely to be able to force a reduction as when bargaining. Others say that the meaning of (the words) *and give to them* is: and advance (money) to them. (Still) others say (that the meaning is): give money to them when they have paid (the price for emancipation) and are free. All this is commendable.

It is related that Ḥuwaiṭib ibn ʿAbd al-ʿUzzā had a slave named aṣ-Ṣabīḥ, who asked his master for a letter of emancipation. He refused, however, whereupon the present verse came down. (Further is related:) The maidservants of the pre-Islamic Arabs (*ahl al-jāhiliyya*) were forced to be prostitutes for their masters. ʿAbd Allāh ibn Ubayy, the chief of 'hypocrisy' (*nifāq*), had six maidservants ... whom he forced into prostitution, and upon whom he imposed all kinds of fees. When two of them complained to the Messenger of God, the present verse came down. ...

(God is) All-forgiving, All-compassionate: concerning the men or concerning the female slaves or concerning both, if they turn in repentance and act justly. ...

10. Holy war

Baiḍāwī on Sūra 2:216f./212–214

> *Prescribed for you is fighting (against the unbelievers), although it be hateful to you. Yet it is possible that you will hate a thing which is better for you; and it is possible that you will love a thing which is worse for you. God knows, and you know not. They will question thee concerning the holy month and fighting in it. Say: 'Fighting in it is a heinous thing, but to bar from God's way—and disbelief in Him—and the holy mosque, and to expel its people*[25] *from it, that is more heinous in God's sight. And persecution is more heinous than slaying.'*

Prescribed for you is fighting (against the unbelievers), although it be hateful to you: although it is repugnant and unbearable to you by nature. ...

Yet it is possible that you will hate a thing which is better for you: What is meant is all that was imposed upon the believers by force, since this is contrary to their nature, even though their integrity depends on it and it is the basis for their well-being.

And it is possible that you will love a thing which is worse for you: What is meant is all that came to be forbidden to the believers, since this is what the soul loved and enjoyed, even though it is led to perdition by it. (The expression) 'it is possible that' (*ʿasā*) is used because the soul (*nafs*), when it exerts itself, turns the affair (*amr*) into its opposite.

God knows what is good for you, *and you know not*: Herein is an indication that the statements (of God) have in mind the predominant well-being (of man), even though man is not aware of this himself.

They will question thee concerning the holy month: It is related that, in the (month of) Jumādā l-Ākhira, which was two months before (the battle of) Badr,[26] the Prophet sent out his paternal cousin 'Abd Allāh ibn Jaḥsh with an expeditionary force, in order to be on the look-out for a caravan of (the tribe of) Quraish in which were 'Amr ibn 'Abd Allāh al-Ḥaḍramī and three (other) men. They killed 'Amr, took two of his men captive, and drove away the caravan, which contained the goods of trade from aṭ-Ṭā'if. This happened at the beginning of (the month of) Rajab, while 'Abd Allāh and his people believed it was (still) the (month of) Jumādā l-Ākhira. Regarding this, the (people of the tribe of) (Quraish said: 'Muḥammad has (unlawfully) regarded the month in which raids and warlike acts are forbidden, so that the fearful can be safe and men can move freely everywhere for the sake of their livelihood, as permissible (for such forbidden acts).' This fell hard upon the members of the expeditionary force, and they said: 'We will not submit until compensation comes down for us.' At this, Muḥammad gave back the caravan along with the captives. According to Ibn 'Abbās (however, it is related) that the Messenger of God accepted the booty when this verse came down. This is supposed to have been the first booty in Islam. Those who questioned (Muḥammad about the holy month) were the unbelievers, who thereby sought to ascribe to him calumny and profanation (of a holy month). Others say (however) that they were the members of the expeditionary force (who asked Muḥammad about the holy month). . . .

Say: *Fighting in it is a heinous thing*: that is, a heinous sin. For the most part, in opposition to 'Aṭā', it is held that this statement is abrogated by the following words of God: 'If they do not leave you alone and offer you peace and stop hostilities, then take them wherever you find them and slay them' (Sūra 4:91/93). In this case the more specific (that is, the prohibition against fighting during the month of Rajab) would be abrogated by the general (that is, the general command to kill the unbelievers). However, there is a contradiction in this. It lies nearest (the truth) to reject (the interpretation) that the present verse declares an absolute prohibition against fighting in the holy month. Although (the word) 'fighting' is indefinite here, it is fixed in scope; and thus, (the fighting here is) not (to be understood as fighting) in general. . . .

IX

DOGMATICS

1. Faith

Zamakhsharī on Sūra 2:256/257

There is no compulsion in religion. What is right has become clear from what is wrong. So whoever disbelieves in idols (aṭ-ṭāghūt) *and believes in God has laid hold of the most firm handle, unbreaking. God is All-hearing, All-knowing.*

There is no compulsion (*ikrāh*) *in religion*: that is, God does not allow belief through compulsion (*ijbār*) and coercion (*qasr*), but through strengthening (*tamkīn*) and free choice (*ikhtiyār*). Accordingly, he has said: 'If thy Lord had willed, whoever is in the earth would have believed, all of them, all together. Wouldst thou then constrain the people until they are believers?' (Sūra 10:99). That is, if he had willed, he would have compelled them to believe; however, he did not do this, but placed faith on the basis of free choice.[1]

What is right has become clear from what is wrong: Faith is distinguished from unbelief through clear indications.

So whoever disbelieves in idols (aṭ-ṭāghūt): whoever freely decides to believe not in Satan or the deities[2] but in God.

Has laid hold of the most firm handle: (This expression) refers to a strong rope that is twisted tightly. (It is the strap) with which one makes certain before a journey that (the load) will not break open. Here knowledge (of faith) which is obtained through insight and deduction is likened to something truly concrete, so that the one who hears this perceives it thus, as if he viewed it directly. Thus his conviction and his certainty concerning it are made firm.

Some say that what is involved here is a proclamation in the sense of a prohibition, namely: 'Exercise no compulsion in your religion!' On the other hand, some people say that this (verse)

82.50
82.50
165.00

is abrogated through God's words: 'O Prophet, struggle with the unbelievers and hypocrites (*munāfiqūn*), and be harsh with them. Their refuge is Jahannam, an evil home-coming!' (Sūra 9:73/74; 66:9). Others say that (the prohibition against compulsion) refers especially to the People of the Book, since they have been immuned themselves (from compulsion) through the payment of tribute (*jizya*).[3] It is related that one of the 'Helpers' (*anṣār*) of the Banū Sālim ibn 'Auf had two sons who had accepted Christianity before the Messenger of God was sent. Both came to Medina and their father was grieved for them and said: 'By God, I will not let you go until you have converted to Islam!' The two refused, however, and then they (all three) came before the Messenger of God with their controversy. The 'Helper' said: 'Messenger of God, should a part of me go into hell-fire while I am watching it?' At this, this present verse came down and the father left the two alone.

2. *Faith and reason*

Zamakhsharī on Sūra 17:15/16

> *Whoever is guided is only guided to his own gain, and whoever goes astray, it is only to his own loss. No soul laden bears the load of another. We never chastise until We send forth a messenger.*

That is, each person bears a burden, but he bears only his own burden and not that of another.

We never chastise: There is among us no principle according to which wisdom requires that we punish people, until after we have sent a messenger (*rasūl*) to them so that we have forced upon them the evidence (for faith) (*ḥujja*). One may now say that the evidence already compelled them before the messengers were sent, since they had the proofs of reason (*'aql*) through which God grants knowledge; however, the people neglected spiritual contemplation (*naẓar*), although they were capable of it. Therefore, they must be punished because they neglected contemplation of that which was given to them (through reason) and thus disbelieved. Yet (they must be punished) not because they disregarded the revealed laws (*ash-sharā'i'*), to which there is no access without God's help (*taufīq*) and which a man can thus obey properly only if he has first obtained faith. To this I answer: The sending of the messengers is among those things which stimulate contemplation and warn him who is slumbering in negligence. Thus, one is not able to say: 'We were neglectful. O that you had sent to us a messenger who would have stimulated contemplation on the rational proofs!'

Baiḍāwī on the same passage

... *We never chastise until We send forth a messenger* who has explained the evidence and rendered accessible the revealed laws, so that we have forced upon them the substance of the evidence. Herein lies an indication that there is no obligation (to believe) before 'the revelation' (of Islam) (*ash-shar'*).[4]

Zamakhsharī on Sūra 67:10

> *They also say: 'If we had only heard or had understood, we would not have been among the inhabitants of the blaze.'*

If we had only heard the warning, like people who strive for the truth, or, if we had only understood it like people who engage in meditative contemplation. Some say: (Here) God has linked hearing with reason because that for which there is a (divine) command (to men) rests on the evidence of hearing and reason. Among the (heretical) innovations (*bida'*) in the interpretation (of this verse) is (the view) that what is meant (here) is: If only we had followed the teaching (*madhhab*) of the 'people of the Tradition' (*ahl al-ḥadīth*) or the teaching of those who interpret (the Qur'ān) according to their own opinion (*ra'y*).[5] (The proponents of such innovations introduce them) as if this verse (first) came down after the appearance of these two points of view (*madhhabain*), as if God had (previously) sent down threats against the adherents of other points of view and those who inquire freely (*mujtahidūn*[6]), and as if the adherents of these (two points of view) felt themselves to be unconditionally among the saved ones, according to the principle that the number of the Companions of the Prophet to whom paradise is promised amounts to ten and that no eleventh has been added.[7] (They do this further) as if most of those who pass over the bridge (*aṣ-ṣirāṭ*) (which leads over hell and into paradise)[8] had never heard anything of the names of these two groups.

Ibn al-Munayyir regarding this

If az-Zamakhsharī means that the statements of religious law are drawn from reason as well as from hearing, (namely) as a method for (distinguishing between) what is considered to be good and what is considered to be evil, then he does not stand far from the inhabitants of hell-fire. If (however) he means that reason leads to the true principles (*'aqā'id ṣaḥīḥa*) and that hearing is appropriate for the statements of religious law, then he agrees with the 'people of the *sunna*'.[9]

3. Free will and predestination

Zamakhsharī on Sūra 18:29/28

> *Say: 'The truth is from your Lord; so whoever wills may believe, and whoever wills may disbelieve.' Surely We have prepared for the evildoers a fire, whose pavilion encompasses them. If they call for succour, they will be succoured with water like molten copper that will scald their faces—how evil a potion, and how evil a resting-place!*

Say: *The truth is from your Lord*: (The word) 'truth' is the subject of something omitted. What is meant is: The truth has come and the excuses (*'ilal*) (on your behalf) have been taken away. There remains for you nothing more than to choose freely whether you want to follow the way of deliverance or the way of destruction. Expressions of command (*amr*) and of 'the granting of a choice' (*at-takhyīr*) are used here, since the man now has the ability to choose freely which of the two (possibilities) he wishes. He is like one to whom it is commanded as an option to choose freely which leader he wishes to follow. . . .

Baiḍāwī on the same passage

. . . *So whoever wills may believe, and whoever wills may disbelieve*: (God means:) I do not worry about the belief of him who believes, nor about the unbelief of him who does not believe. Yet this in no way means necessarily that the servant is solely responsible for his act himself. Even though this happens through his wish, still his wish is not limited to his wish (but is subject to the wish of God)[10]....

Zamakhsharī on Sūra 6:148f./149f.

Those who associate (others with God) will say: 'Had God willed, neither we nor our fathers would have associated (anything with Him), nor would we have forbidden anything.' So also did the people before them count (the message) false, until they tasted Our might. Say: 'Have you any (revealed) knowledge? Bring it forth for us then. You follow only opinion, and you are only conjecturing.'
Say: 'To God belongs the convincing argument. Had He willed, He would have guided you all.'

Those who associate (others with God) will say: Here is announced what they will say (later). And when they have (then) said this, God says: 'Those who associate (others with God) will say: "Had God willed, neither we nor our fathers would have served anything apart from Him"' (Sūra 16:35/37). They suppose in their unbelief and disobedience that their idolatry and that of their fathers, as well as the fact that they have forbidden what God has allowed, have occurred through the wish and the will of God, and that without his wish nothing of this kind would occur. This is in exact agreement with the preaching of the Mujbira.[11]

So also did the people before them count (the message) false, that is: They have declared (the entire truth) to be a lie.[12] God has imprinted (upon the mind) something from reason and sent down something in his books that proves him to be free and exempt from willing and desiring disgraceful things.[13] The messengers have declared this. If someone now (however) ascribes the existence of the disgrace of unbelief and disobedience to the wish and will of God, then he declares (the truth) without restrictions to be a lie, since he accuses God, his books, and his messengers to be false and has disavowed the evidence of reason and hearing.

Until they tasted Our might: until (at last) we have sent down upon them the punishment for their false accusation.

Say: *Have you any (revealed) knowledge* of an unquestionable (*ma'lūm*) fact with which one can argue convincingly for what you assert?

Bring it forth for us then: This is meant ironically and serves as a proof of the fact that words of that kind cannot possibly have in themselves any basis of evidence.

You follow only opinion, when you maintain this.

And you are only conjecturing: You surmise that the facts of the matter are according to your assertion or lying accusation. . . .

Say: *To God belongs the convincing argument*. This means: If the facts are as you assert, namely that the condition in which you find yourselves is in accordance with the wish of God, then, according to your own teaching, God has the convincing argument against you (on his side).

Had He willed, He would have guided you all: you and your opponents in the religion. If you link your religion with the wish of God, you must also link the religion of your opponents with the wish of God. Therefore, assist them and do not be an enemy to them and do not oppose them, since the wish (of God) builds a common bond between you and their situation!

Baiḍāwī on the same passage

Had God willed, neither we nor our fathers would have associated (anything with Him), nor would we have forbidden anything: If according to his pleasure he had desired the opposite of our situation, as indeed he says: 'Had He willed, He would have guided you all', then neither we nor our fathers would have done what we did. They meant by this that they act in a manner which is thoroughly just and agreeable with God (because God has wished it so), and that they did not will it but it was God who has willed these disgraces for them, thus producing a plea for committing these acts, so that they blame God and thus furnish evidence for the (view of the) Mu'tazila. (This interpretation) is supported by God's words: *So also did the people before them count* (*the message*) *false*: that is, just as they accuse you (Muḥammad) of lying when you proclaim that God has prohibited polytheism and has not forbidden what they have forbidden, so (also) those who lived before them accused the messengers of lying. . . .

Zamakhsharī on Sūra 2:6f./5f.

As for the unbelievers, alike is it to them whether thou hast
warned them or hast not warned them, for they do not believe.
God has set a seal on their hearts and on their hearing; and on
their eyes is a covering. And there awaits them a mighty
chastisement.

After first (in the previous verses) mentioning his friends and sincere servants, together with the characteristics which make them worthy of his goodwill, and (after) demonstrating that the Book (of God) signifies right guidance and benevolence for them, God now continues by mentioning their opponents who are unbelievers of arrogant obstinacy, for whom right guidance remains of no use and benevolence (*luṭf*) remains without effect. For these it is the same whether the Book exists or not and whether the Messenger warns or remains silent. . . .

If (the phrase) *as for the unbelievers* is specific (rather than referring to an unspecified group of unbelievers), then this may be because these unbelievers are known. It would then refer to certain individuals like Abū Lahab, Abū Jahl, al-Walīd ibn al-Mughīra, and other unbelievers like them. The specification, however, could also extend to the (entire) group (of unbelievers) and thereby include every person who persists firmly in his unbelief and will not be dissuaded from it later, as is the case with those mentioned and others. That the specification (in fact) extends to (all) those who persist in their unbelief supports the statement reported here that the unbelievers are people for whom it is the same whether they are warned or not. . . .

The (term) 'set a seal' (*khatama*) and the (term) 'keep secret' (*katama*) are cognate expressions, since when a man reassures himself of something by putting a seal on it, then he keeps it secret and conceals it so that no-one else can obtain entrance to it or learn anything about it. . . .

If one asks what the sealing of the heart and the hearing as well as the covering of the eyes mean, then I answer: In reality, there is here neither a sealing nor a covering. Rather there is a trope (*majāz*) whereby both kinds of the trope are taken into consideration, namely, metaphor (*istiʿāra*) and simile (*tamthīl*).[14] A metaphor is present under the following conditions: The heart and the hearing of the unbelievers are represented as things through which one has assurance as if through sealing; that is, because the truth does not penetrate into the heart and does not reach into its interior, since the unbelievers turn away from the truth and regard themselves as too great to receive and believe it, and because the hearing of the unbelievers rejects the truth when they hear it, they do not listen attentively, and they are unwilling to listen to it. And the eyes of the unbelievers are presented as something over which a covering and a curtain are placed, and concerning which perception is made impossible, because the eyes of the unbelievers do not perceive the signs of God which have been presented and the indications (of God's power) which have been manifested, as do the eyes of those who ponder over and reflect upon them.

A simile is presented when the heart, hearing, and eyes are likened to things that are separated from what they should perceive because of a partition, that is, because the unbelievers do not use them for the religious purposes for which they were created and entrusted to men. . . .

One may now say: Why is the (act of) sealing ascribed to God? When it is ascribed to him, this suggests that the unbelievers are prevented from receiving the truth and finding access to the path which leads to it. This would be shameful; but God is exalted high above doing anything shameful,[15] since he knows the disgraceful character of what is shameful and knows that he does not require it. He has (himself) declared that one must keep his nature free (from the attribution of such a characteristic), in that he has said: 'I wrong not My servants' (Sūra 50:29/28), 'We never wronged them, but they themselves did the wrong' (Sūra 43:76), 'God does not command indecency' (Sūra 7:28/27),[16] and similar statements which are declared in the revelation.

To this I answer: The intention here is to characterize the heart as something which is as if it had been sealed.[17] When the (act of) sealing is ascribed to God, it is thereby indicated that this characteristic (of unbelief), when excessively steadfast and persistent, is something innate (in the unbeliever) and not (merely) a passing characteristic. One also says: 'So and so is created with a talent for such and such and is endowed with it', when one means that he is very persistent in it. How can anyone suggest this (that is, that God himself may have sealed the hearts of the unbelievers), when the present verse came down in order to reproach the unbelievers with the loathsomeness of their character and the offensiveness of their conduct, and the explicit threat of a mighty punishment is added!

Perhaps in its present form, thus (in the form) *God has set a seal on their hearts*, the statement is used figuratively. Thus one says: 'The mountain torrent has flowed away with someone', when this person has perished, and: 'The condor bird has flown away with someone', when this person has been absent for a long time. (In reality) the mountain torrent and the condor bird have no part in the destruction and the long absence of the ones in question. On the contrary, what is involved here is a simile in which it is stated that the situation of the one who perished is like that of one with whom the mountain torrent has flowed away, and the situation of the one who has been absent for a long time is like that of one with whom the condor bird has flown away. Likewise, it is here set forth that the condition of the heart of the unbelievers in its aversion to the truth is like the condition of a heart that God has sealed, similar to the heart of the barbarians which in its lack of good sense corresponds directly to the heart of wild animals. Or (it is here set forth that the condition of the heart of the unbelievers is) like the condition of a heart over which God's seal is placed, so that it pays no attention to anything and does not understand anything. (Actually) God has not contributed towards the aversion of the heart to the truth and the disinclination to receive the truth, for he is exalted high above such things.

Perhaps the ascribing (of the act of sealing the heart) is itself also transferred to God (in a metaphorical way) from something other than God. Then the sealing (of the heart) would be attributed to the name of God according to a kind of trope, while in reality it is due to someone other than him. This is to be explained in the following manner: The action has various points of reference. It touches the subject, the (outer) object, the inner object, the time, the location, and that which causes the action. Actually, the action is to be ascribed to the subject; yet, it is (also) ascribed, sometimes in the figurative usage of the metaphor, to the (other) things just mentioned. This can happen because these things are like the subject in so far as they (also) have a relation to the action. This is just like when a man who is like a lion in his daring is metaphorically called a lion. Thus one says (metaphorically) of the object (of an act) 'a satisfied life' (instead of 'a life with which one is satisfied') . . . and of one who is responsible for bringing about an act: 'The amīr has built the city' (instead of 'The amīr has caused the city to be built'). . . . (In the present case) it is now in reality Satan or the unbeliever (himself) who has sealed (the heart). However, since it is God who has granted to him the ability and the possibility (to do it), the sealing (of the heart) is ascribed to him in the same sense as an act which he has caused.

There is (yet) a fourth possible meaning (*wajh*): Since the unbelievers belong firmly and finally among those who do not believe and for whom the signs and warnings do not suffice, and for whom neither the proofs of (divine) benevolence (*alṭāf*) already received nor those that are at hand, should they be granted to them, are of any use, and when there is positive knowledge that they will not come to believe through obedience and free choice (*ikhtiyār*), then there remains no other path to faith than that God compel and coerce them. And if now no other path to faith remains than that God compel and coerce them, but he (nevertheless) does not compel and coerce them, so that the goal which lies in the endeavour (towards faith) may not slip away, then the renunciation is referred to as force and coercion through the sealing (of the heart). By this means it is to be made known that they are those whose determination in favour of disbelief and whose persistence therein approach the limit from which one can be spared only through force and coercion. Here the extreme degree is reached, as is exhibited by their stubborn lingering in falsehood and in their serious condition in error and unrighteousness.

(Finally) the following remains as a fifth possible meaning: What is involved (here) is an ironic response of something that the unbelievers (themselves) had said. That is, they said: 'Our hearts are veiled from what thou callest us to, and in our ears is heaviness, and between us and thee there is a veil' (Sūra 41:5/4). A similar ironic response appears in God's words: 'The unbelievers among the "people of the Book" and the idolaters would never desist (from their unbelief) until the clear sign (*bayyina*) should come to them' (Sūra 98:1). . . .

Zamakhsharī on Sūra 37:95f./93f.

Abraham[18] *said: 'Do you serve what you hew,*
when God created you and what you make?'

When God created you and what (mā) you make: that is, when he created you and the idols which you have made. Thus, God says: '(Recall the time) when Abraham said to his father and his people: "What (good) are these idols to which you are cleaving?" . . . They said: "Hast thou come to us with the truth, or art thou one of those who play?" He said: "Nay, but your Lord is the Lord of the heavens and the earth, who originated them"' (Sūra 21:56/57). What is meant is: 'who originated the idols'.

One may now ask: How can one and the same thing be created by God and made by them, (namely) in such a manner that his creation and their act extend to it together? To this I answer: This is just like when one says: The carpenter makes the door and the chair, and the goldsmith makes the bracelet and the necklace. What is meant by this is the production of the shape and form of these things, but not their substances. Now the idols also consist partly of substances and partly of shapes, and the creator of their substances is God, while the producers of their shapes are those who give them shape, since they carve them (into shape) and remove some parts of them until the shape that they want is attained.

One may ask (further): Why do you deny that the (word) *mā* (with the verb that follows in this verse) functions as a verbal noun (*an takūna mā maṣdariyya*) (in the sense of 'that you make', or 'your making') and not a relative pronoun (in the sense of 'what'), and that the sense of the verse is: 'God has created you and your act', as is maintained by the Mujbira?[19] To this I answer: What first of all proves the weakness of this question is the evidence of reason and the Book that the meaning of the present verse obviously does not permit (the interpretation suggested by) this question and clearly stands in opposition to it. God argues against the idolaters, beginning with the assumption that both the one who worships (the idols) and what is worshipped are God's creation. (But) how can the (one) creation worship the (other) creation, when the one who worships is the (same) one who made the form and shape of what is worshipped? If this were not (the intended meaning), then the worshipper could not in any way have formed and shaped what is worshipped (but God would have to have done it). Were one therefore to say that the meaning is: 'God has created you and your act', then God could not have argued against the idolaters. Consequently, this interpretation does not fit (the text).

(In addition there is still) something else: God's words *what you make* are an interpretation of his words *what you hew*. Moreover, the (term) 'what' in 'what you hew' is certainly relative, and anyone who treats the parallel 'what' otherwise can only be one who acts arbitrarily and clings fanatically to his doctrine, without concerning himself with the (laws of) rhetoric and without understanding the structure (*naẓm*) of the Qur'ān.

One could object (to me as follows): I take the *mā* as relative (but interpret it) in such a way that I am not forced to the same conclusion as you; that is (I take it to mean): 'and what you make as your act'. To this I answer: No, the problem involved in the two necessary conclusions would be resolved for one who is as strict as you, only by dissociating from submission to the truth. When you take the *mā* as relative, but only in order to mean 'the act', you do not argue against polytheism, just as is the case when you take it as functioning like a verbal noun (*maṣdariyya*). Moreover, you sever thereby the connection which exists between *what you make* and *what you hew*, since a contradiction then exists between what is meant in the two cases. (That is) you then interpret 'what you hew' to mean material objects which represent the deities, and you interpret 'what you make' to mean the abstract properties which constitute the acts. This, however, would break up the construction and arrangement of the (statements of the) Qur'ān, just as if you took the *mā* as functioning like a verbal noun.

Baiḍāwī on the same passage

He said: Do you serve what you hew: what you hew as idols.

When God created you and what you make (mā ta'malūna): that is, that which you make (*mā ta'malūnahu*). The substance of the idols was produced through God's creation, while the shape of the idols, although coming about through the act of the idolaters so that the idols are presented as their works, is (actually) produced through the fact that God destined the idolaters to do it and created the motives and dispositions on which their act depends. Or (it means): your act, (that is) in the sense of 'your accomplished (work)'. Thus it corresponds to *what you hew*. Or (it means: your act) in the sense of the origination (of the action). That is, when their act is produced through God's creation, then this accomplished (work) which is done, which depends on their act is especially suited to this (act). In this sense, our companions (of mind), under the assumption that God created the acts, hold fast to this. And it is for them to favour this (manner of explanation) above the two mentioned above, because an expression of opinion or a more figurative usage is present in both of these.[20]

Jalāl ad-Dīn as-Suyūṭī (Tafsīr al-Jalālain) on Sūra 8:24

> *O believers, respond to God and the Messenger when He calls you unto that which will give you life; and know that God stands between a man and his heart, and that to Him you shall be mustered.*

O believers, respond to God and the Messenger: through obedience.

When He calls you unto that which will give you life: (unto something) of the religion, for it is the source of eternal life.

And know that God stands between a man and his heart: so that it can be believing or unbelieving only according to God's will.

And that to Him you shall be mustered: so that he gives you the reward for your deeds.

X

MYSTICAL AND PHILOSOPHICAL QUR'ĀNIC EXEGESIS

1. The outer and inner meanings

Ghazzālī on interpretation according to individual opinion[1]

. . . The Prophet said: 'Whoever interprets the Qur'ān according to his own opinion (*bi-ra'yihī*) is to receive his place in the hell-fire.' The people who are acquainted with only the outer aspect of exegesis (*tafsīr*) have for this reason discredited the mystics in so far as they have been involved with exegesis, because they explain (*ta'wīl*) the wording of the Qur'ān other than according to the Tradition of Ibn 'Abbās and the other interpreters. They have thus advocated the view that what is involved here is unbelief. If the advocates of (the traditional) exegesis are correct, then the understanding of the Qur'ān consists in nothing else than that one knows its interpretation outwardly. But if they are not right, then what is the meaning of the Prophet's words: 'Whoever interprets the Qur'ān according to his own opinion is to receive his place in the hell-fire'?

One should note: When someone maintains that the Qur'ān has no other meaning than that expressed by the outer aspect of exegesis, then by doing so he manifests his own limitation (*ḥadd*). With this confession about himself he hits upon what is absolutely correct (for his own situation); however, he errs in his opinion that the entire creation is to be regarded as being on his level, that is, restricted to his limitation and situation. Rather, the commentaries and Traditions show that the meanings contained in the Qur'ān exhibit a wide scope for experts in the field. Thus, 'Alī said (that a specific meaning can be grasped) only when God grants to one ('*abdan*) understanding for the Qur'ān. (But) if nothing else is present than the interpretation which has been handed down, then this is not understanding. (Further) the Prophet said that the Qur'ān had a literal meaning (*ẓāhir*), an inner meaning (*bāṭin*), a terminal point (of understanding) (*ḥadd*), and a starting point (for understanding) (*muṭṭala'*).... According to the opinion of some scholars, every verse can be understood in sixty thousand ways, and what then still remains unexhausted (in its meaning) is more numerous (*akthar*). Others have maintained that the Qur'ān contains seventy-seven thousand and two hundred (kinds of) knowledge, since every word constitutes one (kind of) knowledge. This then increases fourfold since every word has a literal meaning, an inner meaning, a terminal point (of understanding), and a starting point (for understanding). ...

Ibn Mas'ūd said: Whoever wishes to obtain knowledge about his ancestors and descendants should meditate upon the Qur'ān. This knowledge does not appear, however, if one restricts the interpretation of the Qur'ān to the outer meaning. All in all, every kind of knowledge is included in the realm of actions and attributes of God, and the description of the nature of the actions and attributes of God is contained in the Qur'ān. These kinds of knowledge are unending; yet, in the Qur'ān is found (only) an indication of their general aspects. Thereby, the (various) degrees (*maqāmāt*) of the deeper penetration into the particulars of knowledge are traced back to the (actual) understanding of the Qur'ān. The mere outer aspect of interpretation yields no hint of this knowledge. Rather, the fact is that the Qur'ān contains indications and hints, which certain select people with (correct) understanding can grasp, concerning all that remains obscure of the theoretical way of thinking and that about which the creatures (*al-khalā'iq*) disagree regarding the theoretical sciences and rational ideas.[2] How is the interpretation and explanation of the outer meaning of the Qur'ān to be sufficient for this? ...

Regarding the words of the Prophet 'Whoever interprets the Qur'ān according to his own opinion', and the prohibition concerning this, ... one can conclude as follows: Either, restriction to the Tradition (*ḥadīth*) and what can be learned (from other sources), and (thus) the renunciation of inference and independent understanding, is meant; or, something else is meant. For the following reasons (*wujūh*), it has been decided that it is wrong to conclude that what is meant is that concerning the Qur'ān one is allowed only the outer meaning, which he has heard:

(1) One would then be restricted to what was stated (in the time of the Prophet) and can be traced back to him (through statements of suitable authorities). But this seldom occurs with (interpretations of) the Qur'ān. ...

(2) The Companions of the Prophet and the exegetes are in disagreement concerning the interpretation of certain verses and advance differing statements about them which cannot be brought into harmony with one another. That all of these statements have been heard from the mouth of the Messenger of God is absurd. One was obliged to learn of one of these statements of the Messenger of God in order to refute the rest, and then it became clear that, concerning the meaning (of the passage of the Qur'ān in question), every exegete expressed what appeared to him to be evident through his inference. This went so far that seven different kinds of interpretations, which cannot be brought into harmony with one another, have been advanced concerning the (mysterious) letters at the beginning of (some of) the sūras. ...

(3) The Messenger of God prayed for Ibn 'Abbās: 'God instruct him in the religion and teach him the interpretation!' But if one had heard the interpretation in the same way (that he heard the recitation of the Qur'ān) and could preserve it in his memory just as it was revealed, then what could this statement (of Muḥammad) mean, since it was intended especially for Ibn 'Abbās? ...

(4) God has said: '... those of them whose task it is to investigate would have come to know the matter' (Sūra 4:83/85). Thus he has granted a disclosure to people with knowledge, and it is certain that the disclosure surpasses what is heard (of the doctrines which have been handed down). All of the reports which we have mentioned concerning the understanding of the Qur'ān stand in opposition to this notion (*khayāl*) (of a restriction of interpretation to what is heard from earlier sources), and consequently it is senseless to make hearing (*samā'*) a condition for the interpretation (*ta'wīl*). (Rather) it is permitted to everyone to draw conclusions from the Qur'ān according to the measure of his understanding and according to the scope of his reason.

The prohibition (against interpreting the Qur'ān according to individual opinion) involves the following two reasons for its having been sent down: The first is that someone may have an opinion (*ra'y*) about something, and through his nature as well as his inclination he may shelter a bias for it and then interpret the

Qur'ān in accordance with his opinion and bias, in order thereby to obtain arguments to prove his view to be correct. Moreover, the meaning (which he links with his view) could not at all appear to him from the Qur'ān if he did not have (preconceived) opinion and bias. This sometimes happens consciously, as perchance in the case of those who use individual verses of the Qur'ān as arguments for the correctness of a (heretical) innovation (*bid'a*) and thus know that this is not in accordance with what is meant by the verse. They want rather to deceive their opponents. Sometimes (however) it (also) happens unconsciously. For instance, when a verse allows various meanings, a man inclines in his understanding to that which corresponds with his own opinion. Then, he settles the issue according to his opinion and inclination and thus interprets according to 'individual opinion'. That is: It is 'individual opinion' which drives one to such an interpretation. If one did not have this opinion, then that possibility of interpretation (to which one is inclined) would not have gained predominance. . . .

The second reason is that someone may come to an interpretation of the Qur'ān prematurely on the basis of the outer meaning of the Arabic language, without receiving the assistance of hearing (*samā'*) and the Tradition for what is involved with passages of the Qur'ān which are difficult to understand, for the obscure and ambiguous (*mubdal*) expressions which are found in the Qur'ān, and for abbreviations, omissions, implications (*iḍmār*), anticipations, and allusions which are contained in it. Whoever has not mastered the outer aspect of exegesis, but solely on the basis of his understanding of the Arabic language proceeds hastily to the conclusion of the meaning (of the Qur'ān), commits many errors and aligns himself thereby to the group of those who interpret (the Qur'ān) according to individual opinion. The Tradition and hearing (*samā'*) are indispensable for the outer aspect of exegesis, first of all in order to make certain thereby against the opportunities for error, but then also in order to extend the endeavour to understand and to reach conclusions. The obscure passages which cannot be understood without hearing are in fact numerous. . . .

Ibn Rushd (Averroes) on the harmony between revelation and knowledge[3]

. . . If speculation based on the arguments of reason is to lead someone to knowledge about something, then this matter must involve either something that is not mentioned in the revelation or something about which it does contain information. If it involves something that is not mentioned (in the revelation) then there is no contradiction (between the speculative knowledge and the revelation), and it is then the same case as when specific decisions are not mentioned in the revelation, and the lawyers must make decisions on the basis of 'deduction by analogy' (*qiyās*). If, on the other hand, the revelation speaks explicitly of the matter (concerned), then the outward expression must either be in agreement with that to which the reasoning leads or not. If agreement is present, there is no need for discussion; however, if no agreement is present, then allegorical exegesis (*ta'wīl*) is required. Allegorical exegesis thereby has the purpose of converting the meaning (*dalāla*) of an expression from the literal meaning (*dalāla ḥaqīqiyya*) to a figurative meaning (*dalāla majāziyya*), without thereby damaging the standard linguistic usage of the Arabs with regard to the formation of metaphors.

. . . The reason why there is an inner and an outer meaning in the revelation is to be sought in the fact that the natural talents of people are different and that their abilities in regard to the affirmative function (*taṣdīq*) (of reason) deviate from one another. And the reason why passages appear in the revelation whose outer meanings show disagreement lies in the fact that those (people) who have a thorough knowledge should be stimulated towards allegorical exegesis which creates harmony between the divergent meanings. There is allusion to this in God's words: 'It is He who sent down upon thee the Book, wherein are clear verses that are the *umm al-kitāb*,[4] and others that are ambiguous. As for those in whose hearts is swerving (from the right way), they follow the ambiguous part, desiring dissension, and desiring its interpretation. But none knows its interpretation except God and those firmly rooted in knowledge' (Sūra 3:7/5).[5]

One may now say: There are statements in the revelation which Muslims agree should be taken according to their outer meaning, and statements (which Muslims agree must be taken according to their inner meaning) which must be interpreted allegorically, and (finally) statements concerning which they disagree. How (then) is it possible that the (scientific) reasoning leads to an allegorical exegesis of something concerning which the Muslims are in agreement in accepting the outer meaning, and that it comes to an outer meaning of something concerning which they are in agreement in accepting the allegorical interpretation? To this I answer: If the agreement had to result on the basis of one sure method, then no agreement could have been produced. If, on the other hand, it resulted on the basis of conjecture, then it could appear. . . .

Kāshānī on Sūra 7:54/52

> *Surely your Lord is God, who created the heavens and the earth in six days, then sat Himself upon the Throne (in order to rule the world), causing the night to cover the day, which it pursues urgently. And (he created) the sun, and the moon, and the stars to be subservient, by His* amr.[6] *Are not the creation and the* amr *His alone? Blessed be God, the Lord of all being.*

Surely your Lord is God, who created the heavens and the earth in six days: that is, who has concealed himself in the (pure) spirit of heaven and the matter of the earth for six thousand years, for God says: 'Surely a day with thy Lord is as a thousand years of your counting' (Sūra 22:47/46). What is meant by this is (the time span) from the creation of Adam to the time of Muḥammad. Creating signifies that God (*al-ḥaqq*) conceals himself in the outer things of creation. And this time span extends from the beginning of the period of the concealment (of God) until the beginning of the manifestation, which falls in the time of the sealing of prophecy (through Muḥammad) and the appearance of lordship (*wilāya*). Thus the Prophet has said: Time is turned back (to the situation) in which it was on the day when God created the heavens and the earth. The beginning of the concealment (of God) in the creation is in fact the end of the manifestation. Since the concealment now ends in favour of the manifestation, then time thus turns back to the beginning of creation, as it has elapsed. The manifestation is perfected through the appearance of the Mahdī[7] after the completion of seven (cosmic) days. Thus one says that this world has a duration of seven thousand years.

Then sat Himself upon the Throne: that is, upon the throne of the heart of Muḥammad, since he revealed himself completely with all his attributes through Muḥammad. . . .

Causing the night of the body and the darkness of nature *to cover the day* of the light of the spirit, *which it pursues urgently*, because (as body) the night is gifted and suited for absorbing the day (as spirit) by adjusting (the body fluids).[8] *And the sun* of the spirit, *and the moon* of the heart, *and the stars* of the senses (are created) *by His amr*. This *amr* is something (*sha'n*) that is mentioned in God's words: 'Every day He is engaged in something' (Sūra 55:29). *Are not* the placing-into-being through *His* power (*alone*) and the decree through (his) wisdom (alone)? Or: Are not the causing-to-originate and the creating-anew His (alone)?

If one takes the heaven and the earth according to the outer meaning (of the text), then the six days are the six dimensions[9] (of the material world). That is, one can give expression to events by (speaking of) days. Thus God says: 'And remind them of the days of God' (Sūra 14:5), when what is meant is: (And remind them) of the creation of the world of matter in the six dimensions! Then he firmly took possession of the Throne[10] so that he interwove into it, by imprinting into it, the forms of the things which grew out of it. The Throne has an outer and an inner meaning. According to the outer meaning, it is the ninth sphere of the heavens, in which all forms of things which come into existence are written down. Their being or non-being depends upon whether they are recorded in it or are erased from it. . . . According to the inner meaning, the Throne is the source of reason (*'aql awwal*), in which the forms of things are written in as universals. . . . This is the place of eternal determination. . . .

2. Allegorical interpretation

Kāshānı on Sūra 20:12

(A voice cried out: 'Moses,) I am thy Lord! Take off thy sandals. Thou art in the holy valley, Ṭuwā.'[11]

Take off thy sandals: namely, your soul and your body, or your two (temporal) forms of existence, since when one is free from soul and body, one is free from both (temporal) forms of existence. That is: As soon as one is free, through the spirit (*rūḥ*) and the inner mystery (*sirr*), from the properties and characteristics of the soul and the body, so that one is united with the holy spirit, then one is free from the soul and the body (also) through the heart (*qalb*) and the breast (*ṣadr*), since the general connection (with them) is severed, their actions are released, and one has escaped their properties and activities. God calls the soul and the body sandals and not garments. If one were not free from intimate contact with both, one could not become united with the sacred sphere. The condition (however, on which it depends) is that of becoming united. God gives to Moses the command that he is to devote himself exclusively to him, in the sense of his words: 'And remember the name of thy Lord, and devote thyself completely to Him' (Sūra 73:8). It is therefore almost as if the connection of Moses with the sandals (of the soul and the body) still exists. This connection permits his feet, that is, the lower self, just as the breast designates the place of the heart, to sink into the ground. Consequently, they stand back away from the spiritual and inner turning-point to the holy, and for this reason God commands Moses to free himself from them in order to enter the realm of the spirit. Appropriately, God gives a reason for the necessity of removing the sandals, in his words: *Thou art in the holy valley, Ṭuwā*, that is, in the world of the spirit, which is free from the actions of linking (through the soul and the body) the characteristics of transient things and the material bonds. This world is called Ṭuwā because the stages of the kingdom of God (*malakūt*) are concealed (*ṭawā*) in it, while the heavenly and earthly bodies stand under it. . . .

Kāshānī on Sūra 20:17/18–22/23

'What is that, Moses, thou hast in thy right hand?'
'Why, it is my staff,' said Moses. 'I lean upon it, and with it I beat down leaves to feed my sheep; other uses also I find in it.'
God[12] *said: 'Cast it down, Moses!'*
And he cast it down, and behold it was a serpent sliding.
God said: 'Take it and fear not. We will restore it to its first state.
Now clasp thy hand to thy side; it shall come forth white, without evil. This is a second sign.'

What is that, Moses, thou hast in thy right hand: This is a reference to the soul of Moses, that is, to that which lies in the hand of his reason. That is, reason is a right hand with which man grasps the gift of God and with which he bridles his soul.

Why, it is my staff, said Moses, I lean upon it: that is, the soul, on which I lean in the world of intuition and the acquisition of perfection, of turning to God, and of the assimilation to his characteristics. That is: These things are possible only through the soul.

And with it I beat down leaves to feed my sheep: that is, with (the soul) I beat down the leaves of profitable knowledge and of practical wisdom from the trees of the spirit, since the power of thinking moves with the soul above the sheep, that is, man's animal powers.

Other uses also I find in it: namely, the acquisition of the (mystical) stages as well as the pursuit of the (ecstatic) conditions, gifts, and (divine) manifestations. ...

God said: Cast it down, Moses: that is, set your soul free from the bridling through reason!

And he cast it down: that is, he set (his soul) free, and its concern was entirely transformed after it acquired a share in bringing to light the manifestations of the attributes of divine force (*qahr*).

And behold it was a serpent sliding (along the ground): that is, a serpent which moved about as a result of fierce anger. The soul of Moses was filled with intense anger and vehement rage. Then as soon as he reached the stage in which the (divine) attributes manifest themselves, as a result of the necessity of his predisposition, his share in the manifestation of (divine) power turned out to be abundant. ... With the fading away of the (divine) attributes, his anger changed into divine (*ilāhī*) anger and divine (*rabbānī*) power. Thus the soul became a serpent which swallows everything it finds.

God said: Take it (up from the ground): that is, bridle it through your reason (so that it becomes again) like it was before.

And fear not concerning it (and let not) your soul overpower and defeat you, so that you fall into the sinful condition of vacillation. Your anger is now faded away and moves according to my command. It was not veiled at the level of the soul, through the light of the heart, so that it might (be allowed to) step forward, after which it was concealed.

We will restore it to its first state: that is, dead and faded away and turned back again to the level of vegetative power, which has no perception and no desire. Because Moses killed the soul in his upbringing with Shu'aib[13] and thus treated it like the vegetative powers, it is designated as a staff. Thus it is said that Shu'aib gave it to him.

Now clasp thy hand to thy side (janāḥ): that is, clasp your reason to the side (*jānib*) of your spirit, which is your right wing (*janāḥ*), so that you are enlightened through the light of divine (*ḥaqqānī*) right-guidance! In the way that reason is suited to the aim of ordering earthly life and is connected to its side, which constitutes the left wing, reason will be dulled and mixed with the power of imagination (*wahm*) (of lower standing). It is then cloudy and obstinate and will neither enlighten nor can it receive the divine (*rabbānī*) gift and the divine (*ilāhī*) truths. Therefore God has commanded Moses to clasp it to the side of the spirit, whereby it becomes pure and receives the holy light.

It shall come forth white: enlightened through the light of divine (*ḥaqqānī*) right-guidance and the rays of holy light.

Without evil: (without) an injury, a blemish, or a sickness (being present), as is brought about through the mingling (of reason) with the powers of imagination and fantasy (*khayāl*).

3. *Parallel interpretation*

Kāshānī on Sūra 8:41/42

> *And you must know that, whatever booty you take, the fifth part of it is God's and the Messenger's, and the near kinsman's and the orphan's, and for the needy and the traveller, if you believe in God and what We sent down upon Our servant (Muḥammad) on the day of salvation* (furqān), *the day the hosts encountered. And God is powerful over everything.*

(The passage beginning) *And you must know that, whatever booty you take, the fifth part of it is God's* (together with the following verses) down to God's words: 'And God is terrible in retribution' (Sūra 8:48/50) allows no allegorical interpretation (*ta'wīl*), because herein an actual occurrence is treated. If one, however, wished to establish parallels (*taṭbīq*)[14] between these words and the individual parts of (human) being, then one could say: 'And you spiritual forces must know that whatever booty you take (in the form) of profitable knowledge and of the laws on which Islam is built, the fifth part of it belongs to God, according to the words of the Prophet: "Islam is based on five things."'[15] What is involved with this fifth part is the acknowledgment that there is no god but God and that Muḥammad is the Messenger of God, for the general unity of being (*tauḥīd*) is at stake here.

And the near kinsman's, which are the inner mystery (*sirr*) (of man) as well as the outstanding theoretical and practical powers of imagination, in addition to the power of thinking and the lower powers of the soul.

And for ... the traveller: This is to be understood as the soul which goes on a journey, wandering in a foreign land, passing through the stations of the journey and turning away from its original resting place. (In this case what is involved is the confession of faith) in that what is thereby concerned is the unity of being which is dismembered in the world of prophecy. The remaining four-fifths are distributed to the limbs, the trunk parts, and the natural powers. ...

XI

SHĪʿITE QURʾĀNIC EXEGESIS

1. The genuine revealed text

Kāshī on Sūra 3:123/119

And God most surely helped you at Badr, when you were utterly abject (adhilla).[1] *So fear God! Perhaps you will be thankful.*

And God most surely helped you at Badr: Here is mentioned something which taught them to trust in God. Badr is an oasis between Mecca and Medina which belonged to a man named Badr and then was named after him.

When you were utterly abject (adhilla): Al-Qummī and al-ʿAyyāshī say according to (the Imām) aṣ-Ṣādiq: They were not abject, for the Messenger of God was among them. (Actually, the following) came down: 'When you were weak (*ḍuʿafāʾ*)'. Al-ʿAyyāshī reports according to aṣ-Ṣādiq that Abū Baṣīr recited the verse (in this way) in aṣ-Ṣādiq's presence. Regarding this, the latter said that God did not send down the verse in this form; (and that actually the following) was sent down: 'when you were few (*qalīl*)'. In a Tradition it is said that God never humbled (*adhalla*) his Messenger, and thus what was sent down was: 'when you were few'. In several reliable reports it is said that they numbered three hundred and thirteen.

So fear God constantly! *Perhaps you will be thankful* for the blessings which he has granted to you.

Kāshī on Sūra 26:227/228

. . . And those who have done wrong will (one day) know what kind of turning upside down they will experience.

Al-Qummī says: God has mentioned their enemies and those who have done wrong against them. He has said (in Sūra 26:227/228): 'Those who have done wrong against the law of the family of Muḥammad will (one day) know what kind of turning upside down they will experience.' This is the way the verse actually came down. . . .

Kāshī on Sūra 5:67/71

> *O Messenger, deliver that which has been sent down to thee from thy Lord; for if thou dost not, thou wilt not have delivered His message. God will protect thee from men. God guides not the people of the unbelievers.*

O Messenger, deliver that which has been sent down to thee (as revelation) from thy Lord: that is, (what has been sent down to you) with regard to 'Alī. According to the tradition of the authorities on doctrine, the verse (actually) came down in this (extended) form.

For if thou dost not, thou wilt not have delievered His message: If you discontinue the delivery of what has been sent down to you concerning the guardianship (*wilāya*) of 'Alī (over the believers), and you keep this secret, then it is as if you delivered none of the message of your Lord concerning that which requires reconciliation. Some also read: 'his message concerning the confession of the unity of God (*tauḥīd*)'.

God will protect thee from men: He will guard you against their inflicting evil upon you.

God guides not the people of the unbelievers: In the *Jawāmi'* (of aṭ-Ṭabarsī) it is said according to Ibn 'Abbās and Jābir ibn 'Abd Allāh that God commanded his Prophet to place 'Alī before men and to inform them of his guardianship (over them). The Prophet, however, was afraid that they would say: '(He is) the protector of his paternal cousin', and that a group of his Companions might find this distressing. The present verse came down regarding this. On the next day, the Prophet then took 'Alī gently by the hand and said: 'Whose protector (*maulā*) I am, their protector (also) is 'Alī.' Then he recited (this verse). . . .

2. *The 'Alids and their opponents*

Kāshī on Sūra 2:269/272

He gives wisdom (al-ḥikma) *to whomever He will, and whoever is given wisdom has been given much good. Yet none remembers except those who have understanding.*

... (What is meant are) people with reason who are free from prejudice through the power of imagination (*wahm*) and eager desire.[2] In the *Kāfī* (of aṭ-Ṭabarsī) and with al-'Ayyāshī it is said according to (the Imām) aṣ-Ṣādiq concerning this verse: (What is involved here is) obedience to God and knowledge about the Imām. According to aṣ-Ṣādiq (this verse involves) knowledge about the Imām and the avoidance of grave sins, for which God has imposed (the punishment of) the hell-fire. Al-'Ayyāshī has reported according to aṣ-Ṣādiq: Wisdom is knowledge and cognizance of the religion. Whoever of you has knowledge (of it) is wise. The death of no believer is dearer to Iblīs than that of one who possesses (this) knowledge. ...

Kāshī on Sūra 1:6f./5–7

Guide us in the straight path,
the path of those whom Thou hast blessed, not of those against whom Thou art wrathful, nor of those who go astray.

Guide us in the straight path: ... In the *Ma'ānī* (of Ibn Bābūya al-Qummī) it is said according to (the Imām) aṣ-Ṣādiq: This is the path of knowledge of God, and there are two paths—one in this world and one in the hereafter. The path in this world is the Imām, who demands obedience. Whoever acknowledges him in this world and follows his guidance passes over that path which in the hereafter consists of the bridge over the hell-fire.[3] Whoever does not acknowledge him in this world, his foot will slip from the path in the hereafter, so that he falls into hell-fire. From aṣ-Ṣādiq (is further related): The path is the Prince of the Believers ('Alī). ...

The path of those whom Thou hast blessed, not of those against whom Thou art wrathful, nor of those who go astray: ...[4] In the *Ma'ānī* (is related) from the Prophet: Those for whom you have shown mercy are the party (*shī'a*) of 'Alī, that is, you have shown mercy for them through the guardianship (*wilāya*) of 'Alī ibn Abī Ṭālib, and they neither suffer the wrath (of God) nor do they go astray. According to aṣ-Ṣādiq, Muḥammad and his descendants are meant. Al-Qummī has related according to aṣ-Ṣādiq: Those who suffer the wrath (of God) are the enemies (of 'Alī), and those who go astray are the doubters who do not acknowledge the Imām. . . .

Kāshī on Sūra 7:44f./42f.

The inhabitants of paradise will call to the inhabitants of the fire: 'We have found what our Lord promised us true. Have you found what your Lord promised you true?' 'Yes', they will say. And then a herald shall proclaim among them: 'God's curse is on the evildoers
who bar from God's way, desiring to make it crooked, disbelieving in the world to come.'

The inhabitants of paradise will call . . . : They say this with joyfulness concerning their (own) situation and with gloating pleasure and sighs concerning the (situation of the) inhabitants of the hell-fire. God does not say: 'what your Lord promised you' in the same way that he says: 'what our Lord promised us', because what is promised which causes pain to the inhabitants of hell-fire is not promised so specifically as the resurrection, the balancing of accounts, and the grace of paradise (which are promised) to the inhabitants of paradise. . . .

And then a herald shall proclaim among them: God's curse is on the evildoers: . . . In the *Kāfī* (of aṭ-Ṭabarsī), and by al-Qummī according to (the Imām Mūsā) al-Kāẓim, and by al-'Ayyāshī according to (the Imām) ar-Riḍā, it is stated: The herald is the Ruler of the Believers ('Alī). Al-Qummī (adds to this): He will announce (this) in a manner which will cause the creatures to listen attentively. In the *Majma'* (of aṭ-Ṭabarsī) and in the *Ma'ānī* (of Ibn Bābūya al-Qummī) it is reported from the Ruler of the Believers: I am that herald. . . .

Kāshī on Sūra 39:60/61

And upon the day of resurrection thou shalt see those who lied against God, their faces blackened. Is there not in Jahannam a lodging for those who are proud?

Referring to this verse, al-Qummī reports from (the Imām) aṣ-Ṣādiq: (What is meant is) one who claims to be Imām but (in reality) is not. Someone asked: Even if he is a Fāṭimid descendant[5] of 'Alī? To this aṣ-Ṣādiq answered: (This applies even) when such is the case. ...

Kāshī on Sūra 14:24/29–26/31

Hast thou not seen how God has coined a simile? A good word is like a good tree; its roots are firm, and its branches are in heaven.
It gives its produce every season by the leave of its Lord. Thus God coins similes for men. Perhaps they will remember.
And a corrupt word is like a corrupt tree—uprooted from the earth, having no firm hold.

... *Like a good tree* which bears good fruit, perhaps the palm. In the *Majma'* (of aṭ-Ṭabarsī) it is said from the Prophet: This good tree is the palm. ...

Thus God coins similes for men. Perhaps they will remember: In the coining of similes lie an admonition and a graphic description of important matters which need to be understood, (and God coins these similes) in order to bring these matters closer to understanding. Al-'Ayyāshī has reported from (the Imām) aṣ-Ṣādiq: This is a simile that God has coined regarding the family of the Prophet and their enemies. In the *Kāfī* (of aṭ-Ṭabarsī) it is said from aṣ-Ṣādiq: When someone asked aṣ-Ṣādiq about the tree in this verse, he answered: The Messenger of God is its root, the Prince of the Believers ('Alī) is its trunk, the imāms among the descendants of both are its branches, the knowledge of the imāms constitutes its fruit, and the believers of their party (*shī'a*) are its leaves. He said (further): When a believer is born, a leaf is formed on it, and when a believer dies, one falls off. In the *Ikmāl* (of Ibn Bābūya al-Qummī) it is said: Al-Ḥasan and al-Ḥusain are its fruits and the nine (later imāms) from the descendants of al-Ḥusain are its branches. In the *Ma'ānī* (of Ibn Bābūya al-Qummī) is (stated): The branch of the tree is (Muḥammad's daughter) Fāṭima, its fruits are their children, and its leaves are their party. ...

Like a corrupt tree: which bears no good fruit, perhaps the colocynth. ... In the *Majma'* (of aṭ-Ṭabarsī) it is said from (the Imām) al-Bāqir that this is a simile referring to the Umayyads. ...

Kāshī on Sūra 24:35[6]

God is the light of the heavens and the earth. His light is to be likened to a niche wherein is a lamp—the lamp in a glass, the glass as it were a glittering star—kindled (with oil) from a blessed tree, an olive that is neither of the east nor of the west, whose oil wellnigh would shine, even if no fire touched it. Light upon light; God guides to His light whom He will. And God coins similes for men, and God has knowledge of everything.

... In the *Tauḥīd* (of Ibn Bābūya al-Qummī) it is said from (the Imām) aṣ-Ṣādiq: What is involved here is a simile that God has coined for us. (Regarding God's words) *God is the light of the heavens and the earth*, aṣ-Ṣādiq says: God is thus. *His light*: Aṣ-Ṣādiq says (this is) Muḥammad. *Is to be likened to a niche*: Aṣ-Ṣādiq says (what is meant is) Muḥammad's breast. *Wherein is a lamp*, aṣ-Ṣādiq says: wherein is the light of knowledge, that is, of prophecy. *The lamp in a glass*, aṣ-Ṣādiq says: The knowledge of the Messenger of God issued from the latter into the heart of 'Alī. ... (The words) *the glass as it were a glittering star, kindled from a blessed tree, an olive that is neither of the east nor of the west*, according to aṣ-Ṣādiq, are coined in reference to the Ruler of the Believers, 'Alī ibn Abī Ṭālib, who was neither a Jew nor a Christian. (Regarding God's words:) *Whose oil wellnigh would shine, even if no fire touched it*, aṣ-Ṣādiq says: The knowledge would wellnigh issue forth from the mouth of the knowing one of the family of Muḥammad (that is, 'Alī), even if Muḥammad had not spoken it. *Light upon light*, aṣ-Ṣādiq says (means): Imām to imām.

Regarding the meaning of the simile, there are further accounts. Thus, it is said in the *Kāfī* (of aṭ-Ṭabarsī) from (the Imām) al-Bāqir in a Tradition, (God's words *God is the light of the heavens and the earth*) mean: I am the (rightly guiding) director of the heavens and the earth. The knowledge that I have given, namely, my light through which the guidance results, *is to be likened to a niche wherein is a lamp*: The niche is the heart of Muḥammad, and the lamp is his light, wherein lies knowledge. God's words: *The lamp in a glass* mean: I want to lay hold of you and what is with you, thus setting forth the executor (*waṣī*)[7] (of your mission) (that is, 'Alī), like the lamp stands in the glass. *As it were a glittering star*: Then will I give to men news of the excellence of the executor. *Kindled (with oil)* from a blessed tree: The root of the blessed tree is Abraham. This is mentioned in God's words: 'The mercy of God and His blessings be upon you, O people of the House! Surely he (that is, Abraham) is worthy of praise and glory' (Sūra 11:73/76),[8] as well as: 'God chose Adam and Noah and the House of Abraham and the House of 'Imrān[9] above all beings (*al-'ālamūn*), the descendants of (the patriarchs all being of the same race and thus interrelated with) one another. God hears and knows' (Sūra 3:33f./30). *That is neither of the east nor of the west* means: You are neither Jews, so that you would perform the prayer facing towards the west, nor Christians, so that you would face towards the east.[10] Rather, you follow the creed of Abraham, of whom God has said: 'No, in truth Abraham was neither a Jew nor a Christian, but a Ḥanīf who was surrendered to God (*ḥanīfan musliman*).[11] Certainly he was never one of the idolaters' (Sūra 3:67/60). God's words *whose oil wellnigh would shine* mean: Your children who will be begotten of you are like oil which is pressed from olives. They wellnigh speak already in prophecy, even though an angel has not yet come down to them.

Al-Qummī has related from aṣ-Ṣādiq who related from his father (al-Bāqir) the following concerning this verse. *God is the light of the heavens and the earth*: Al-Bāqir says that God begins with his own light. *His light*, that is, his guidance in the hearts of the believers, *is to be likened to a niche wherein is a lamp*: The niche is the inside of the body of the believer, the light glass (*qindīl*) is his heart, and the lamp is the light that God has placed therein. *Kindled (with oil) from a blessed tree*, al-Bāqir says: The tree is the believer. *An olive (tree) that is neither of the east nor of the west*, al-Bāqir says: (What is meant is an olive tree that stands) on the ridge of a mountain. 'Neither of the east' means that the tree has no sunrise side, and 'nor of the west' means that it has no sunset side. When the sun rises, it rises over the tree, and when it sets, it sets over it. *Whose oil wellnigh would shine*: (The tree is a believer) in which the light that God has placed in his heart wellnigh shines even though he had not spoken. *Light upon light*: command upon command and precept upon precept (*sunna*). *God guides to His light whom He will*, al-Bāqir says: God guides whom he will to himself according to his command and precept. *And God coins similes for men*, al-Bāqir says: This is a simile that God has coined for the believer. The believer walks in five kinds of light: His entrance (into the world) is a light, his exit is a light, his knowledge is a light, his word (*kalām*) is a light, and his entrance into paradise on the day of resurrection is a light. . . .

3. Ismā'īlite Qur'ānic interpretation

Ḍiyā' ad-Dīn on Sūra 13:31

*And still the unbelievers are smitten by a shattering (*qāri'a[12]*) for what they wrought, or it alights near their dwelling, until God's promise is fulfilled. And God will not fail the tryst.*

And still the unbelievers: that is, (those who do not believe) in the rank of the veil of lights.[13]

Are smitten by a shattering for what they wrought: What is involved here is an allusion to the appearance of the (coming) public imāms.

Or it alights near their dwelling: Here is a reference to the location of the (Ismā'īlite) community on the Yemenite peninsula, especially (referring to the time) since the end of the generation of the Chosen One,[14] when the enemies among the inhabitants of this place became afraid of the imāms of rightful guidance, while the community—according to God's will—has grown.

Until God's promise is fulfilled: that is, (until) in the time of the public imāms, whose time of elevation is looked forward to expectantly, (the promise) of al-'Ain[15] (is fulfilled), whereby the (divine) rule (*amr*) makes its appearance and the truth gains power.

God will not fail the tryst (al-mī'ād)[16]: He is exalted above doing so.

Ḍiyā' ad-Dīn on Sūra 22:17

Surely they that believe, and those who are Jewish, the Sabaeans, the Christians, the Zoroastrians, and those who associate (other gods with God)—God shall distinguish between them on the day of resurrection. Surely God is witness over everything.

Surely they that believe: What is meant are the descendants of that group of converts in each age who believe in the rank of the masters of guidance and in their veils,[17] who recruit for them.

Those who are Jewish (alladhīna hādū): that is, ('those who turn away', *hādū*) from the executor.[18] What is meant are the Jews of this (Islamic) community (*umma*), (that is) the descendants of the hateful ones who went before them in each early period.

The Sabaeans: These are the ones who strive (*ṣāba*) after indecision in this community. They belong to the descendants of the descendants of those who remain undecided, since they found themselves in harmony neither with the guardianship of the executor, nor with that of his opponents. For these people behave just the same in this world.

The Christians: These are the extremists of his community, who are descended from the evil ones among those who went before them as extremists in the earlier periods.

The Zoroastrians: These are the 'hypocrites' (*munāfiqūn*) of this community, who are descended from the evil ones among the descendants of the hypocrites in the past.

And those who associate (other gods with God): These are those who associate (other gods with God) among this community, who are descended from the descendants of those who at one time acknowledged the rank of the executor as well as that of his opponents. Although this evil group will be hurled down the cliff of hell, certain parts of their evil fumes must be preserved in the corners, so that they become the same kind of leaven for the people of later generations, bringing ruin to these.

Then God says: *God shall distinguish between them on the day of resurrection*, that is: when he appears and steps forward openly out of the circle of the *qāʾim*.[19]

Surely God is witness over everything means: (He is) witness over them and discloses what has proceeded from them.

XII

MODERN QUR'ĀNIC EXEGESIS

Polygamy

Muḥammad 'Abduh and Muḥammad Rashīd Riḍā on Sūra 4:3

If you fear that you will not be able to act justly towards orphans (who are to be the first choice in marriage, then instead of them) marry two, three, or four of such women as seem good to you, but if you fear you will not be equitable, then (marry) only one, or what your right hands own (as slaves). Thus it will be more likely that you will not be partial.

... The Ustādh-Imām[1] (Muḥammad 'Abduh has said): Polygamy is mentioned in connection with the words (of the present verse) concerning orphans and with the prohibition against spending all their wealth, even though it be through marriage. He said: If you feel within yourself the fear that by marrying the orphaned girl (*al-yatīma*) you will spend all her wealth, then you may (choose) not (to) marry her, since here God has given to you a possibility of avoiding (your duty) concerning (marriage to) the orphan. He has given you the choice of marrying other wives, up to (the number of) four. If you fear, however, that you will not be able to treat two or more wives justly, you must restrict yourself to one. Moreover, (justifiable) fear that a proper act will not be done is present whenever there is adequate presumption and adequate doubt, indeed even when there is adequate suspicion. The law may nevertheless justify suspicion since where knowledge of this kind of thing exists there is seldom freedom from it. The marriage of two or more wives is therefore allowed as an option (only) to one who has the conviction in himself that he will deal justly, (indeed) in such a way that he has no doubt about it, or that he suspects it but shelters (only) a small doubt about it.

Muḥammad 'Abduh has said: After God said *But if you fear you will not be equitable, then (marry) only one*, he gives a reason for this in his words: *Thus, it will be more likely that you will not be partial*, that is, thus you will come more closely to the condition in which neither injustice nor oppression will occur. Consequently, God has made the condition that one keep far from injustice to be the basis for his giving of a law (concerning marriage). This confirms the fact that justice is enjoined as a condition and that duty consists in striving for it. Further, it shows that justice is something difficult to attain. God says in another verse of this sūra: 'You will not be able to treat your wives equally, regardless of how eager you are (to do so)' (Sūra 4:129/128). This refers to justice in the inclination of the heart, since otherwise the two verses taken together would have the result that there would be no permission for polygamy at all. And then also the meaning of his words in (another) part of the verse just cited, (namely) 'Yet do not follow your inclination to the extreme (thus completely severing your relations with any of them) so that you leave her as it were deserted' (Sūra 4:129/128), would not be clear. God forgives the servant when something in the inclination of his heart goes beyond his power, even as, towards the end of his life, the Prophet felt a stronger inclination for 'Ā'isha than for his other wives. To be sure, he did not treat her with any distinction above them, that is, not without their consent and authorization. He used to say: 'God, this is my share of what lies in my power. Do not call me to account for what does not lie in my power!' That is: (This is my share) regarding the inclination of the heart.

Muḥammad 'Abduh has said: Whoever considers the two verses correctly acknowledges that permission for polygamy in Islam applies (only) with the most severe restriction. Polygamy is like one of those necessities which is permitted to the one to whom it is allowed (only) with the stipulation that he act fairly with trustworthiness and that he be immune from injustice (*al-jaur*). In view of this restriction, when one now considers what corruption results from polygamy in modern times, then one will know for certain that a people (*umma*) cannot be trained so that their remedy lies in polygamy, since, in a family in which a single man has two wives, no beneficial situation and no order prevail. Rather, the man and his wives each mutually assist in the ruin of the family, as if each of them were the enemy of the other; and also the children then become enemies to one another. The corruption of polygamy carries over from the individual to the family and from the family to the (entire) people.

Muḥammad 'Abduh has said: Polygamy had advantages in the early period of Islam, among the most important at that time being that it brought about the bond of blood relationship and of relationship by marriage, so that the feeling of tribal solidarity was strengthened. Also, at that time it did not lead to the same harm (*ḍarar*) that it does today, since at that time the religion was firmly rooted in the souls of women and men, and the insult (*adhan*) of taking an additional wife (*ḍarra*) did not go beyond her rival (in its effect). Today, on the other hand, the harm (*ḍarar*) of every additional wife (*ḍarra*) carries over to her child, its father, and its other relatives. The wife stirs up enmity and hatred among them; she incites her child to enmity against his brothers and sisters, and she incites her husband to suppress the rights of the children which he has from the other wives. The husband, on the other hand, follows in the folly of the wife whom he loves the most, and thus ruin creeps into the entire family. If one wished to enumerate specifically the disadvantages and mishaps that result from polygamy, then one would present something that would cause the blood of the believers to curdle. This includes theft and adultery, lies and deceit, cowardice and deception, indeed even murder, so that the child kills the father, the father kills the child, the wife kills the husband, and the husband kills the wife. All this is tangible and is demonstrated from the (records of the) courts of justice.

It may suffice here to refer to the (poor) education of the (modern) woman, who knows neither the worth (*qīma*) of the husband nor that of the child and finds herself in ignorance concerning herself and her religion, knowing of religion only legends and errors which she has snatched up from others like herself and which are not found either in the scriptures or in (the sayings of) the prophets who have been sent. If women had the benefit of a proper religious education, so that religion had the highest power over their hearts and would prevail over jealousy, then no harm would grow out of polygamy for the people today, but the harm would remain limited as a rule to the women (who are concerned). However, since the matter now stands as we see and hear it, there is no possibility of educating the people so long as polygamy is widespread among them. Thus, it is the duty of scholars to investigate this problem, (that is) especially the Ḥanafite scholars, in whose hand the matter lies (in the Ottoman empire and its sphere of influence), and whose opinion is determinative (here). They do not deny that religion was sent down for the use and benefit of mankind and that it belongs to the principles of religion to prevent harm and injury. Now if at a (certain) time (that is, the present), corruption results from something that was not connected with it earlier, it is without doubt necessary to alter the laws and to adapt them to the actual situation, that is, according to the principle that one must prevent the deterioration beforehand in order then to bring about the well-being (of the community). Muḥammad 'Abduh has said: Hence, it is recognized that polygamy is strictly forbidden when the fear exists that one cannot act fairly.

This is what the Ustādh-Imām (Muḥammad 'Abduh) said in the first lecture in which he interpreted the present verse. In the second lecture he then said: It has been said before that permission for polygamy is restricted since a stipulation is imposed which is so difficult to realize that it represents the same as a prohibition against polygamy. Further, it has been said that to him who fears that he is unable to act equitably it is forbidden to marry more than one wife. This is not, as has been done by some students (of al-Azhar University), to be understood in the sense that a marriage settlement is null and void when it has been completed under such circumstances, since the prohibition (given here) is not so firm that it could require the negation of the marriage settlement.[2] The husband may indeed fear that he will act unjustly, but yet not do so. And he may act unjustly, but then repent and act equitably and thus lead a legitimate life. . . .

I (Muḥammad Rashīd Riḍā) say: Add to this that polygamy is at variance with the natural fundamental rule (*aṣl*) in the nature of marriage, since the fundamental rule is that the man is to have a single wife and that he is her mate just as she is his. Polygamy is, however, a necessity that befalls human society (under certain circumstances, that is) especially in warlike peoples (*al-umam al-ḥarbiyya*) like the Islamic community. Polygamy is permitted to them only in the case of necessity, and then only with the stipulation that neither injustice nor oppression will occur thereby. This problem requires further discussion. So the wisdom of the plurality and number (of wives) is discussed, and there must be discussion as to the extent to which the administrators of the law are in a position to impede the perversions of polygamy through restraint when the harm done through polygamy becomes widespread, as is seen to be thc case in Egypt. For those men who marry more than one wife are numerous here, while in Syria and Turkey this is not the case; and at the same time, the customs in Egypt ordinarily are more corrupted than there. We have published a legal opinion (*fatwa*) concerning the wisdom of polygamy in the seventh volume of (the journal) *Al-manār*. It reads as follows:

The wisdom of polygamy

Question ... from Najīb Āfandī Qonawī, a student in America: Many American physicians and others ask me about the verse: *Then marry two, three, or four of such women as seem good to you, but if you fear you will not be equitable, then (marry) only one.* And they say: 'How can a Muslim join together four women (to form a family unit)?' I have answered them, so far as I understand this verse, in support of my religion, and have said: It is impossible to treat two (wives) equitably. For if one marries a new (wife), the old one must be resentful. How is one to treat them equitably? But God has commanded that one treat (them) equitably. Therefore, it is best when one has (only) one (wife). I have said this and usually those who inquire are satisfied with this answer. However, I would appreciate your interpretation and explanation of this verse, and I would like to know what you say to those who marry two or three (wives).

Answer: The general public in the West regard the problem of polygamy to be the most serious deficiency in Islam, because this general public are influenced by their customs, their religious traditions, their excessive esteem for women, and by what they have heard and learned about the conduct of many Muslims who marry several wives only for the release of their animal desires, without holding to the restrictions that have been imposed upon them concerning permission for it. (Further, the general public in the West are of this opinion because they are influenced) by what appears to them to be corruption in a family which consists of one husband and several wives, whose children confront each other with jealousy, strife, and hatred. This kind of view, however, does not suffice in order to resolve so serious a problem as this for human society. Rather, before making a decision one must reflect about the nature of man and woman, about (the question) of whether there is a larger number of men or women, (further) about the problem of domestic life and the care of men for women or vice versa, or the independence of both marriage partners from each other, and (finally) about the history of human development, in order to know whether people in the stage of nomadic life were satisfied for each man to have (only) a single wife. After all this, one has to see whether the Qur'ān has made the problem of polygamy a religious matter worthy of striving after or a concession that is allowed in the case of necessity and under limiting restrictions.

You who are occupied with the medical sciences know best among mankind the distinction between the nature of man and that of woman as well as the most important difference between the two. According to what we all know, man has by nature a greater desire for woman than she has for him. There is (only) seldom an impotent man who (because of this impotence) by nature has no desire for women; but there are many women who by nature have no desire for men. If the woman were not to become enamoured with being loved by the man, and if she did not undertake considerable reflection regarding esteem by the man, then there would be many more women today who would forgo marriage. This passion in the woman is something other than the inclination that grows out of the natural craving for procreation in her and in the man. This passion is sheltered also by the old woman and by those who cannot hope for a wedding with the customary adornments of the virgin bride. In my opinion, the most important reason for it is a social one, consisting of the fact that many centuries have established in the nature and belief of women the desire to have the benefit of the protection and care of men, (further) in the fact that the provision of the man for the woman arises according to the measure of esteem which she has for him and the inclination which he has for her. Women felt this in primitive times (by necessity) and have continued it so that it has become a hereditary factor with them. This is so much the case that, even when a woman hates a man, it hurts her if he turns away from her and treats her contemptuously, and it hurts the woman when she sees a man—even a stricken old man or a monk who has turned away from the world—who feels no inclination for the woman, does not succumb to her charms, and does not show a reaction to her glamour. Hence it follows that the procreative instinct is stronger in the man than in the woman, and this is a primary premise (for the solution of the problem).

Thus, divine wisdom exists concerning the inclination that each of the two marriage partners, the male as well as the female, feels for the other, for the inclination which leads to marriage exists in procreation, through which the species is preserved, just as the wisdom concerning the necessity for food exists in the preservation of the individual. Now a woman is capable of procreation during only half of the natural human lifetime, which amounts to a hundred years. This is because the power of the woman in general after fifty years is no longer sufficient for pregnancy, and thus menstruation and the (forming of the) eggs cease(s) in the womb. The wisdom in this is evident and the medical people can explain it better in detail.

Whenever there is no freedom for the man to marry more than a single woman, (then) half of the natural lifetime of the men among the people will be prevented from procreation, which is the purpose of marriage; (that is, this is true) if one assumes that the man marries (a woman) of the same age. Some men, however, lose more than fifty years, (which is the case) if they marry older (women) and if they reach the natural age (of a hundred years), just as some few (years) are lost if they marry younger (women). In each case (a man) loses a part of his time (for procreation). Even if he were to marry a fifteen-year-old (girl) when he was fifty years old, (still) fifteen years would be lost to him. If illness, premature old age, or death can befall men before the attainment of the natural age, they can also strike women before the change of life. A Western scholar has given attention to this distinction (in the ability for procreation). He has asserted: If we allow a single man to remain together for a single year with a hundred women, then we could receive a hundred offspring in the year. On the other hand, if we allow a hundred men to remain together with a single woman for a full year, then we would receive a single person at the most from their offspring. Probably, however, this woman would not bring into the world a single (person), because each of the men would destroy the (fertile) field of the others. Whoever has given attention to the importance of sufficient offspring within the laws of nature and for the condition of the people, to him the importance of this distinction will be clear. Herewith is given a second premise.

Then also, female births are more numerous than male ones in most regions of the earth. (Footnote appearing in the Arabic text: One may well dispute whether females are more numerous in most regions of the earth; however, it is true for England and for the survivors of a war in any state). And one sees that men, although they are fewer in number than women, are exposed to death and obstacles to marriage to a greater degree than women, including above all, military service and wars as well as the inability to bear the burdens and expenses of marriage. This is required according to the law of order in nature and the custom of the tribes and their peoples—although there are exceptions. When the man who is suited for marriage is not allowed to marry more than a single (wife), then this inevitably results in a situation in which a greater number of women are left without offspring, and they are prevented from reproducing, as is demanded of them by nature and the people. (Further, what results is a situation in which) they are required to suppress the procreative instinct in their nature, from which develop many physical and psychological illnesses, whereby these unfortunate ones become a burden and a misfortune for the people, after they (previously) had been a benefit to them. Or (what results is a situation in which) they surrender their good reputation and acquiesce to unchastity. This then leads to cases of misfortune, especially if they are poor, and no-one who has any human feelings can be satisfied with this. Such cases of misfortune are in fact so common in Western countries that people have thereby been weakened and have set their researchers to work to find a remedy for it. To some of them it has become clear that the only remedy lies in the sanction of polygamy. It is noteworthy that this view is advocated by several women authors in England, about whom we have written in an article in the fourth volume of (the journal) *Al-manār*. . . . This is noteworthy since women are the very ones who by nature shrink back from such a thing, since they reach opinions more according to sentiment and feeling than according to evidence and (concern for) the common good. What is more, to Western men, as a result of (the views of) their women, the question of polygamy has become a problem which is full of emotion, so that they do not find themselves in the position of the philosopher who in an impartial manner investigates the advantages of polygamy and the basis on which a necessity for it exists, striving (only) for the disclosure of the truth. This is a third premise.

From here on I want now to devote myself along with the reader (*bika*) to an exploration of the principle of married life and to examine this institution with him, as it is seen by reason and presented by nature. This principle states that the man must be the breadwinner for the wife and the manager of the household, because his body and his intellect are strong and he is better suited to (maintenance of) livelihood and protection (than the woman). This is the meaning of God's words: 'Men are the managers of the affairs of women because God has exalted the one above the other, and because they spend their wealth (on the women).[3] Righteous women are therefore obedient (to their husbands), guarding in their absence what God desires to be guarded' (Sūra 4:34/38). (Further, the principle of married life together means) that the woman has to lead the household and bring up the children, because she is gentle and patient and because she . . . is in the middle between the man and the child regarding feeling and thinking. She is thus fully suited to occupy a position in the middle in order to prepare the boy gradually for manhood and to guide the girl into that condition of mildness, gentleness, and ability concerning her natural activity as must be done. In clarifying this problem, one could say that the family is a small state, just as families together make up the large state. Then, in this state the woman would be responsible for the guidance of internal matters and educational matters, while the man would be responsible for the management of finances, public works, war, and external matters.

Since it now corresponds to the order of nature that the woman represents the 'valuable part' of the family and remains restricted to it in her activity—according to her nature and on account of the obstruction through pregnancy, delivery, and the care of the children, she is took weak for another activity and to that extent dependent upon man—the independent life is too difficult a task for her, to say nothing of domination and authority over the man. And if it is correct that the woman must stand under the care of man and 'the men must stand over the women', as indeed is obviously the case, what should we do then when the women are more numerous than the men? Must it not correspond with order in human society that a single man be permitted to care for a number of women, especially when a corresponding requirement exists, (for instance) when what is involved are people who have survived war which has claimed the men and left behind many women without breadwinners and helpers? Many people add (as an argument in favour of polygamy) that it is easy for the man to take many people to help with his work outdoors. On the other hand, the household is comprised solely of its members, and it is often urgently necessary that the woman have help with her many tasks, as is indicated by the laws of economics regarding the division of labour. But it is impossible that a (strange) man should (be hired to) help the woman in the family, because this would lead to corruption. Thus, it is good to have more women in the family to promote its prosperity. So say some people. Herewith is given a fourth premise.

If the reader will now turn with me to an examination of human development regarding marriage (*zawāj*) and the family, or coupling (*izdiwaj*) and reproduction, he will find that among no people is the man satisfied with a single woman, as is also the case with most animals. This is not the place to explain the natural reasons for this phenomenon. It has been shown through research that in primitive tribes the women were the common property of the men according to the mutual agreement that the woman was then the manager of the family, since as a rule the father (of the children) was not known. Now, gradually as man evolved upward he recognized the disadvantage of this common possession and mingling, and he inclined towards a restriction (*ikhtiṣāṣ*). The first restriction in the tribe then was that the women of the tribe came to the men of that tribe and not to the men of another tribe. Mankind developed upward further until they reached the point that the individual man was limited to several women, but without being restricted to a specific number. Rather, he acted according to his capabilities. Thereby the history of the family moved into a new stage, in which the father became the pillar of the genealogy and the support of the family, as some recent scholars in Germany and England have shown in books about the history of the family. From this point Westerners have reached the conviction that the end of the development is that the individual man is to be restricted to a single woman. This also is undisputed and should be the basic principle in the family.

But what do Westerners say concerning the natural and social phenomena that require that the man be concerned about the proper welfare of women and about the welfare of the people, as well as concerning his appropriate natural gift for several women? Can they report to us that the men among any people are content with this restriction and are satisfied with monogamy until today? Is there in Europe among a hundred thousand men a single one who has not committed adultery? Certainly not, since, because of his nature and his hereditary factor, the man cannot be satisfied with a single woman, for the woman is not disposed to it every time the man wishes to cohabit with her, just as she is not disposed every time to fertility and the natural gain from this cohabitation, namely offspring. On the contrary, for the woman (the desire for) sexual intercourse with the man is limited to specific times and is impossible at other times. According to normal gifts, the natural need of the woman for sexual intercourse with the man consists (only) in the time after menstruation. During the period of menstruation as well as during pregnancy (*ḥaml*) and child-bearing (*ithqāl*) the nature of the woman declines sexual intercourse.

I believe as follows: If the woman had not accustomed herself to giving satisfaction to the man and enjoying his esteem, and if the thought and conception of carnal pleasure which appeared in its time had not been brought to maturity through effort and repetition—which essentially is the case considering the influences which upbringing and general customs exert—then women would deny themselves to men on most days on which they are pure and ready for conception, which of course is the beginning of procreation. From this statement one understands the following: When a man is content with a single woman, then this leads necessarily to the fact that according to his nature he is stimulated by her on many days in which she is not disposed to have sexual intercourse with him. The most evident of these (times) are during the days of menstruation, pregnancy, and childbirth (*nifās*), while it is less evidently the case during the days of nursing (*raḍā'*), and especially on the first day of menstruation and the last day before. Thus, on these days, as a result of the superior strength of habit, the man struggles against his nature. On the other hand, when a woman is content with a single man, then a hindrance exists here neither from the side of her nature nor from the benefit of procreation; indeed, it is suitable to procreation, since the woman is never disposed to sexual intercourse when the man is not, that is so long as both are of normal constitution. We are of course not speaking here of sickness, since both marriage partners are then alike, and duty and the good practice of marriage require that each marriage partner should occupy himself with the care of the other when one is affected by some misfortune, without thereby pursuing his desire. With reference to (the statements of) some European scholars it should be mentioned that the large number of married men sometimes found among primitive tribes may be a result of the small number of girls, since at that time the men used to bury (newborn) girls alive.[4] This is a fifth premise.

If, after all this, the reader will consider with me the history of the Arab people before Islam, then he will find that this had developed to the extent that legal marriage constituted the basic principle for the rise of the family and that the man represented the pillar of the family and the root of the genealogy. However, polygamy was neither limited according to number nor bound to any (restrictive) stipulation. Sexual intercourse of several men with a single woman was regarded as unchastity worthy of blame. In spite of its frequency (at that time) this remained almost limited to female slaves and was (only) seldom practised by free women, possibly because the man consented to the woman's cohabiting with another man of her choosing in order to receive a child. Unchastity was not considered to be shameful or dishonourable for the man who committed it. (Thus) only with free women was it seen as shameful. In view of this situation, it would have been very difficult for men to accept Islam and act according to it if polygamy had not been allowed. Had this not happened then adultery would be regarded as legal in the Islamic countries just as it is allowed in the countries of the West. Herewith is given a sixth premise.

Even when one is aware of these problems, one must not forget that the final aim in the development of social order and family happiness consists in building each family on only two marriage partners of which each grants to the other a large measure of love, faithfulness, trust, and exclusive devotion. Thus, they bear sorrow together in the rearing of children, so the children will be brought up well and will provide joy for them, as they (as parents) form a good example for them in harmony, concord, love, and faithfulness. This is a seventh premise.

When one considers all these premises correctly and knows them according to branch and root, the following conclusion or the following conclusions become clear: The basis for happiness in marriage and family life consists in the man having (only) a single wife. This is the final aim of human development in its kind and the perfection into which the people grow up and with which they should be satisfied. Over against this, however, stands the fact that not all men can reach this stage and that conditions (often) require that a particular man care for more than a single woman. This can be to the benefit of the particular men as well as of the particular women. Thus, a man may marry a barren wife and then for the sake of posterity be obliged to (marry) another woman. Here it is then to the benefit of the (first) wife or to the benefit of both together, provided he does not separate from her and she declares herself agreed that he should marry another woman, especially in the case of a king or prince. Or, the woman may reach the change of life when the man is in the position to have more than a single wife and to care for many children and to rear them, and he perceives that he still could witness offspring with another woman. Or, he may perceive that one woman does not suffice for him to continue blameless (in marriage fidelity), since his temperament drives him to frequent sexual intercourse while it is the opposite with her, or she absolutely cannot endure it, or her menstrual period extends for a long time and lasts up to fifteen days in a month. Then the man sees himself faced with the alternative of marrying a second woman or being forced into unchastity; but the religion (Islam) prohibits the possibility and wholesomeness of unchastity, which signifies a greater evil for the wife than when one adds to her another (woman) and at the same time treats both properly, as is the stipulation in Islam for the sanction (of polygamy). For this reason unchastity is regarded as legal in countries in which polygamy is forbidden.

Polygamy is sometimes also of benefit for the people (as a whole), as perhaps when a large surplus of women exists in a society, as for example in England and in any country that has suffered a devastating war to which the men are carried off, up to many thousands, leading to a large surplus of women and forcing the women to seek employment and to be concerned for their means of livelihood. In such cases most of them have as an object of value in exchange for earnings nothing other than their sexual parts. If she surrenders these, then no observer can remain unaware of the misery that results from this surrender for the woman who is without a breadwinner, if she is forced to grieve for herself and a fatherless child, especially just after the birth and during the time of nursing, but also during the entire period of infancy. When many women writers of England have spoken of the necessity of polygamy, they have done this (only) after first gaining insight into the situation of the girls who work in the factories and other public places and (after seeing) what shame, what need, and what misery these girls have suffered. Now since the grounds for allowing polygamy lie in the extent of the necessities for which it is permitted, and since men as a rule are inclined to it in order to satisfy their eager desire rather than to promote the (general) welfare, and (finally) since perfection (in family life), which is to be aspired to as a basic principle, knows no multiple marriage, polygamy has been approved in Islam, but not as an obligation nor as something that would be recommended as desirable in itself. It is tied to the stipulation that is declared in the noble verse (Sūra 4:3—'But if you fear you will not be equitable, then [marry] only one') and is confirmed and repeated (in the statement: 'Thus, it will be more likely that you will not be partial'). One should contemplate this verse thoughtfully. . . .

NOTES

INTRODUCTION

1 These were the states of Maʿīn, Ṣabaʾ, Qatabān, and Ḥaḍramaut.

2 Ancient southern Arabic, which is known to us through inscriptions, is certainly similar to the northern dialects of Arabia; however, it is even more closely related to ancient Ethiopic.

3 Such states include the kingdoms of the Nabateans in northwestern Arabia, the Palmyrians in the region of Syria, the Lakhmids in the vicinity of Babylonia, and the Ghassānids in Syria, which were tolerated and supported to some extent as buffer states by the surrounding empires. Also, the kingdom of the Kindites existed temporarily in interior Arabia.

4 These were the springtime month of Rajab and the late summer and fall consecutive months of Dhū l-Qaʿda, Dhū l-Ḥijja, and al-Muḥarram. While in ancient times the Arabs sought to assimilate their year to the solar year by inserting extra months occasionally, the Islamic calendar is reckoned strictly according to the lunar year of 354 days (see p. 265, note 25). The months named above are the seventh, eleventh, twelfth, and first months of the year.

5 The names of these goddesses, whose cults were by no means limited to the Meccans, mean: 'the goddess' (cf. Allāh), 'the most powerful one', and 'fate'. The Arabs know other derivations for these names, whose supporters referred to them collectively as *banāt Allāh* (daughters of Allāh). See pp. 141 ff.

6 The word *jinn*, which according to the Muslim lexicographers is derived from *ijtanna* (to be covered), has been connected with the Latin 'genius' by European scholars. Whoever was in league with such a spirit came to be designated as *majnūn* (see p. 9). In contrast to some of the philosophers. Muḥammad and official Islam have acknowledged the existence of the jinn (see p. 9). The jinn could become believers and participate in salvation (see Sūra 72:2 and also p. 169).

7 The word *ḥanīf* appears in the Qur'ān especially in reference to Abraham as one who supported the worship of God alone, thus anticipating Islam. See p. 11, and also pp. 98 f., 99 f., and 245.

8 On the distinction between prophets and messengers, which is not entirely clear, see pp. 54 f. The word *nabī* is derived from the Hebrew *nāḇī* as

well as from the Aramaic *naḇīyā*. Regarding *rasūl* (messenger) cf. the word 'apostle' in Christian usage.

9 Regarding the sons of Muḥammad who died early, see p. 82 and p. 272, note 32. Except for Khadīja, who was Muḥammad's only wife until the time of her death, only the Coptic slave Māriya bore a child through him.

10 See pp. 49 ff.

11 See pp. 62 f.

12 [First published in the *Edinburgh Review* for July 1866, and reprinted in *A Reader on Islam*, ed. Arthur Jeffery (The Hague: Mouton, 1962), p. 20. As an example of an attempt to imitate *saj'* in German, Gätje quotes the following translation of Sūra 96:1–8 by Hubert Grimme:

> Trag vor in des Herren Namen,
> der euch schuf aus blutigem Samen!
> Trag vor! Er ist der Geehrte,
> der mit dem Schreibrohr lehrte,
> was noch kein Menschenohr hörte.
> Doch der Mensch ist von störrischer Art,
> nicht achtend, dass Er ihn gewahrt.
> Doch zu Gott führt einst die Fahrt.]

13 The term *maulā* designates not only the protector or patron, but also the one protected and the client. The *wilā'*-relationship has its special significance in the emancipation of slaves, where the emancipator becomes the patron of the one emancipated. See p. 210.

14 Literally: 'mother of the book'. This is believed to exist on a heavenly tablet (see pp. 51 f. and p. 268, note 18). Regarding another meaning which is associated with the concept in the Medinan period (see p. 28) of the revelation, see pp. 55 f. and p. 269, note 30.

15 Cain and Abel are not mentioned by name in the Qur'ān, but are referred to as 'sons of Adam'.

16 Among the prophetic forerunners of Muḥammad, one finds some who do not appear in the Bible, such as Hūd (see p. 274, note 41) and Ṣāliḥ (see p. 72 and p. 271, note 8).

17 The word *umma*, meaning '(religious) community, corporate body, people', is a Hebrew as well as Aramaic loan-word (Syriac: *ummthā*). In the Qur'ān it usually designates the national, linguistic, or religious communities which are the subjects of special divine treatment (see pp. 92 ff.). The borrowing of words from the Jewish-Christian sphere is characteristic for this new religion, as is also the practice of giving new meanings to ancient Arabic concepts.

18 The word *mu'jiza* has come to designate the 'verification miracle' of the prophets. It does not appear in the Qur'ān; however, the idea that the people could produce nothing equivalent to the Qur'ān is clearly expressed (Sūra 17:88/90). The individual segments of the revelation in the Qur'ān are called 'signs' (*āyāt*, sing. *āya*). This term then came to be used in the sense of 'verse (of the Qur'ān)'. The verification miracle of the prophets is to be distinguished from the later concept of *karāma*, the gift of miracles which is attributed to the saints (see p. 20).

19 Later, however, within the scope of a glorified image of the Prophet numerous miraculous deeds were attributed to Muḥammad. See p. 81 and p. 271, note 16.

20 In the Qur'ān the People of the Book are only the Jews and Christians. To be sure, the Sabaeans (*ṣābi'īn*) and the Zoroastrians (*majūs*) are mentioned in the Qur'ān and already in early Islam they came to be included among the People of the Book on the basis of specific Traditions. Some scholars consider the Sabaeans to be the Mandaeans, a Jewish-Christian sect in Mesopotamia. Others identify them with the ancient Carrhae, a pagan sect in Ḥarrān influenced by Hellenism, whom many scholars have mentioned and who continued to be among the possessors of the Book for a still longer time in Islam. In the Qur'ān itself the Mandaeans are no doubt intended.

21 See p. 4 and p. 263, note 7.

22 The ritual prayer is to be distinguished from personal prayer (*du'ā*). The word *ṣalāt*, like the term *zakāt*, is derived from the Aramaic. Also, in the meaning of the Arabic words *ṣaum* or *ṣiyām* as 'fast' one sees Jewish–Christian influence at work.

23 The term *ṣadaqa* is also used for 'alms'; however, this term usually refers to the freewill gift as distinguished from the obligatory alms tax called *zakāt*.

24 In contrast to the duty of the individual (*farḍ al-'ain*), this is a duty of 'sufficiency' (*farḍ al-kifāya*). One other duty of this kind is, for example, the participation of a sufficient number of believers at Friday worship in the mosque.

25 See p. 263, note 4. Perhaps Muḥammad thereby held to a calendar commonly used in the moon cult. The year 1 of the Islamic era begins with 16 July 622 of the Gregorian calendar.

26 The word *imām* means 'example, leader, model, guiding principle' (see pp. 93 and 25). It then became the designation for the leader of the common prayer in the mosque, then it came to be used by the Sunnites as a title of honour for distinguished scholars (see p. 248), and in Shī'ite circles it has become in some respects a synonym of *khalīfa* (caliph).

27 Regarding the terms *sunna* and *jamā'a*, see p. 16 and p. 273, note 2. The Sunnites claim that they follow the 'custom' (*sunna*) of the Prophet and eschew any deviation in both dogmatic and practical matters.

28 The word *ḥadīth* originally meant 'announcement, narrative, story' and then came to be used as the designation for the individual Tradition and also for the collection of Traditions as a whole.

29 See pp. 66 f.

30 The word *fiqh* (properly 'intelligence, understanding') gradually came to be the name for jurisprudence in Islam. In older theological language the term *fiqh* was used, in contrast to *'ilm* (knowledge), to mean that knowledge which was based on independent intellectual activity regarding questions about which the Qur'ān and the Tradition did not contain decisive statements. The word *fiqh* also could then designate theology in the sense of an interpretation of the content of faith and corresponding statements in the form of confessions of faith.

31 That one could later see *ra'y* in a positive sense, so far as it does not rest on prejudice, is shown by al-Ghazzālī (see pp. 228 f.), who in contrast to orthodoxy also claims for himself the right of individual investigation (*ijtihād*, properly 'effort', see below).

32 The word *taqlīd* properly means 'putting on a necklace' (*qilāda*), and then also it came to mean 'clothing with authority' and the unquestioning adoption of doctrines, whereby one wished to distinguish between legitimate and illegitimate authoritative beliefs (see pp. 139 f.).

33 For the Mu'tazilites as well as later orthodox believers, namely the Ash'arites (see pp. 19 f.), were supporters of coercion, because they did not acknowledge absolute freedom of will. Zamakhsharī frequently refers to his opponents on this point as 'the Mujbira'.

34 *'Iṣma* properly means 'shelter, preservation' etc., and then became a term for sinlessness and infallibility, in the sense of a shelter with which God protects his prophets. This characteristic is attributed to Muḥammad and according to some scholars also to the other prophets. The theologians have diverging opinions regarding the nature, extent, and beginning of this sinlessness (whether it existed already before the call to prophethood, etc.).

35 The term *shafā'a* appears in the Qur'ān mainly in the negative sense, in contexts where it is stated that there shall be no intercession on the Last Day. However, some positive statements are also made, providing a Qur'ānic basis for the later doctrine of the intercession of the Prophet, which became acknowledged through consensus.

36 See p. 264, note 18.

37 [On the spelling of the name al-Ghazzālī, see *Journal of the Royal Asiatic Society* (1902), pp. 18–22; and for arguments in favour of the spelling 'al-Ghazālī', see W. Montgomery Watt, *Muslim Intellectual: A Study of al-Ghazālī* (Edinburgh University Press, 1963), pp. 181–3.]

38 The word *bid'a* has primarily a negative meaning and is used variously after its introduction into traditional accepted thought. However, innovations which are praiseworthy and do not run contrary to traditional sources of belief are also recognized, as for example the use of Arabic philology for the understanding of the Qur'ān.

39 With reference to this term one speaks also of the movement of the *salafiyya*.

40 See p. 264, note 18.

41 Thus, for example, a fragment could be integrated into the text because at the time of the compilation it was written on the back of a sheet or other material containing a text from another context on the front side. [It should be pointed out here that this is one of Richard Bell's theories, which significantly affected the format of his two-volume translation of the Qur'ān. For W. Montgomery Watt's critique of this proposal as a dominant factor in the compilation of the Qur'ān, see Watt's work entitled *Bell's Introduction to the Qur'ān* (Edinburgh University Press, 1970), pp. 101–7.]

42 Separate schools of Qur'ānic readers developed in Kūfa and other cities which received copies of the Qur'ān prepared by the 'Uthmānic redaction commission.

43 According to the orthodox view, abrogation applies only to regulations and not to statements which are subject to the criterion of truth (see pp. 158 and 180). Whether or not a verse of the Qur'ān can be regarded as having been abrogated on the basis of a Tradition is disputed (see p. 59).
44 See p. 266, note 41.
45 See pp. 17 and 31f.
46 Since the tenth century a system of seven canonical readings of the Qur'ān, which later were expanded, have been known. [See Watt, *Bell's Introduction to the Qur'ān*, pp. 47–50.]
47 For example, the passage 'which however became disunified' after the statement 'The people were one community (*umma*)' in Sūra 2:213/209, which is found in the reading of 'Abd Allāh ibn Mas'ūd (see p. 93).
48 For instance, 'Alī is said to have read 'And Noah called to *their* (unbelieving) son' instead of 'And Noah called to his (unbelieving) son' in Sūra 11:42/44 (see pp. 104 f.), thus affirming that this was not Noah's own son, but a child that his wife had brought into the marriage. It would be shocking if the actual son of a prophet were unbelieving. Theological motives have led to alterations in the text especially within the sphere of the Shī'a. (See pp. 39 and 239 ff.).
49 [For readers of this English edition, the Qur'ān translation by Arthur J. Arberry (which is followed in the present work) and the more recent translations by Pir Salahud-Din and Muḥammad Zafrulla Khan should also be mentioned. See bibliography.]
50 See p. 264, note 18.
51 [It should be noted that, although in later usage the term *ummī* for theological reasons came to mean 'unlettered' or 'illiterate' and was especially applied to Muḥammad, in the Qur'ān there is no evidence to suggest that this meaning was known during Muḥammad's lifetime. The Qur'ānic meaning of the term *ummī* seems to be 'native', 'belonging to the (Arab) community', or possibly 'belonging to the common people'. See Rudi Paret, *Der Koran: Kommentar und Konkordanz* (Stuttgart, 1971), pp. 21–2.]
52 See pp. 17 and 24.
53 See p. 265, note 30.
54 The word *tafsīr* is used also for commentaries on scientific and philosophical works, in which case it is interchangeable with *sharḥ* (explanation, interpretation).
55 [As distinguished from Ṭabarī's other major work, a multi-volume history of the world, commonly cited as *Annals*.]
56 This is not always apparent in the texts of Ṭabarī translated here, because most of these must be summarized in the interest of space and readability.
57 See perhaps pp. 123 f.
58 See pp. 65 f., 95 and 125.
59 Sūra 3:7/5. On this topic, see pp. 55 ff. and p. 232.
60 [German: 'elendes Gewebe von Lügen und Dummheiten', a description given by Theodor Nöldeke, *Geschichte des Qorāns*, 2nd ed (edited by Friedrich Schwally), II, p. 180.]
61 On this title, see Sūra 83:27. The Tasnīm is regarded as a spring in paradise.

62 See pp. 249 f.

I. REVELATION

1 Sūra 28:7/6
2 Sūra 37:102/100 f.
3 According to Zamakhsharī neither the attribute of speech nor that of signt can be ascribed directly to God. See pp. 19, 36, 162 f., etc. Regarding the present verse, see also pp. 158 f.
4 Sūra 4:164/162 (see p. 46) and 19:52/53. According to the Tradition, in the case of Moses God created the speech in the bush on Mount Sinai (see p. 175).
5 Baiḍāwī accepts the doctrine of *bi-lā kaifa* and regards speech as a positive attribute of God (see p. 19).
6 Literally, *it*.
7 Arabic, *bait al-muqaddas* or *bait al-maqdis* (house of holiness). This is a translation of the Hebrew *bēth ham-miqdāsh*, which designated the Temple of Solomon and then, along with other designations, became a name for Jerusalem.
8 The last part of this saying has become proverbial.
9 Ramaḍān is the ninth month of the Islamic lunar year. The name indicates that in ancient times this month fell in the hot part of the year. See p. 263, note 4.
10 The exact date of the Night of Destiny is not known. It is regarded as certain that it is one of the last five odd-numbered nights of Ramaḍān. [See, however, K. Wagtendonk, *Fasting in the Koran* (Leiden: E. J. Brill, 1968), pp. 97–122, where it is argued that the *lailat al-qadr* was originally the *lailat al-mi'rāj* (the night of Muḥammad's ascension to heaven) which falls on the 27th of Rajab.]
11 By Torah (*taurāt*) is probably meant here the entire Hebrew Bible, as it is sometimes designated by the Jews themselves.
12 Literally, *in it*.
13 The eighth month of the Islamic lunar year. What is meant is the night before the 15th of Sha'bān.
14 A *rak'a* is the bending at the waist with the preceding erect position and the two following prostrations in the ritual prayer (*ṣalāt*).
15 A tribe of Syrian-Arab nomads with large holdings in livestock.
16 See pp. 48 f.
17 The concept of seven heavens (see Sūra 2:29/27, etc.) is an ancient oriental idea. One might think of the seven planetary deities of the Babylonians.
18 In the doctrine of the well-preserved tablet are combined two separate concepts. On the one hand, the tablet contains the divine revelation in its 'original text' (*umm al-kitāb*), which is preserved here against alterations (see Sūra 85:22). On the other hand, the tablet is also the receptacle for the unalterable divine decisions and decrees (see p. 52 and p. 264, note 14). The expression 'original text' (*umm al-kitāb*) is also used in the latter sense (see p. 184).

19 ['It' here may refer either to the 'Arabic Qur'ān' mentioned in v. 3/2 or to the 'clear Book' in v. 2/1.]
20 *Abāna* (participle: *mubīn*) means not only 'to be clear', but also 'to make clear, to clarify, to separate, to distinguish'.
21 *La'alla* usually appears as a designation for something hoped for or feared.
22 See p. 264, note 14 and p. 268, note 18.
23 See pp. 7 f. and p. 264, note 14, etc.
24 See p. 9 and p. 264, note 18, etc.
25 See pp. 105 ff.
26 Referring to Muḥammad.
27 In the Tradition the messengers are not all mentioned by name, to say nothing of the prophets.
28 Namely, al-Lāt, al-'Uzzā, and Manāt (see pp. 3 and 141 ff.), who are represented in Sūra 53:23 as 'mere names'. That Muḥammad was once near to permitting his opponents to influence him in the recitation of the revelation is shown in Sūra 17:73f., 75f. (see pp. 73f.).
29 See pp. 36 and 232.
30 Thus, here not all verses of the Qur'ān are part of the *umm al-kitāb* as above pp. 51 f. See p. 264, note 14.
31 The following examples comprise two pairs, each of which contains one clear verse and one ambiguous verse.
32 See pp. 156 ff.
33 See pp. 162 f. and also p. 156. As a Mu'tazilite, Zamakhsharī refused to attribute actual visibility to God; thus, the 'gazing' must have a special meaning.
34 According to Mu'tazilite doctrine, God commands nothing evil. See p. 222.
35 [This is an allusion to Sūra 74:27–31/34. Bell, *Qur'ān*, p. 618, regards the long passage, vv. 31/31–34, as a later, Medinan addition and explanation of the number nineteen in v. 30. For additional literature on this topic, see Paret, *Kommentar*, p. 494.]
36 [It should be noted that both Paret and Arberry adopt the alternative interpretation. Paret: 'Aber niemand weiss es (wirklich) zu deuten ausser Gott. Und diejenigen, die ein gründliches Wissen haben, sagen: "Wir glauben daran."' And Arberry: 'And none knows its interpretation, save only God. And those firmly rooted in knowledge say, "We believe in it."' Cf. the translation of the same passage at the beginning of this section, where Gätje has adopted the interpretation of Zamakhsharī.]
37 According to Ignaz Goldziher (*Die Richtungen der islamischen Koranauslegung*, p. 24), this is the correct reading, while *nansa'hā* and *tansahā* are to be attributed to theological considerations (see pp. 29 f.). That God commits something to oblivion cannot be reconciled with the immutability of the divine will. [It should be noted that, although Zamakhsharī adopts the reading *nansa'hā* at this point, both the official Cairo edition and the Flügel edition have *nunsihā*.]
38 Although soothsaying exhibits a certain similarity to the Qur'ān in its rhymed prose and also, as a rule, in diction and themes (see pp. 3 and 6),

poetry is distinguished from the Qur'ān even externally through its strict metric construction and specific requirements concerning rhyme. There are also important distinctions in themes; see below.

39 Literally, *him*.

40 That is, the good news which Muḥammad brings.

41 There are differing Traditions concerning Muḥammad's ability to read and write (see p. 7). When Muḥammad is represented here as illiterate, what is being said is that he could not have acquired knowledge from earlier revealed books. The word *ummī*, which is connected with *umma* (see p. 264, note 17), however, does not have the meaning 'gentilis', but 'vulgaris'. [See also p. 267, note 51.]

42 *Rajaz* is a relatively simply organized metre, in which in ancient times not only the verses but also the hemistichs had to rhyme.

43 Regarding the jinn, see p. 263, note 6.

44 For the Mu'tazilites, reason is a source of understanding which stands next to revelation on an equal basis. See pp. 19, 36, 216 ff, etc.

45 According to the Mu'tazilite view, God is required to punish evil and reward good, since a statement to this effect has been issued. See pp. 19 and 36.

46 In this connection some have called attention to the practice of wrapping oneself in a shroud among the ecstatics and visionaries. However here, as also at the beginning of Sūra 73, one could just as well think of someone who has covered himself in his mantle for the night and now has been summoned to arise.

47 See p. 5.

48 See p. 5.

49 The word *abb* is also derived from the Aramaic (cf. the Syriac *ebbā*).

50 See p. 109. Either the travellers who found Joseph in the cistern or Joseph's brothers could be meant here. In the following text from Ṭabarī, the separate Traditions are omitted.

51 The *uqiyya* (ounce), as was found in Mecca in early Islamic times, amounted to 125 grams.

52 *Iḥyā 'ulūm ad-din* (Istanbul, 1318–22 A.H./1900–4) I, p. 254.

53 *Ibid.*, I, pp. 17 f.

54 To which belong certain parts of speculative theology (*kalām*) and philosophy (*falsafa*).

55 On the following, see pp. 16 ff.

56 [On the Qur'ānic usage of the term *ummī* and the later development of its meaning, see p. 267, note 51.]

57 [A 'defective chain' is one in which two or more successive links in the chain of authorities could not have had contact with each other, usually because they did not live at the same time and place.]

II. MUḤAMMAD

1 [Gätje, following Paret, renders this phrase: *was von der Thora vor mir da war* (what was there of the Torah before me), thus eliminating the problem

that the term Torah in the Qur'ān is usually interpreted as referring to the entire Hebrew Bible which was not complete at the time of Jesus.]

2 Or: 'with a highly praiseworthy name' (*ismuhū aḥmadu*). Apparently, Muḥammad had already referred this verse to himself and this is an allusion to his name (which means 'the praiseworthy one, the one who is praised').

3 Here Jesus is seen as not being the son of a Jew.

4 Referring to the battle at Uḥud (March 625), in which Muḥammad was injured.

5 'Abd Allāh ibn Ubayy was at the head of the Medinan 'hypocrites', while Abū Sufyān was the leader of the pagan Meccans against Muḥammad.

6 Literally, *they*.

7 Literally, *him*.

8 Ṣāliḥ, the prophet of the ancient Arab tribe of Thamūd (see pp. 118 f.), had as his miracle of verification of prophethood a she-camel (Sūra 7:73/71), which according to the Tradition was born out of a rock. Concerning Jesus' miracle of verification of prophethood, see pp. 123 ff.

9 Literally, *they*.

10 Literally, *they*.

11 Literally, *it*.

12 See p. 10. According to the Tradition, the event described in the following is said to have occurred in the ninth year after the Hijra.

13 See pp. 3, 141 ff., etc. The main sanctuary of al-Lāt was a four-sided boulder in the Valley of Wajj near aṭ-Ṭa'if.

14 [Paret translates *al-masjid al-aqṣā* as 'fernen Kultstätte', and Arberry renders this expression 'Further Mosque'. The English translation here follows Gätje who follows Zamakhsharī.]

15 That is, God.

16 Together with the ascension (*mi'rāj*) of Muḥammad mentioned below, the night journey to Jerusalem (*isrā*), concerning which there are various Traditions, is regarded by Muslims as a kind of miracle, although Muḥammad himself says in numerous passages in the Qur'ān (e.g., Sūra 13:7/8; 17:93/95) that he is nothing but an ordinary person (see also pp. 70 ff.). However, other miraculous deeds also came to be attributed to Muḥammad (see p. 81).

17 In Arabic this word is indeterminative, although here according to Zamakhsharī it has a specific meaning.

18 The concept *ash-sha'm* is more extensive than that of modern Syria and included Palestine also.

19 The German 'Moschee' [and the English 'mosque'] come from the Arabic *masjid* [through the French 'mosquée']. What is meant is the mosque at Mecca, which lies within the greater area of jurisdiction of Mecca (see p. 2).

20 Burāq (who is not mentioned in the Qur'ān) is the amazing animal on which Muḥammad is believed to have undertaken the night journey and the ascension.

21 The idea of an ascension to heaven by Muḥammad is connected with the

vision portrayed in Sūra 53:1 ff. (see p. 166). There are differing Traditions about the ascension and its relationship with the night journey.

22 Or: 'the house which was (well) maintained' (see Sūra 52:4). What is referred to here is an abode that is situated over the Ka'ba in one of the various heavens.

23 See Sūra 53:14. According to later interpretation this tree stands in the seventh heaven and shades paradise. [Also, the rivers of pure water, milk, wine, and honey mentioned in Sūra 47:15f./16f. are said to flow from the roots of this tree. See pp. 180 ff.]

24 According to another interpretation, this is the farthest spot in the seventh heaven, from which the angels pay homage to God.

25 Literally, *they*.

26 That is, Muḥammad.

27 *Laḥd*, in contrast to the simple vertical grave (*ḍarīḥ*), is a grave with a niche for the corpse in the lateral wall.

28 Literally, 'through hearing'. See pp. 217 f.

29 Mecca was conquered in January 630, while Sūra 48:1–17 was proclaimed well after the Treaty of Ḥudaibiya which Muḥammad concluded with the Meccans in March 628 (see p. 12).

30 The successful military expedition against the Jews in Khaibar probably occurred in May 628. After this, the Jews of Fadak submitted voluntarily.

31 The Persians had inflicted a heavy defeat upon the Byzantines in 613/14 and had carried off the cross from Jerusalem. Emperor Herakleios I forced the Persians to an armistice in 628 and in 629 carried the cross back to Jerusalem.

32 This son, who died young, was born to Muḥammad by the Coptic slave Māriya as his only child after the death of Khadīja. Regarding the other sons, none of whom lived beyond tender childhood, the Traditions differ to some extent as to number and names. See p. 5.

33 See pp. 129 f.

34 Regarding the doctrine of God's support (*taufīq*), see pp. 19, 153 ff., etc.

35 Muḥammad had set free and adopted his slave Zaid ibn Ḥāritha, one of the first adherents of Islam. Zaid then married Muḥammad's cousin Zainab bint Jaḥsh, from whom he separated, however, when Muḥammad took a liking for her (in 627).

36 The waiting period after divorce lasts for three menstrual periods or three months for non-menstruating women. Pregnant women may first enter into a new marriage forty days after the delivery.

37 According to Islamic law one should celebrate the wedding during a feast.

38 Regarding the coexistence of reason and revelation, see pp. 19, 36, 216 ff., etc.

39 Honorary title for the wives of Muḥammad.

40 Literally, *them*.

41 The amount of the *mahr al-mithl* is set according to the position, age, beauty, and other characteristics of the woman.

42 *Dār al-ḥarb*, in contrast to *dār al-islām*, is the non-Islamic territory, which gradually has to be conquered.

43 That is, the wives of Muḥammad.

44 All together, Muḥammad is believed to have had fourteen legitimate wives; but the identity of these is in part disputed. Moreover, some had already died.

III. SALVATION HISTORY

1 Literally, *they*, meaning the followers of earlier revealed religions.
2 Regarding the term *umma* as '(religious) community', see p. 264, note 17. In contrast to this Qur'ānic term is the word *jamā'a* with the meaning 'community (of believers)' which belongs to later linguistic usage.
3 Regarding this addition, see p. 267, note 47.
4 Cf. Sūra 2:124/118, where Abraham is represented as an example (*imām*) for the people. One should also notice the similarity between the words *umma* and *imām*.
5 Ascribing to the word *umma* the meaning of *imām* is not the same as interpreting it *pro toto*, as is done here.
6 In the Qur'ān, both the 'Children of Israel' (*banū isrā'īl*) and the Jews (*yahūd*) are mentioned. Evidently, at a later period, Muḥammad designated the contemporary Jews as *yahūd* and the ancestors as Children of Israel. [The contexts of Ṭabarī's references to the 'Jews among the Children of Israel', as well as 'these groups of the Children of Israel' suggest that Jews and Christians are both regarded as 'among the Children of Israel'. See pp. 99 and 124.]
7 See p. 11 and especially pp. 130 ff.
8 In Islam the fast is prescribed only during the daytime during the month of Ramaḍān and on the other fast days which are commanded.
9 See p. 263, note 7.
10 See Sūra 4:125/124.
11 See pp. 130 ff.
12 The Qur'ān mentions Abraham in a number of passages and includes several stories about him, including the story of the offering of his son (Sūra 37:102 ff./100 ff.), although it is not stated whether this son is Ishmael or Isaac. Regarding Abraham as the one who built or purified the Ka'ba and as harbinger of Islam, see pp. 11 and 100 ff.
13 See Sūra 9:30 and pp. 126 f.
14 Noah enjoys special popularity in the Qur'ān and in the Muslim legends. He came as a prophet and warner to his people, who however displayed widespread unbelief. Muḥammad is strongly portrayed in the role of this prophet. Regarding the flood, see pp. 8 and 147 f.
15 Jesus is the herald of the Last Judgment. See p. 129.
16 In addition to this son, Qur'ānic exegetes also know the biblical sons of Noah, namely Shem, Ham, and Japheth.
17 Regarding the beginning of this sūra, see above pp. 52 f. See also p. 65. Joseph belongs among the favourites of Islamic legends, which in part appeal to the haggadic sources for information. [This entire section on Joseph and his brothers comes from Baiḍāwī's commentary.]
18 Literally, *He*.

19 Baiḍāwī appeals here to a philosophical interpretation of dreams, based on a later development of Aristotelian psychology.
20 Regarding the temptation of Adam and Eve, see Sūra 2:35f./33f. and 7:19 ff./18 ff. (see pp. 170 f.).
21 Here the traditional doctrine concerning dreams is placed with the philosophical teaching about dreams.
22 See pp. 99 f.
23 See Sūra 21:68f.
24 See p. 273, note 12.
25 See p. 53.
26 Actually eleven names are mentioned here, if one regards Benjamin as a full brother. Dinah is, of course, a girl in the Bible.
27 This is prohibited in Sūra 4:27/23.
28 The parasang measured about six kilometres [or three and a half miles].
29 See Sūra 19:12/13 and 30/31.
30 [A term meaning 'mighty, powerful, highly esteemed'; but in this context it is a title meaning 'overlord'.]
31 Corrupted from Potiphar.
32 Shu'aib is a prophet who is often mentioned in the Qur'ān. Later interpreters identify him with Jethro, the father-in-law of Moses.
33 Literally, *He*.
34 Literally, *He*.
35 See p. 271, note 18.
36 Not mentioned by name in the Qur'ān, but alluded to in Sūra 5:23/26, where he is meant in a reference to the two devout men, Joshua and Caleb.
37 In contrast to Job, not mentioned by name in the Qur'ān.
38 That is, the story of Joseph.
39 Literally, *them*.
40 According to the Qur'ān, Solomon understood the language of birds and animals (Sūra 27:16), he ruled the wind and the spirits (34:12 f./11 f., etc.), and his army consisted of spirits, people, and birds (27:17). He plays a leading role in the legends and is regarded as one of the four world rulers, of whom two were unbelievers (Nimrod and Nebuchadnezzar) and two were believers (Alexander the Great and Solomon).
41 Regarding the Thamūd, see p. 271, note 8. The 'Ād, according to tradition, lived after the time of Noah and were a powerful people to whom the prophet Hūd was sent.
42 Literally, *he*.
43 Paret translates: 'Katastrophe' here and also in Sūra 13:31 (see p. 246) and 101:1–3/1–2 (see p. 176). [Arberry translates: 'Clatterer' in 69:4 and 101:1–3/1–2, and 'shattering' in 13:31.]
44 According to Sūra 11:67/70 it was the 'cry', and according to Sūra 41:17/16 it was the 'thunderbolt of the chastisement of humiliation', which came upon the Thamūd (see also p. 166).
45 The tenth month of the Islamic year.
46 In the confrontation between Lot and the inhabitants of Sodom, Muḥammad saw a similar contrast to that between himself and the pagan Meccans. According to the Qur'ān, the people of Lot were destroyed by a rain of stones (11:82/84) or a sandstorm (54:34). See also, however, p. 166.

47 [The term *ar-rūm*, which occurs only once in the Qur'ān, at the beginning of Sūra 30, which is called *Sūrat ar-rūm*, refers to the Eastern Roman Empire and means 'the Byzantines'. Baiḍāwī, however, refers here to Alexander the Great at *rūmī* (actually, 'Byzantine').]

48 Dhū l-Qarnain is also the nickname of the Lakhmid king, Mundhir III. In the Qur'ān, however, the name Dhū l-Qarnain clearly refers to Alexander the Great, who above all was known through the so-called 'Alexander saga'. This name may stem from an unknown version of this legend.

49 [See p. 274, note 40.]

50 That is, Jesus.

51 [Reading *al-mashraqa* (which means both 'eastern' and 'sunny') here and where indicated in the text above, instead of *al-mashrafa* (elevated spot) which appears in both places in Ṭabarī's text (Cairo edition, 1373 A.H./1954).]

52 Some have seen in the account to which these verses belong a reference to various stories of the New Testament, such as the vision of Peter in Acts 10:10 ff. and the story of the feeding of the multitude in Matthew 14:17 ff., and 15:32 ff. If this Qur'ānic account refers to the Eucharist, then the statements about it are confused. In the following text by Ṭabarī, the numerous individual Traditions are again omitted.

53 As a Mu'tazilite, Zamakhsharī refuses any anthropomorphism in statements about God (see pp. 19 and 36, etc.).

54 The *dajjāl*, who does not appear in the Qur'ān itself, is derived from Christian views. See the false Christ of Matthew 24:24 (Syriac: *mshīḥē daggālē*).

IV. ISLAM, THE 'BOOK RELIGIONS', AND PAGANISM

1 See pp. 246 f.

2 See p. 265, note 20.

3 See p. 11.

4 The present verses date from the time when Muḥammad had already broken with the Jews, but still felt united with the Christians.

5 Paret translates: *die sich (Gott) ergeben haben* ['who had surrendered themselves (to God)'. Gätje translates: *die den Zustand des Islams angenommen haben* (who had embraced Islam)]. See the commentary of Zamakhsharī.

6 Note the special view-point of the Mu'tazila, who deny real attributes to God (see p. 19).

7 In the earliest period of Islam every person guilty of unchastity was stoned. Later this punishment was mitigated through Muḥammad to flogging (Sūra 24:2 ff./3 ff.). The second caliph, 'Umar, however, is said to have recalled very clearly the 'stoning verse', which is missing in the present text of the Qur'ān, and as a result, from then on certain categories of people found guilty of unchastity also were stoned.

8 See the following verses of the sūra.

9 The words *jibt* and *ṭāghūt*, which here designate the objects of idolatry, apparently came into Arabic from Ethiopic. [Although Zamakhsharī

interprets the term *aṭ-ṭāghūt* to mean Satan, the consensus of Western scholars is that it is a general generic term meaning 'idols'. See Arthur Jeffery, *The Foreign Vocabulary in the Qur'ān* (Baroda, 1938), pp. 202 f. and additional references in Paret, *Kommentar*, p. 55.]

10 Or: *pronounce to be forbidden.*

11 See p. 11.

12 Although the term *yad* specifically means 'hand', it also has the meaning 'power, control, influence, authority, assistance, etc.'

13 Regarding *taqlīd* as the opposite of *ijtihād*, see pp. 17 f.

14 Literally, *their calling* [as in Arberry. Gätje, following Paret, has: 'die Gebete ihrer Verehrer'.]

15 That is, those who regard such beings as divine and worship them.

16 See p. 3, and p. 263, note 5, etc.

17 This event occurred after the capitulation of Mecca in the year 630. The goddess al-'Uzzā was connected especially with the Ghaṭafān, whose pasture area was east of Khaibar and on the edge of the Ḥijāz. The main sanctuary, however, is believed to have been in the valley of Nakhla.

18 The main sanctuary of Manāt, a black stone, was located among the Hudhailites in Qudaid, to the north of Mecca on the way to Medina. This goddess was worshipped by many Arab tribes.

19 Actually the expression *al-ukhrā* might be occasioned by the rhyme.

20 See p. 198.

21 These tribes were dispersed over various parts of the Arabian peninsula. To some extent these gods were also worshipped by other tribes.

22 Regarding Iblīs, see p. 278, note 11.

23 Knots, spittle, and blowing were used in ancient Arab paganism in both harmful and non-harmful magic. In Islam the death penalty was imposed for sorcery. Although the efficacy of sorcery is clearly acknowledged in the present sūra, Zamakhsharī as a Mu'tazilite who opposed unbelief, questions its real existence.

V. GOD

1 Or, *they comprehend nothing of the knowledge concerning it* (see pp. 157 f.). [Gätje translates simply: *Sie aber wissen nichts davon* (they however know nothing of it).]

2 That is, the heavens and the earth.

3 This verse is well known as the so-called 'Throne Verse'. Many exegetes identify the chair, which is mentioned here, with the throne (*'arsh*) of God (see pp. 148 ff., 164 ff., etc.); however, others, as is indicated by Zamakhsharī, think that the chair (*kursī*) is a kind of footstool before the throne. Significantly for Zamakhsharī as a Mu'tazilite again is the attempt to keep the conception of God free from anthropomorphic features.

4 Literally, *it*. Regarding the Flood, see pp. 8 and 102 ff.

5 See pp. 233 ff.

6 This creation story, which is treated variously in the Qur'ān, is based on the account in the Hebrew Bible. While the total time required for the

creation is mentioned, the individual stages are not clearly specified, and thus the views of the exegetes also vary. See the following.

7 This viewpoint (see p. 19) is adopted by Baiḍāwī, in contrast to Zamakhsharī (see pp. 146 ff.).

8 According to verse 9/8 of the sūra (see pp. 149 f.). Then in verse 10/9 the provisioning of the earth and the (entire) four-day period are treated. While Baiḍāwī is of the opinion that at first the heavens were created in two days and then the earth and its provisions were created in a further four days, Zamakhsharī includes the creation of the heavens in the two periods of the creation and provisioning of the earth.

9 The term *takhyīl* refers to something which is represented as existing, although in reality it cannot exist. The simile, on the other hand, is used to relate something which is imagined. In general, Muslim scholars regard the Qur'ān as exalted above the fantastic illusions discussed here by Zamakhsharī as a means for avoiding anthropomorphic conceptions of God.

10 The first man here is Adam. According to Zamakhsharī, the water (*mā'*) here is the sperm. See the commentary to Sūra 23:12f.

11 Literally, *heart* (*al-af'ida*).

12 In accordance with the traditional editions of the Qur'ān [including both the Flügel and official Cairo editions], Paret reads *khalaqahū* and translates: (*Er*) *der alles, was er geschaffen hat, gut gemacht hat* ([He] who made good everything which he created). Zamakhsharī also records this interpretation.

13 Paret: *darin, dass die Winde wechseln; in den Wolken, die zwischen Himmel und Erde in Dienst gestellt sind* (in which the winds turn about; in which the clouds are placed in service between heaven and earth). This interpretation is also recorded in Baiḍāwī.

14 On the doctrine of divine support and benevolence, see p. 19. Concerning this verse, see also pp. 240 f.

15 Literally, *them*.

16 The Arabic *adraka* can mean 'attain, reach, overtake' as well as 'grasp (physically or mentally), comprehend, perceive, understand', etc. Concerning this verse, see also p. 56, where Zamakhsharī interprets the 'reaching' clearly in the sense of 'seeing'.

17 *Aḥāṭa* means primarily 'surround, comprise, encircle', but then also 'know thoroughly, grasp fully, understand'. What is meant here is thorough comprehension.

18 Here and also in the other contexts below, various individual Traditions are omitted.

19 See pp. 162 f. and also p. 56.

20 See p. 146 [and p. 276, note 1].

21 See p. 180 and p. 267, note 43.

22 See pp. 45 f.

23 See p. 166.

24 Zamakhsharī also does this (see p. 162).

25 Ṭabarī then attempts to refute in detail the divergent views.

26 See pp. 56 and 156 f.

27 [Paret translates the term *fāqira* as 'eine Brandkerbe' (a burning perforation); Arberry translates, 'the Calamity'; and Gätje, following Zamakhsharī, translates, 'eine (Wirbelsäulen)erkrankung' (a [back-breaking] sickness). The term *fāqira* is usually associated with *faqār* (spine, vertebrae); however, Bell notes that the verb *faqara* is used for 'making an incision in the snout of a camel in which to insert the leading-rope, and, as faces are here spoken of, this is appropriate' (*Qur'ān*, p. 622, note 1). Bell thus translates this verse: 'One would think holes were being bored in them.']

VI. ANGELS, SPIRITS, AND MANKIND

1 Regarding the Throne of God and Zamakhsharī's interpretation of it, see pp. 146 f. and p. 276, note 3.
2 The name of one of the archangels, who probably goes back to the Hebrew Serāfīm, just as the Arabic word for 'angel' (*malak*, *mal'ak*, originally 'messenger') apparently stems from the Hebrew. In contrast with Gabriel and Michael, Isrāfīl is not mentioned by name in the Qur'ān.
3 Regarding the relationship between faith and reason according to the Mu'tazilites, see pp. 19, 36, 216 ff., etc.
4 The angels are created out of light, the spirits (*jinn*) out of fire, and man out of earth (see pp. 169 f.).
5 Or: *It*, that is, the Qur'ān.
6 That is, Muḥammad.
7 The vision described here belongs to the complex of events associated with the so-called ascension of Muḥammad (see p. 271, note 16).
8 Regarding the destruction of the people of Lot and the Thamūd, see pp. 118 f.
9 Regarding Iblīs, see p. 278, note 11.
10 See 53:13. [Diḥya was a Companion of the Prophet renowned for his outstanding beauty. See 'Diḥya' in *Ency. of Islam*.]
11 Iblīs is one of the Qur'ānic names for the devil. The word is apparently derived from *διαβολος*. God had commanded the angels to bow down before Adam after he was created, which all except Iblīs did (Sūra 38 : 71ff.; see also 2:34/32, 7:12/11, etc.). However, since on the other hand Iblīs is also designated as one of the spirits (*jinn*) (18:50/48), there are varying views concerning the relationship between Iblīs and the angels and spirits.
12 Literally, *He*.
13 See verse 76/77 of the sūra and 7:12/11. The spirits are also created out of fire (see p. 169 ff.), while the angels are said to be created out of light.
14 In the Qur'ān, angels (Sūra 4:172/170) as well as certain favoured people, like Jesus (3:45/40) are designated as 'those who stand near (God)' (*muqarrabūn*). In general, the theologians, in contrast to the Mu'tazilites and the philosophers, grant the prophets, among whom Adam also belongs, a higher rank than the angels (see p. 171).
15 Regarding the jinn, see p. 263, note 6.
16 The term *jānn* is, in fact, derived from *jinn* and is identical with it.

17 Here and in the following, Baiḍāwī has derived ideas from Greek philosophy.
18 See also Sūra 20:120 f./118 f. According to the Qur'ān, Eve is created out of Adam; but there is no reference to the rib. Both live in paradise, but are driven out after the Fall. Adam then repents and is restored to his elevated rank.
19 See p. 278, note 14.

VII. ESCHATOLOGY

1 See p. 278, note 14.
2 That is, the unbelievers.
3 According to the widespread view, which Zamakhsharī does not, however, accept, God awakens man into a kind of life while he is in the state of death within the grave.
4 Like most Muslims, Zamakhsharī thinks of a corporeal resurrection, whereas some of the philosophers believed only in the resurrection of the soul.
5 The plural appears in the Arabic since what is referred to are the individual 'skins' of various men. [However, see Zamakhsharī's commentary below.]
6 See p. 268, note 4.
7 Paret translates: *Katastrophe*. See p. 274, note 43.
8 In this case the meaning is: 'whose mother is (the hell) Hāwiya.' Concerning the plunge into hell, see also p. 282, note 8.
9 See pp. 187 f. According to the predominant view, unbelief negates good works to the extent that a direct reward, and thus admittance into paradise, is excluded. The views differ in details while the Mu'tazila, on the basis of their view of necessary divine justice (see p. 19), also accept the conclusion that every other grave sin negates good works and is worthy of punishment. Orthodoxy advocates a more generous view-point.
10 Literally, 'the garden' (*al-janna*). The name is thus related to the biblical Garden of Eden. [Note that the Qur'ānic verse here has the plural 'gardens of delight' (*jannāt an-na'īm*). The Qur'ān also speaks of 'gardens of Eden' (*jannāt 'adn*) (Sūra 9:72/73, 18:31/30, etc.).]
11 See p. 158 and p. 267, note 43.
12 That is, the godfearing.
13 Name of a mountain near Mecca and also other mountains.
14 Whom Zamakhsharī regards as the opponents of free will (see p. 266, note 33).
15 *Jahannam*. The word comes from Hebrew through Ethiopic.
16 [Literally, *it*.]
17 Literally, *our misery*.
18 See p. 268, note 18.
19 The evidence cited by Ṭabarī is again only partly reproduced here.
20 See Sūra 40:50/53, where it is mentioned that the prayer of unbelievers fails completely.

21 See pp. 173 f.

VIII. DUTIES AND PROHIBITIONS

1 According to Islamic law, the following actions are punishable: (1) Injuries against life and limb, which justify blood revenge or the claim for expiatory money. (2) Offences for which a specific, unalterable punishment is prescribed either in the Qur'ān or in the Tradition, that is, unchastity, slander with regard to this, the partaking of wine, theft, highway robbery, and according to some, also apostasy, for which the death penalty is given. (3) All other violations against the command of God. Here the punishment is determined by judges.

2 That is, in this world.

3 Recitation of the Qur'ān is considered to be meritorious.

4 That is, the gold and silver which are hoarded.

5 See Sūra 2:177/172 and 9:60, where those who are to receive alms are listed. See also p. 210 f.

6 [Literally, 'seeking the face of God' (*turīdūna wajha-llāh*).]

7 [Or: 'doubled' (*al-muḍʿifūn*).]

8 In Islam one distinguishes between interest involving a business transaction (exchange in return for an object of higher value) and interest involving a loan. Regarding the former, opinions differed at first; however, the view has prevailed that one may charge no interest in business transactions. On the other hand, according to all legal schools any explicit arrangement to charge interest in a loan agreement is unconditionally prohibited. However, many a stratagem (*ḥiyal*) has been employed in order to come to gain, while not violating the letter of the law.

9 That is, he is not required to give up his past earnings through interest.

10 That is, by entering into new interest transactions.

11 See p. 280, note 1, and also p. 275, note 7.

12 That is, if instead of retaliation through killing, only blood money is demanded.

13 That is, by the brother of the deceased person or by one's brother in faith (a fellow-Muslim). See the commentary.

14 This is a reference to the so-called battle of Basūs between the tribes of Bakr and Taghlib, which was caused by an act of violence on the part of the powerful Taghlib chief, Kulaib. It apparently ended towards the beginning of the sixth century.

15 Only the Mālikites do not consider the dog unclean.

16 The term *khamr* apparently stems from the Aramaic. In ancient Arabia there was only a small amount of wine-growing; thus wine was imported from the Syrian-Palestinian and Mesopotamian regions. However, the people used to make all kinds of drinks out of varieties of dates, fruits and the like, which had a more or less intoxicating effect after preparation and aging. Among these belongs *nabīdh* (which is mentioned below), regarding which there is disagreement as to whether it falls within the broader scope of *khamr*.

17 [*Maisir* was actually a specific game of chance practised in Arabia at the time of Muḥammad. It involved the use of arrows for casting lots as a method for dividing a butchered camel. Such arrows were also used for divining purposes and were sometimes associated with certain idols. Arberry translates this term as 'arrow-shuffling'. For references to literature on *maisir*, see Paret, *Kommentar*, p. 46.]
18 In Medina this dry or liquid measure amounted to 12,617 litres; however, the amount and weight varied considerably. Ultimately this was not true regarding the *raṭl* (also mentioned here), which weighed between about 300 and 3,000 grammes.
19 See Sūra 2:260/262.
20 The emancipation of slaves was considered as meritorious. Two kinds of emancipation are the so-called *tadbīr*, the declaration of the master that after his death the slave is to be free, and the method described here, where emancipation is based on an agreement. Perhaps the name *kitāba*, which is derived from *kataba* (to write), comes from the fact that the agreement is fixed in writing. Compare, however, Zamakhsharī's meaning.
21 The slaves have no individual rights until they obtain these with the letter of emancipation.
22 Regarding the word *maulā*, see p. 264, note 13. The former master, as patron, can be an heir to the one who is set free if there are no male blood relatives of the male line.
23 The 'public treasury' is supplied through the alms tax, as well as through other taxes, inheritances, and similar sources, and can be provided directly to the needy and the other people who are entitled to receive it.
24 A rich person is not allowed to accept alms for himself.
25 That is, the Meccan believers.
26 Jumādā l-Ākhira is the sixth month of the Islamic year. In the following month of Rajab a sacred truce was maintained in ancient Arabia. The battle of Badr, which brought Muḥammad a victory over the Meccans, occurred in March 624 according to our chronology. The attack upon 'Amr ibn 'Abd Allāh al-Ḥaḍramī occurred near Nakhla.

IX. DOGMATICS

1 This interpretation means that no-one can be forced into proper faith against his will.
2 See p. 275, note 9.
3 See pp. 11 and 138 f.
4 As a Mu'tazilite, Zamakhsharī considers reason to be a source for religious understanding in addition to the knowledge of revelation that is obtained through hearing or instruction (see pp. 19, 36, etc.). Baiḍāwī deviates consciously from this view-point.
5 See, among others, pp. 32 and 228 ff.
6 See pp. 17 f., 21, 22, etc.
7 According to Muslim tradition Muḥammad promised paradise to ten of his Companions already in their lifetime.

8 According to the Muslim view, when the people are resurrected they must walk across a bridge which stretches over hell, and the damned will fall off into hell, while the blessed pass over into paradise. See p. 241.
9 See p. 14 and p. 265, note 27.
10 While Zamakhsharī as a Mu'tazilite interprets the passage in the sense of free will (see p. 19), Baiḍāwī accepts the Ash'arite view-point of the determinism of the will (see pp. 19 f.). Another interpretation of the passage in the sense of determinism is: 'If God wills, then. . . .'
11 See p. 266, note 33.
12 The Arabic text does not state what it is that is said here to be a lie.
13 See p. 266,
14 The distinction between the metaphor and the simile here is that with the metaphor something is ascribed directly to the subject, which in reality does not belong to it, while with the simile the subject is likened to something else which in fact has the same properties.
15 See p. 219.
16 See p. 56.
17 The possibilities, which have not previously been enumerated, are: (1) The hearts are sealed firmly since God created them thus. (2) The sealing of the hearts is like a sealing which God has actually created in other subjects. (3) God has created the possibility of the sealing, but did not undertake the sealing itself.
18 Literally, *He*.
19 As a Mu'tazilite, Zamakhsharī ascribes to the people themselves individual responsibility for their acts (see p. 19), while the Mujbira (see p. 266, note 33) assert that the acts of people are created and determined by God. According to their view the translation would be: 'When God created you and your doing (i.e., making or acting).'
20 The situation is thus not described in full, as Baiḍāwī interprets it in this case. In the Arabic the object is not specified.

X. MYSTICAL AND PHILOSOPHICAL QUR'ĀNIC EXEGESIS

1 *Iḥyā 'ulūm ad-dīn* (Istanbul, 1318–1322 A.H./1900–4), I, pp. 268 ff. Here, Ghazzālī modifies the concept of interpretation according to individual opinion (see pp. 31 f., etc.) and reserves to himself an individually expressed opinion (see p. 266, note 31). In the acceptance of an outer and an inner meaning, he is influenced by the mystics, acknowledging however the necessity for outer exegesis as the preliminary stage for inner interpretation.
2 Ghazzālī places the intuitive certainty of faith above reason, while in the following text Ibn Rushd takes reason to be a higher authority, to which Qur'ānic exegesis has to be adapted.
3 Ibn Rushd, *Kitāb faṣl al-maqāl*, ed. George F. Hourani (Leiden, 1959), pp. 13 f.
4 [See p. 268, note 18.]

5 See pp. 55 ff. and also 36. [Note that both Paret and Arberry end the sentence with 'except God', thus beginning a new sentence with 'Those firmly rooted in knowledge say: . . . .' See p. 269, note 36.]
6 Paret translates: 'Befehl' (see p. 148) [and Arberry translates: 'command']. The word *amr* has various meanings and signifies 'command, power, dominion' as well as 'matter, affair'. It can also be used in the sense of Logos.
7 The Mahdī ('rightly guided one') is to appear at the end of time as one who restores faith within the world. The Sunnites have other views of the Mahdī than the Shī'ites (see p. 15) and identify the Mahdī in part with Jesus.
8 Compare with this the ancient concept of *εὐκρασία*. Here, as well as in the other texts of Kāshānī, many Greek and especially neo-Platonic influences are at work.
9 That is, above, below, to the right, to the left, before, and behind.
10 Regarding the Throne of God, see p. 276, note 3.
11 [Referring to Moses at Mount Horeb (or Sinai). The significance of the 'holy valley' and the name Ṭuwā have not been satisfactorily explained. See Paret, *Kommentar*, p. 331. Bell (*Qur'ān*, p. 294) suggests a connection with the Syriac *ṭūrā* (Mount).]
12 Literally, *He*.
13 See p. 274, note 32.
14 [The term *taṭbīq* is actually a verbal noun (*maṣdar*) meaning 'adaptation, accommodation', from the verb *ṭabbaqa* (to cover up, to make congruent). Gätje translates *taṭbīq* as 'Parallelisierung', which is also his title for this section of the chapter. See also pp. 40f.]
15 What is meant are the five 'Pillars of Islam' (see p. 11), of which the confession of faith is one.

XI. SHĪ'ITE QUR'ĀNIC EXEGESIS

1 Paret translates *adhilla* as: 'ein bescheidener, unscheinbarer Haufe' (a modest, insignificant group). The word had a negative sense and is thus represented in the commentary as a false reading. Regarding the battle of Badr, see p. 281, note 26.
2 Regarding this, see Kāshānī, above, p. 237. On the interpretation of this verse, see p. 153.
3 See p. 282, note 8.
4 Omitted here is the often-cited interpretation that those who are blessed by God are the Muslims, those against whom God is wrathful are the Jews, and those who have gone astray are the Christians.
5 Regarding the Fāṭimids and their relation to the Imāmites, to whom al-Kāshī belongs, see p. 15.
6 This verse is known as the 'Light Verse' and has received special attention in mystical interpretation of the Qur'ān.
7 Referring to 'Alī, who was to put into effect Muḥammad's will. See p. 284, note 18.

8 [Arberry translates: 'Surely He is All-laudable, All-glorious', thus following the usual interpretation that the pronoun *hu* refers to God and not Abraham. Arberry's translation: 'O people of the House' indicates that he has adopted Paret's suggestion that this is a reference to the Ka'ba. See Bell, *Qur'ān*, p. 212, and Paret's later statement in his *Kommentar*, pp. 239–40.]

9 'Imrān is the father of Moses, Aaron, and Miriam, who in the Qur'ān seems to be identified with the mother of Jesus, so that 'Imrān is identified also as the grandfather of Jesus.

10 Regarding the *qibla*, or direction of prayer, see pp. 11 and 130 ff. In various Traditions the direction of prayer facing Mecca is said to be that of Abraham.

11 See pp. 99 f. [Arberry translates: 'A Muslim and one pure of faith'.]

12 Regarding *qāri'a* as pounder', see pp. 118 f. and 176.

13 The ideas in this text are not fully clear to me. It is evidently thought here that the lights have veiled certain higher stages of emanation in forms to which Muḥammad and 'Alī belong.

14 That is, Muḥammad.

15 '*Ain* is Arabic for 'eye, source, self, substance, individuality', etc. In mysticism, it designates the original or real self. The present text uses the word as an equivalent for God, although at the same time also bringing into play other associations.

16 [The term *mī'ād* (from *wa'ada*, 'to make a promise, to arrange a rendezvous') means both 'promise' and 'rendezvous, appointed time'.]

17 According to Ismā'īlite doctrine, the prophets and imāms are special people who are regarded as 'mediator-veils'.

18 In Shī'ite texts the term *waṣī* appears frequently in reference to 'Alī as the executor of Muḥammad's will (see p. 283, note 7). At times, however, the prophets and also the imāms had an 'executor'. With the imāms this is generally the immediate successor.

19 The term *qā'im* (one who arises) evidently designates here that being whose appearance marks the beginning of the resurrection.

XII. MODERN QUR'ĀNIC EXEGESIS

1 *Ustādh* means 'master, teacher' and is a title for university teachers, but is also used for other scholars and eminent people. The title *imām* (see p. 265, note 26) has been conferred upon eminent scholars by the Sunnites since early times.

2 The dissolving of marriage in Islam generally occurs through repudiation by the man (called *ṭalāq*). This can be effected with or without specific conditions. There is also the *mubāra'a*, a mutual declaration of separation which includes waiving all claims to property and other compensation, and the *khul'*, divorce at the request of the wife, who must pay compensation. Only under specific circumstances can a judge declare the marriage void (*faskh*) on a motion of the wife. Another basis for separation according to the penal code is the so-called curse: the man swears on oath that

the wife has committed adultery and if necessary she swears the opposite. The marriage can also become void of itself (for example, through apostasy).

3 [Regarding the statement 'because they spend their wealth', Paret adds in parentheses: 'als Morgangabe für die Frauen?' (as dowries for the women?). The same suggestion is made by Bell, *Qur'ān*, p. 74.]

4 See pp. 143 and 198.

SELECT BIBLIOGRAPHY

(Prepared for the English edition and annotated by A. T. Welch.)

General and introductory works

Brockelmann, Carl. *Geschichte der arabischen Litteratur*. 2nd edn. 2 vols. Leiden: E. J. Brill, 1943–9; three Supplement vols (to the 1st edn), 1937–42. (Not really a 'history of Arabic literature', but a catalogue of manuscripts and printed works on various topics, with brief descriptions and biographical information.)

The Encyclopaedia of Islam. 1st edn, ed. M. Th. Houtsma *et al*., 4 vols and Supplement, Leiden and London, 1913–38. New Edition, ed. H. A. R. Gibb, J. H. Kramers *et al*., Leiden: E. J. Brill, 1960—(completed to letter K in 1975). (Authoritative, concise articles on all aspects of Islamic life, thought, and history; indispensable reference work.)

Gibb, Hamilton A. R. *Mohammedanism: An Historical Survey*. 2nd edn. London and New York: Oxford University Press, 1953; reprinted with revisions, 1961; Galaxy Book paperback, 1962. (A revision of D. S. Margoliouth's *Mohammedanism* first published in 1911, but still an excellent, concise introduction to Islam.)

Gibb, Hamilton A. R., and Kramers J. H., eds. *Shorter Encyclopaedia of Islam*. Leiden: E. J. Brill, 1953, 1974. (Over 600 articles selected and reprinted from *The Encyclopaedia of Islam*.)

Jeffery, Arthur, ed. and trans. *Islam: Muhammad and His Religion*. New York: Library of Liberal Arts, 1958. (Valuable collection of translations from the Qur'ān and the Muslim traditional literature dealing with the life of Muḥammad and Muslim beliefs and practices.)

———. *A Reader on Islam: Passages from Standard Arabic Writings Illustrative of the Beliefs and Practices of Muslims*. The Hague: Mouton, 1962; Atlantic Highlands, NJ: Humanities Press, 1962.

Pearson, J. D. *Index Islamicus, 1906–1955: A Catalogue of Articles on Islamic Subjects in Periodicals and other Collective Publications*, with Supplements for 1956–60, 1961–5, and 1966–70. Cambridge: W. Heffer, 1958, 1962, 1967, 1972, respectively. (A helpful guide to periodical literature on all Islamic subjects; arranged topically.)

Rahman, Fazlur. *Islam*. London: Weidenfeld & Nicolson, 1966; New York:

Holt, Rinehart & Winston, 1966; Doubleday Anchor Book paperback, 1968. (Combines standard 'Western approach' to the introduction to Islam with insights from the Muslim perspective.)

Sezgin, Fuat. *Geschichte des arabischen Schrifttums.* 5 vols published to date, vol. 6 in press, Leiden: E. J. Brill, 1967–75. (The first volume, the most important for general Islamic studies, is a catalogue of Arabic manuscripts and printed books on Qur'ānic studies, *ḥadīth*, history, jurisprudence, theology, and mysticism.)

Watt, W. Montgomery. *What is Islam?* The introductory volume in the Arab Background Series, ed. N. A. Ziadeh. London: Longmans, 1968; New York: Praeger, 1968. (Possibly the best general introduction to Islam available in Engish.)

Arabia before Islam

Grohmann, Adolf. 'Al-'Arab', first section: 'The Ancient History of the Arabs', *Encyclopaedia of Islam.* New Edition, I, pp. 524–7.

Ibn al-Kalbī, Hishām. *The Book of Idols.* Translation of the *Kitāb al-aṣnām* with introduction and notes by Nabih Amin Faris. Princeton University Press, 1952. (Survey of religious beliefs and practices of 'pre-Islamic' Arabia written in the late eighth or early ninth century.)

Moscati, Sabatino. *Ancient Semitic Civilizations.* Translation of *Storia e civiltà dei Semiti.* London: Elek, 1957; New York: Putnam, 1958; Capricorn Giant Series paperback, 1960.

Nöldeke, Theodor. 'Arabs (Ancient)', *Encyclopaedia of Religion and Ethics.* Edinburgh: T. & T. Clark, 1908, 1925. Vol. I, pp. 659–73.

O'Leary, E. de Lacy. *Arabia before Mohammed.* London: Kegan Paul, Trench, Trübner, 1927; New York: E. P. Dutton, 1927; reprint, New York: AMS Press, n.d.

Rentz, George. 'Djazīrat al-'Arab', *Encyclopaedia of Islam.* New Edition, I, pp. 533–56.

Ryckmans, A. *Les religions arabes préislamiques.* 2nd edn. Louvain: Publications Universitaires, 1951.

Wellhausen, Julius. *Reste arabischen Heidentums.* 2nd edn. Berlin: G. Reimer, 1897; reprinted in Berlin, 1927.

Muḥammad

Andrae, Tor. *Mohammed: The Man and His Faith.* Trans. Theophil Menzel. London: Allen & Unwin, 1936; New York: Harper Torchbook, 1960. (Valuable introduction to the life of Muḥammad emphasizing the development of his religious experience and the nature of the revelation.)

Buhl, Frants. *Das Leben Mohammeds.* 2nd edn. Heidelberg: Quelle & Meyer, 1955. (Possibly the best and most detailed Western account of the life and works of Muḥammad.)

Ibn Hishām, 'Abd al-Mālik. *The Life of Muḥammad.* Ed. and trans. Alfred Guillaume. London and New York: Oxford University Press, 1955;

Oxford paperback, 1967. (Translation of the standard classical Arabic biography of Muḥammad, Ibn Hishām's early ninth-century revision of Ibn Isḥāq's early eighth-century work.)

Paret, Rudi. *Mohammed und der Koran: Geschichte und Verkündigung des arabischen Propheten.* 2nd edn. Stuttgart: W. Kohlhammer, 1966.

Watt, W. Montgomery. *Muhammad at Mecca.* Oxford: Clarendon Press, 1953.

———. *Muhammad at Medina.* Oxford: Clarendon Press, 1956.

———. *Muhammad: Prophet and Statesman.* London: Oxford University Press, 1961. (In part, a summary and refinement of the two larger volumes; available in paperback.)

Wessels, Antonie. *A Modern Arabic Biography of Muḥammad: A Critical Study of Muḥammad Ḥusayn Haykal's 'Ḥayāt Muḥammad'*. Leiden: E. J. Brill, 1972. (An analysis of a modern 'historical-critical' Arabic biography of Muḥammad first published in book form in 1935; 10th edn 1969.)

General and political history of the Islamic world

Brockelmann, Carl. *History of the Islamic Peoples.* With a review of events 1939–47 by Moshe Perlmann. Translated from the German by Moshe Perlmann and Joel Carmichael. New York: G. P. Putnam's Sons, 1947; London: Routledge & Kegan Paul, 1949; Capricorn Books paperback, 1960. (Concise and detailed account emphasizing names, dates and political history, and including information on all peoples predominantly Muslim.)

Gabrieli, Francesco. *Muhammad and the Conquests of Islam.* Translated from the Italian by Virginia Luling and Rosamund Linell. New York: McGraw-Hill, 1968. (Short history with helpful maps and beautiful illustrations; available in paperback.)

Grunebaum, G. E. von. *Classical Islam: A History, 600–1258*, Translated from the German by Katherine Watson. London: Allen & Unwin, 1970; Chicago: Aldine Publishing Co., 1970.

Hitti, Philip K. *History of the Arabs: From the Earliest Times to the Present.* 10th edn. London: Macmillan Co., 1970; New York: St Martin's Press, 1970; available in paperback. (Comprehensive account with emphasis on early period. Provides valuable information from Arabic sources not available elsewhere in English.)

Holt, P. M., Lambton, Ann K. S. and Lewis, Bernard, eds. *The Cambridge History of Islam.* Vol. 1: *The Central Islamic Lands.* Vol. 2: *The Further Islamic Lands, Islamic Society and Civilization.* Cambridge University Press, 1970.

Spuler, Bertold *et al. The Muslim World: A Historical Survey.* Translated from the German by F. R. C. Bagley. 4 Parts. Leiden: E. J. Brill, 1960–9 (vols 1–3); vol. 4 in preparation.

Literary and cultural history of the Islamic world

Arberry, Arthur J. *Aspects of Islamic Civilization: As Depicted in the Original Texts.* London: Allen & Unwin, 1964; paperback, Ann Arbor: University of Michigan Press, 1967.

———, ed. *Religion in the Middle East*. Vol. 2: *Islam*. London: Cambridge University Press, 1969. (A survey of the development of Muslim faith and practice and various Muslim sects in the Middle East, central Asia, India, Pakistan, and parts of Africa during the last hundred years; includes discussion of social, economic and cultural factors influencing Islam.)

Dunlop, D. M. *Arab Civilization to A. D. 1500*. Arab Background Series, ed. N. A. Ziadeh. London: Longmans, 1971; New York: Praeger, 1971. (Survey of the development of Arabic literature, historiography, geography, philosophy, science, and medicine.)

Gibb, Hamilton A. R. *Arabic Literature: An Introduction*, 2nd (rev.) edn, Oxford: Clarendon Press, 1963.

———. *Studies on the Civilization of Islam*. Ed. Stanford J. Shaw and William R. Polk. London: Routledge & Kegan Paul, 1962; Boston: Beacon Press, 1962.

Grunebaum, G. E. von. *Medieval Islam: A Study in Cultural Orientation*. 2nd edn. University of Chicago Press, 1953; available in paperback.

———. *Modern Islam: The Search for Cultural Identity*. Berkeley: University of California Press, 1962; New York: Vintage Books, 1964.

Kremer, Alfred von. *The Orient under the Caliphs*. Trans. Salahuddin Khuda Bukhsh from *Culturgeschichte des Orients unter den Chalifen* (Vienna, 1875–7). University of Calcutta, 1920; reprint, Beirut: United Publishers, 1973.

Kritzeck, James, ed. *Anthology of Islamic Literature: From the Rise of Islam to Modern Times*. New York: Holt, Rinehart & Winston, 1964; Mentor Book paperback, 1966.

Levy, Reuben. *The Social Structure of Islam*. Cambridge University Press, 1957, 1969 (1st edn, called *The Sociology of Islam*, London: Williams & Norgate, 1930.)

Mez, Adam. *The Renaissance of Islam*. Trans. Salahuddin Khuda Bukhsh and D. S. Margoliouth. London: Luzac & Co., 1937; reprint, Hildesheim: Georg Olms, 1968, and New York: AMS Press, n.d.

Rice, David Talbot. *Islamic Painting: A Survey*. Edinburgh University Press, 1971; Chicago: Aldine Publishing Co., 1971.

Watt, W. Montgomery. *The Majesty That Was Islam: The Islamic World 661–1100*. Sidgwick & Jackson Great Civilizations Series. London: Sidgwick & Jackson, 1974.

Muslim intellectual history

ʻAbduh, Muḥammad. *The Theology of Unity*. Trans. Isḥāq Musaʻad and Kenneth Cragg. London: Allen & Unwin, 1966. (Translation of the 18th edn of *Risālat at-tawḥīd*, 1957, by the 'father of twentieth century Muslim thinking in the Arab world'; first published 1897, 2nd edn revised by Rashīd Riḍā, 1908.)

Arberry, Arthur J. *Sufism: An Account of the Mystics of Islam*. London: Allen & Unwin, 1950; paperback, New York: Harper & Row, 1970.

de Boer, T. J. *The History of Philosophy in Islam*. 2nd edn. Trans. Edward R. Jones. London: Luzac & Co., 1933; Dover Publications paperback, 1967.

Donaldson, D. *The Shi'ite Religion: A History of Islam in Persia and Irak*. London: Luzac & Co., 1933.

Gardet, Louis, and Anawati, M. *Introduction à la théologie musulmane*. Paris: Librairie Philosophique J. Vrin, 1948.

Goldziher, Ignaz. *Muslim Studies*. 2 vols. Translation of *Muhammedanische Studien* (1889–90) by C. R. Barber and S. M. Stern. London: Allen & Unwin, 1967, 1971.

———. *Vorlesungen über den Islam*. 2nd edn revised by Franz Babinger. Heidelberg: C. Winter, 1925.

Guillaume, Alfred. *The Traditions of Islam: An Introduction to the Study of the Hadith Literature*. Oxford: Clarendon Press, 1924; Beirut: Khayats, 1966.

McCarthy, Richard J. *The Theology of al-Ash'arī*. Beirut: Imprimerie Catholique, 1953.

Macdonald, Duncan B. *Development of Muslim Theology, Jurisprudence and Constitutional Theory*. London: Routledge, 1903, 1915; New York: C. Scribner's Sons, 1903; reprint, New York: Russell & Russell, 1965.

———. *The Religious Attitude and Life in Islam*. 2nd edn. University of Chicago Press, 1912; reprint, Beirut: Khayats, 1965, and New York: AMS Press, n.d.

Watt, W. Montgomery. *The Formative Period of Islamic Thought*. Edinburgh University Press, 1973; Chicago: Aldine Publishing Co., 1973.

———. *Islamic Philosophy and Theology*. Islamic Surveys Series, no. 1. Edinburgh University Press, 1962; Chicago: Aldine Publishing Co., 1962.

———. *Islamic Political Thought: The Basic Concepts*. Islamic Surveys Series, no. 6. Edinburgh University Press, 1968; Chicago: Aldine Publishing Co., 1968.

———. *Muslim Intellectual: A Study of al-Ghazali*. Edinburgh University Press, 1963; Chicago: Aldine Publishing Co., 1963.

Wensinck, A. J. *The Muslim Creed: Its Genesis and Historical Development*. Cambridge University Press, 1932; reprint, London: Frank Cass, 1965.

Jurisprudence

Coulson, Joel J. *Conflicts and Tensions in Islamic Jurisprudence*. University of Chicago Press, 1969.

———. *A History of Islamic Law*. Islamic Surveys Series, no. 2. Edinburgh University Press, 1964.

Fyzee, A. A. A. *Outlines of Muhammadan Law*. 3rd edn. London and New York: Oxford University Press, 1964.

Schacht, Joseph. *An Introduction to Islamic Law*. Oxford: Clarendon Press, 1964.

———. *The Origins of Muhammadan Jurisprudence*. Oxford: Clarendon Press, 1950; reprinted several times with corrections and additions.

Editions of the Arabic text and translations of the Qur'ān

Ali, Abdullah Yusuf. *The Holy Qur-an: Text, Translation and Commentary*. Lahore: Shaikh Muhammad Ashraf, 1934, 1973. (One of the most reliable oriental translations of the Qur'ān in terms of reflecting the Arabic text; however, later theological views are sometimes read into the translation and defended in copious notes. Follows the verse numbering of the Egyptian 'standard edition' of the Qur'ān, except for occasional deviations.)

Al-muṣḥaf ash-sharīf, or *Al-qur'ān al-karīm*. Cairo: Maṭba'a al-Amīriyya, 1344 A.H.; often reprinted. (Egyptian 'standard edition' of the Qur'ān authorized by the king of Egypt in 1924; gradually replacing use of Flügel's edition among Western scholars.)

Arberry, A. J. *The Koran Interpreted*. London: Allen & Unwin, 1955; New York: Macmillan, 1955; available in paperback. (Widely used English translation of the Qur'ān by a well-known British Arabist. Accurately reflects the Arabic text, including ambiguity in some places. Follows Flügel verse numbering, but only every fifth verse is numbered. Divisions of the text reflect influence of Bell's translation.)

Bell, Richard. *The Qur'ān Translated, with a critical re-arrangement of the Surahs*. 2 vols. Edinburgh: T. & T. Clark, 1937, 1939. (Valuable translation and critical study that attempts to reconstruct the complicated history of the text of the Qur'ān before the sūras reached their final form. Follows Flügel verse numbering and is based largely on the Flügel text.)

Blachère, Régis. *Le Coran*. 2nd edn. Paris: G.-P. Maisonneuve & Larose, 1966; reprinted 1973. (Standard French translation of the Qur'ān with valuable notes. Variant readings are sometimes given alongside the reading of the 'Uthmānic text, and verses believed to be later interpolations are indented. Except for these changes, the sūras appear in the traditional order. In the first edition, published from 1949–51, the text of the Qur'ān was rearranged in a supposed chronological order, based largely on the Nöldeke/Schwally dating of the sūras.)

Flügel, Gustav, ed. *Corani textus arabicus*. Leipzig: Sumtibus Caroli Tauchnitii, 1834; reprint, Ridgewood, NJ: Gregg Press, 1965. (Continues to be the Arabic text of the Qur'ān most widely used in Europe, even though it is recognized as an inferior text and the verse numbers differ from the Egyptian standard edition.)

Khan, Muhammad Zafrulla. *The Quran*. London: Curzon Press, 1971. (Arabic text with introduction and smooth English translation that is often more a paraphrase. Also, the translation sometimes misrepresents the Arabic text by reading in later theological views. Follows an Indian/Pakistani system of verse numbering, which often runs one number ahead of the Egyptian standard edition because the *basmalah* is counted as verse 1.)

Paret, Rudi. *Der Koran: Übersetzung*. Stuttgart: W. Kohlhammer Verlag, 1962. (The best translation of the Qur'ān so far in any Western language. Incorporates explanatory interpolations into the text along with transliterations of key Arabic terms; also has helpful notes. Designed to be used with Paret's *Kommentar und Konkordanz*. Includes both Egyptian and Flügel verse numbers.)

Pickthall, Mohammed Marmaduke. *The Meaning of the Glorious Koran: An Explanatory Translation.* London: A. A. Knopf, 1930; New York: New American Library, 1953; London: Allen & Unwin, 1957; Arabic and English edn, New York: Orientalia, 1970. (Translation by a well-known British writer who converted to Islam, often reflects traditional Muslim interpretation rather than literal meaning of Arabic text. Follows the Egyptian verse numbering.)

Salahud-Din, Pir. *The Wonderful Koran: A New English Translation.* Eminabad, Pakistan: Raftar-i-Zamana Publications, n.d. (A smooth, eminently readable English rendering of the Qur'ān. A unique feature of this translation is that in cases where the Arabic text is ambiguous or contrary to later theological views, interpretatations or explanatory phrases from the classical commentaries are incorporated into the translation, with the sources indicated in footnotes. Usually, but not consistently, follows the same Indian/Pakistani verse numbering as that of Khan.)

Commentaries and general studies on the Qur'ān

(Arabic commentaries are listed in last section below.)

Abbott, Nabia. *Studies in Arabic Literary Papyri.* Vol. 2, *Qur'ānic Commentary and Tradition.* University of Chicago Press, 1967.

'Abd al-Bāqī, Muḥammad Fu'ād. *Al-mu'jam al-mufahras li-alfāẓ al-qur'ān al-karīm.* Cairo, 1364 A.H./1945; new edn, 1968. (Concordance to the Egyptian standard edition of the Qur'ān; includes brief contexts of each key term in the Qur'ān.)

Baljon, J. M. S. *Modern Muslim Koran Interpretation (1880–1960).* Leiden: E. J. Brill, 1961. (Brings up to date the last chapter in Goldziher's *Richtungen.*)

Beeston, A. F. L. *Baiḍāwī's Commentary on Sūrah 12 of the Qur'ān: Text, Accompanied by an interpretative rendering and notes.* Oxford: Clarendon Press, 1963.

Birkeland, Harris. *The Lord Guideth: Studies on Primitive Islam.* Oslo: I Kommisjon Hos H. Aschehoug & Co., 1956. (Historical-critical commentary on Sūras 93, 94, 105, 106, and 108; example of excellent Qur'ānic exegesis.)

Blachère, Régis. *Introduction au Coran.* 2nd edn. Paris: Besson & Chantemerle, 1959. (Standard French introduction to the Qur'ān.)

Cragg, Kenneth. *The Event of the Qur'ān: Islam in its Scripture.* London: Allen & Unwin, 1971.

———. *The Mind of the Qur'ān: Chapters in Reflection.* London: Allen & Unwin, 1973.

Flügel, Gustav. *Concordantiae Corani Arabicae.* Leipzig: Tauchnitii, 1842; reprint, Ridgewood, NJ: Gregg Press, 1965. (Concordance to Flügel's edition of the Arabic text of the Qur'ān.)

Goldziher, Ignaz. *Die Richtungen der islamischen Koranauslegung.* Leiden: E. J. Brill, 1920, 1952. (The 'classical' work on Muslim interpretation of the Qur'ān; must now be read with Baljon and Jansen.)

Horovitz, Josef. *Koranische Untersuchungen*. Leipzig: Walter de Gruyter & Co., 1926. (Unsurpassed study of key terms and concepts of the Qur'ān.)

Jansen, J. J. G. *The Interpretation of the Koran in Modern Egypt*. Leiden: E. J. Brill, 1974.

Jeffery, Arthur. *The Foreign Vocabulary of the Qur'ān*. Baroda: Oriental Institute, 1938.

———, ed. *Materials for the History of the Text of the Qur'ān*. Leiden: E. J. Brill, 1937. (Lists of variant readings collected from early Arabic sources and classical commentaries.)

Jomier, Jacques. *Le commentaire coranique du Manâr: tendances modernes de l'exégèse coranique en Égypte*. Paris: G.-P. Maisonneuve, 1954.

Margoliouth, D. S. *Chrestomathia Baidawiana: The Commentary of el-Baiḍāwī on Sura III Translated and Explained for the Use of Students of Arabic*. London: Luzac & Co., 1894.

Nöldeke, Theodor. *Geschichte des Qorāns*. 2nd edn, by Friedrich Schwally, G. Bergsträsser and O. Pretzl. 3 vols. Leipzig: Dieterich'sche Verlagsbuchhandlung, 1909–38; Hildesheim and New York: Georg Olms Verlag, 1970. (Standard Western introduction to the Qur'ān; available only in German.)

Paret, Rudi. *Grenzen der Koranforschung*. Stuttgart: W. Kohlhammer Verlag, 1960.

———. *Der Koran: Kommentar und Konkordanz*. Stuttgart: W. Kohlhammer Verlag, 1971. (Not so much a 'commentary and concordance' as extended notes to Paret's translation. Arranged verse by verse and containing cross references, transliterations of key Arabic phrases, and extensive bibliographical references. Indispensable aid to study of the Qur'ān.)

Penrice, John. *A Dictionary and Glossary of the Kor-ân, with Copious Grammatical References and Explanations of the Text*. New York: Biblo & Tannen, 1969; first published, 1873.

Stanton, H. U. Weitbrecht. *The Teaching of the Qur'ān, with an Account of its Growth and a Subject Index*. New York: Biblo & Tannen, 1969; first published, 1919.

Watt, W. Montgomery. *Bell's Introduction to the Qur'ān: Completely revised and enlarged*. Islamic Surveys Series, no. 8. Edinburgh University Press, 1970. (Best introduction to the Qur'ān available in English.)

Studies on specific Qur'ānic themes and topics

Crollius, Ary A. Roest. *The Word in the Experience of Revelation in Qur'ān and Hindu Scripture*. Rome: Università Gregoriana Editrice, 1974.

Horovitz, Josef. *Jewish Proper Names and Derivatives in the Koran*. Hildesheim: Georg Olms Verlag, 1964. (Reprinted from *Hebrew Union College Annual*, II, 1925, pp. 145–227.)

Izutsu, Toshihiko. *Ethico-Religious Concepts in the Qur'ān*. Montreal: McGill University Press, 1966.

———. *God and Man in the Koran: Semantics of the Koranic Weltanschauung*. Tokyo: The Keio Institute of Cultural and Linguistic Studies, 1964.

Jomier, Jacques. *The Bible and the Koran*. Translated from the French by Edward P. Arbez. New York: Desclee Co., 1964.

Moubarac, Y. *Abraham dans le Coran*. Paris: Librairie Philosophique J. Vrin, 1958.

Nwyia, Paul. *Exégèse coranique et langage mystique: Novel essai sur le lexique technique des mystiques musulmans*. Beirut: Dar al-Machreq, 1970.

O'Shaughnessy, Thomas. *The Development of the Meaning of Spirit in the Koran*. Rome: Pont. Institutum Orientalium Studiorum, 1953.

———. *The Koranic Concept of the Word of God*. Rome: Pontificio Instituto Biblio, 1948.

———. *Muhammad's Thoughts on Death: A Thematic Study of the Qur'anic Data*. Leiden: E. J. Brill, 1969.

Parrinder, Edward Geoffrey. *Jesus in the Qur'ān*. London: Faber & Faber, 1965; New York: Barnes & Noble, 1965.

Rahbar, Daud. *God of Justice: A Study in the Ethical Doctrine of the Qur'ān*. Leiden: E. J. Brill, 1960.

Rudolph, Wilhelm. *Die Abhängigkeit des Qorans vom Judentum und Christentum*. Stuttgart: W. Kohlhammer, 1922.

Sabbagh, T. *Le métaphore dans le Coran*. Paris: Librairie d'Amérique et d'Orient Adrien-Maisonneuve, 1943.

Sidersky, David. *Les origines des légendes musulmanes dans le Coran et dans les vies des prophètes*. Paris: Paul Geuthner, 1933.

Wagtendonk, K. *Fasting in the Koran*. Leiden: E. J. Brill, 1968.

Editions of Arabic texts used for the present translations

'Abduh, Muḥammad, and Rashīd Riḍā, Muḥammad. *Tafsīr al-qur'ān al-ḥakīm*. 11 vols. Cairo, 1325–53 A.H./1907–34.

Fleischer, H. O., ed. *Beidhawii commentarius in Coranum*. 2 vols. Leipzig, 1846–8.

al-Ghazzālī, Abū Hāmid Muḥammad. *Iḥyā' 'ulūm ad-dīn*. 4 vols. Istanbul, 1318–22 A.H./1900–4.

Ibn-al-Munayyir's *Al-instiṣāf*, printed under the text of az-Zamakhsharī's *Tafsīr al-kashshāf*.

Ibn Rushd, Abūl-Walīd Muḥammad (Averroes). *Kitāb faṣl al-maqāl*. Ed. George F. Hourani. Leiden, 1959.

al-Kāshānī, 'Abd ar-Razzāq. *Tafsīr ash-Shayikh Muhyī' ad-Dīn ibn 'Arabī*. Vols 1 and 2. Cairo, 1283 A.H./1866–7.

al-Kāshī, Muḥammad Murtaḍā. *Aṣṣāfī fī tafsīr kalām Allāh*. Teheran, 1283 A.H./1866–7.

al-Maḥallī, Jalāl ad-Dīn, and as-Suyūṭī, Jalāl ad-Dīn. *Tafsīr al-Jalālain*, in: *Al-futūḥāt al-ilāhiyya bi-tau ḍīḥ tafsīr al-Jalālain li-daqā'iq al-khafiyya ta'līf Sulaymān ibn 'Umar al-'Uyaylī ash-Shāfi'ī*. 4 vols. Cairo, 1377 A.H./1957–8.

ar-Rāzī, Fakhr ad-Din. *Mafātīḥ al-ghayib al-mushtahir bi-t-tafsīr al-kabīr*. 8 vols. Cairo, 1308 A.H./1890–1.

Strothmann, Rudolph, ed. *Ismaelitscher Kommentar zum Koran*. Parts 11–20. Commentary by Ḍiyā' ad-Dīn ibn Hibat Allāh. Göttingen, 1955.

aṭ-Ṭabarī, Abū Ja'far Muḥammad ibn Jarīr. *Jāmi' al-bayān fī tafsīr al-qur'ān*. 30 vols. Bulaq, 1323 A.H./1905.

az-Zamakhsharī, Jadullah Maḥmūd ibn 'Umar. *Tafsīr al-kashshāf 'an ḥaqā'iq ghawāmiḍ at-tanzīl wa-uyūn al-'aqāwīl fī wujūh at-ta'wīl*. Ed. Muṣṭafā Ḥusain Aḥmad. 4 vols. 2nd edn, Cairo, 1373 A.H./1953–5.

GENERAL INDEX

This index contains key topics, personal and place names, certain key Arabic terms, and also several special features. Arabic forms of Biblical and other well-known names are given in parentheses after the English entries. Brief comments and biographical data are supplied in numerous cases. References are given to variant readings (*qirā'āt*) and occasions of revelation (*asbāb an-nuzūl*) mentioned in the commentaries translated in this work. The italic numbers given with certain Arab names indicate pages where passages translated from their commentaries begin. Initial definite articles (al-, ad-, etc.) are disregarded in the alphabetical listing.

INDEX TO QUR'ĀNIC REFERENCES

(Passages with commentaries are set in italics.)

£10